♡ TOUGH LOVE ♡

High School Confidential

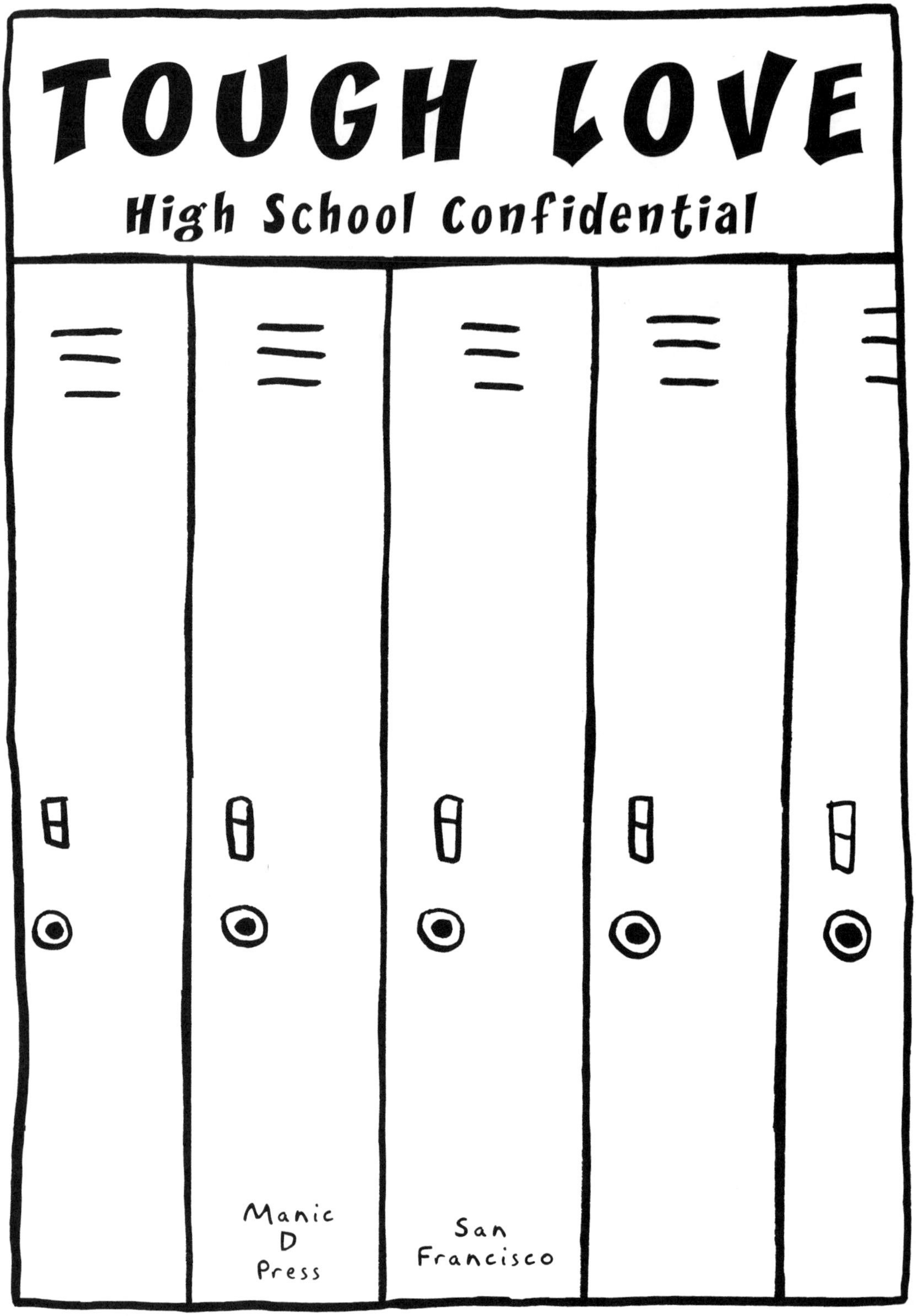
TOUGH LOVE
High School Confidential
Manic D Press
San Francisco

written and illustrated by **Abby Denson**

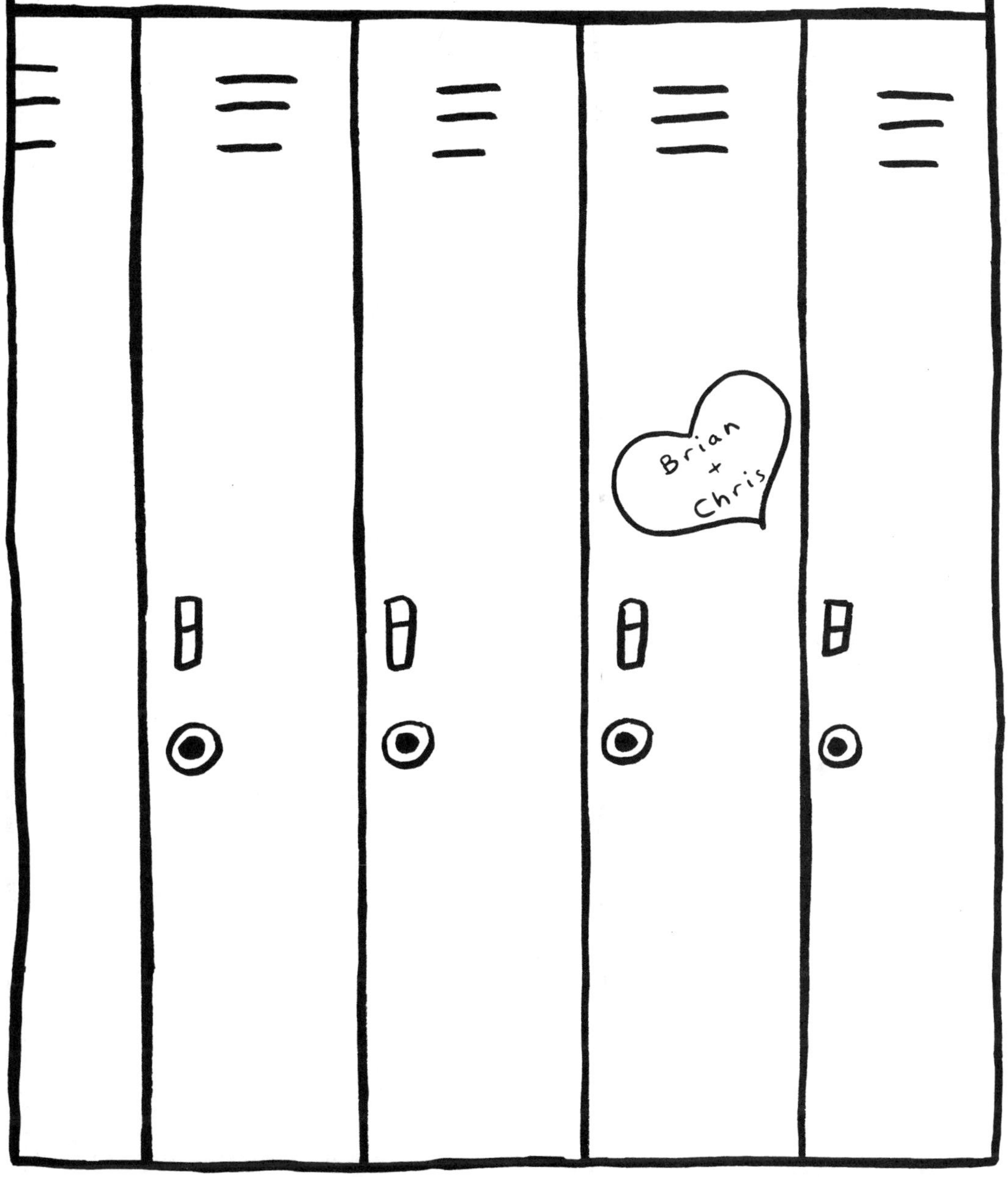
Brian
+
Chris

Tough Love: High School Confidential. Copyright 2006 by Abby Denson.
All rights reserved. Published by Manic D Press, Inc.
PO Box 410804, San Francisco, CA 94141. www.manicdpress.com

Production thanks to: Jason Staloff, Michael Denson, Matt Loux,
Dave Roman, Marc Wilkofsky, John Green, Raina Telgemeier, Dick Demenus,
Daniel Genalo, Don Peterson, Ron Thomson, and Derek Davis.

ISBN 1-933149-08-6 / ISBN 978-1-933149-08-0
Library of Congress Control Number: 2006926615

Visit Abby Denson online - www.abbycomix.com

Dedicated to my grandfather,
Alvin Deutsch, aka Pop Pop, whose unwavering
love and support made this book possible.

Chapter 1

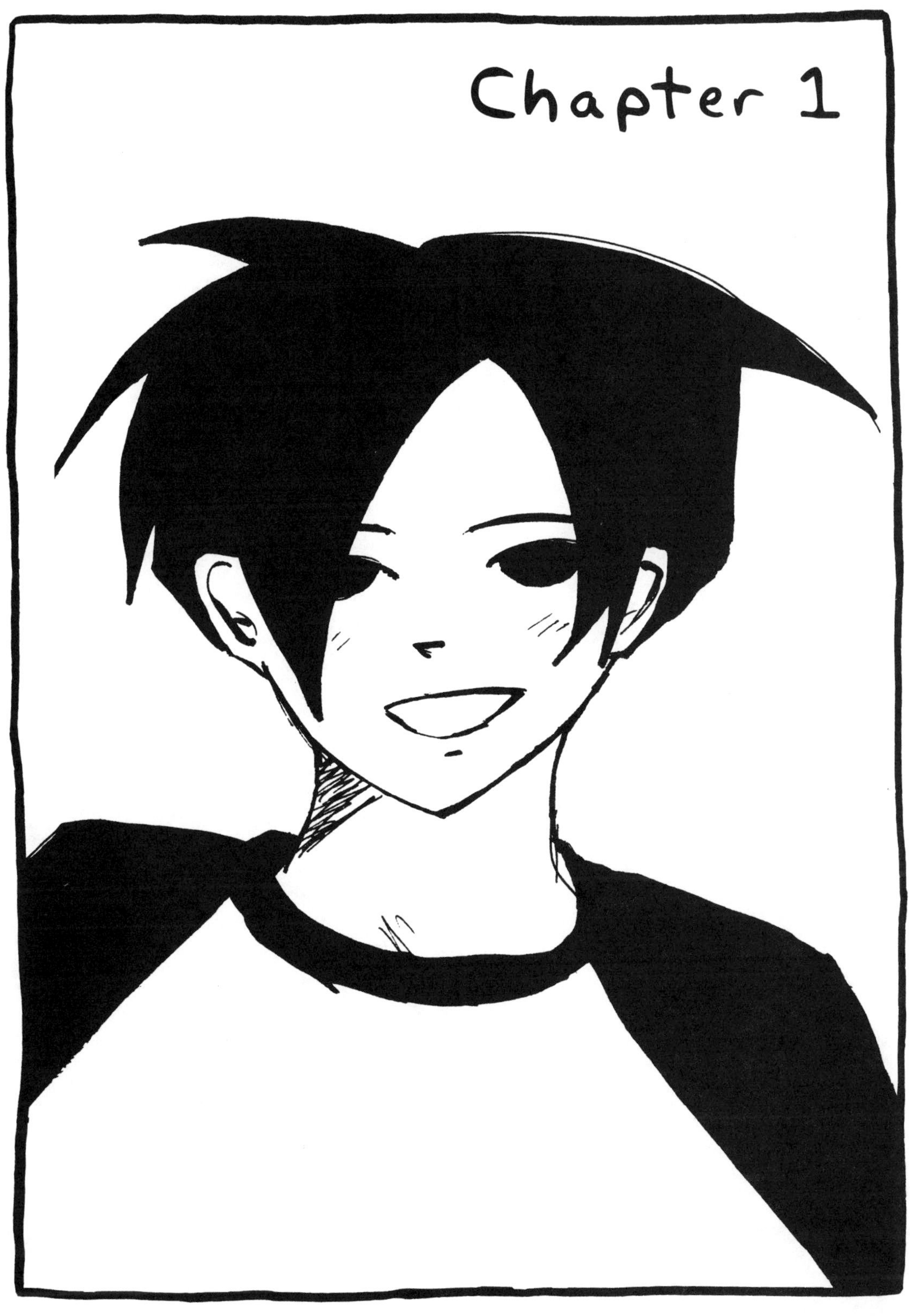

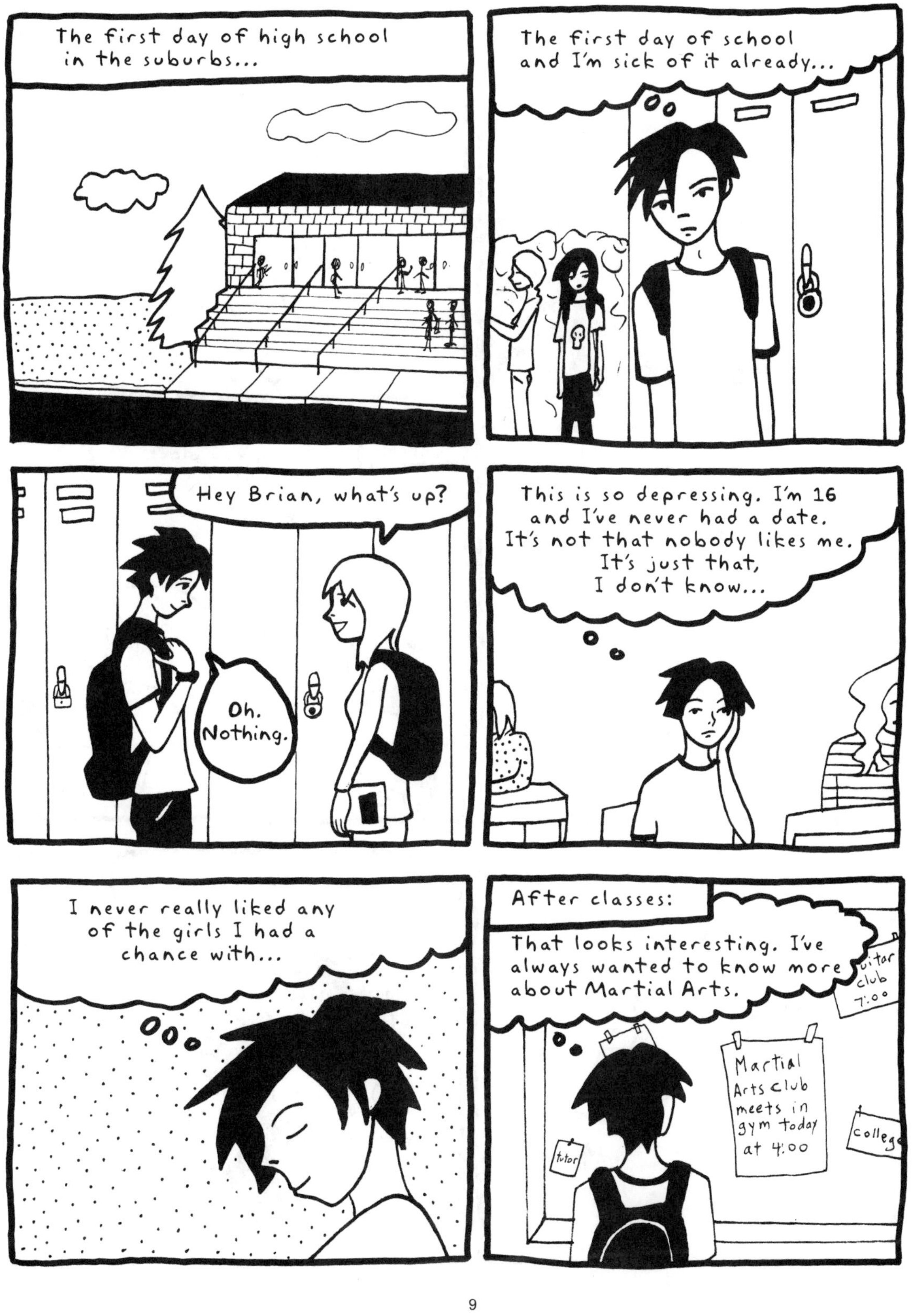

The first day of high school in the suburbs...
The first day of school and I'm sick of it already...
Hey Brian, what's up?
Oh. Nothing.
This is so depressing. I'm 16 and I've never had a date. It's not that nobody likes me. It's just that, I don't know...
I never really liked any of the girls I had a chance with...
After classes:
That looks interesting. I've always wanted to know more about Martial Arts.
Martial Arts club meets in gym today at 4:00
tutor
college
club 7:00

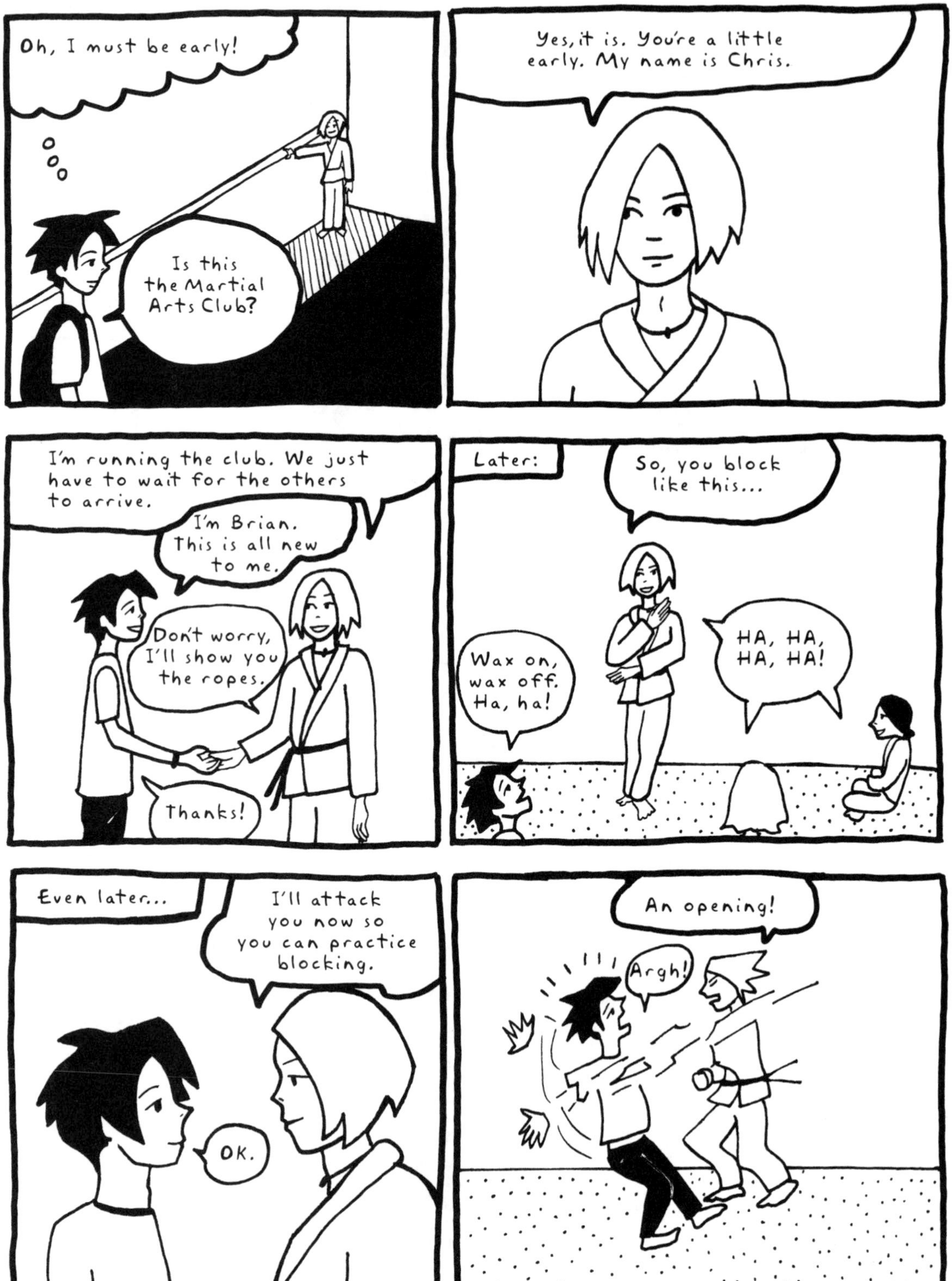
Oh, I must be early!
Is this the Martial Arts Club?
Yes, it is. You're a little early. My name is Chris.
I'm running the club. We just have to wait for the others to arrive.
I'm Brian. This is all new to me.
Don't worry, I'll show you the ropes.
Thanks!
Later:
So, you block like this...
Wax on, wax off. Ha, ha!
HA, HA, HA, HA!
Even later...
I'll attack you now so you can practice blocking.
OK.
An opening!
Argh!

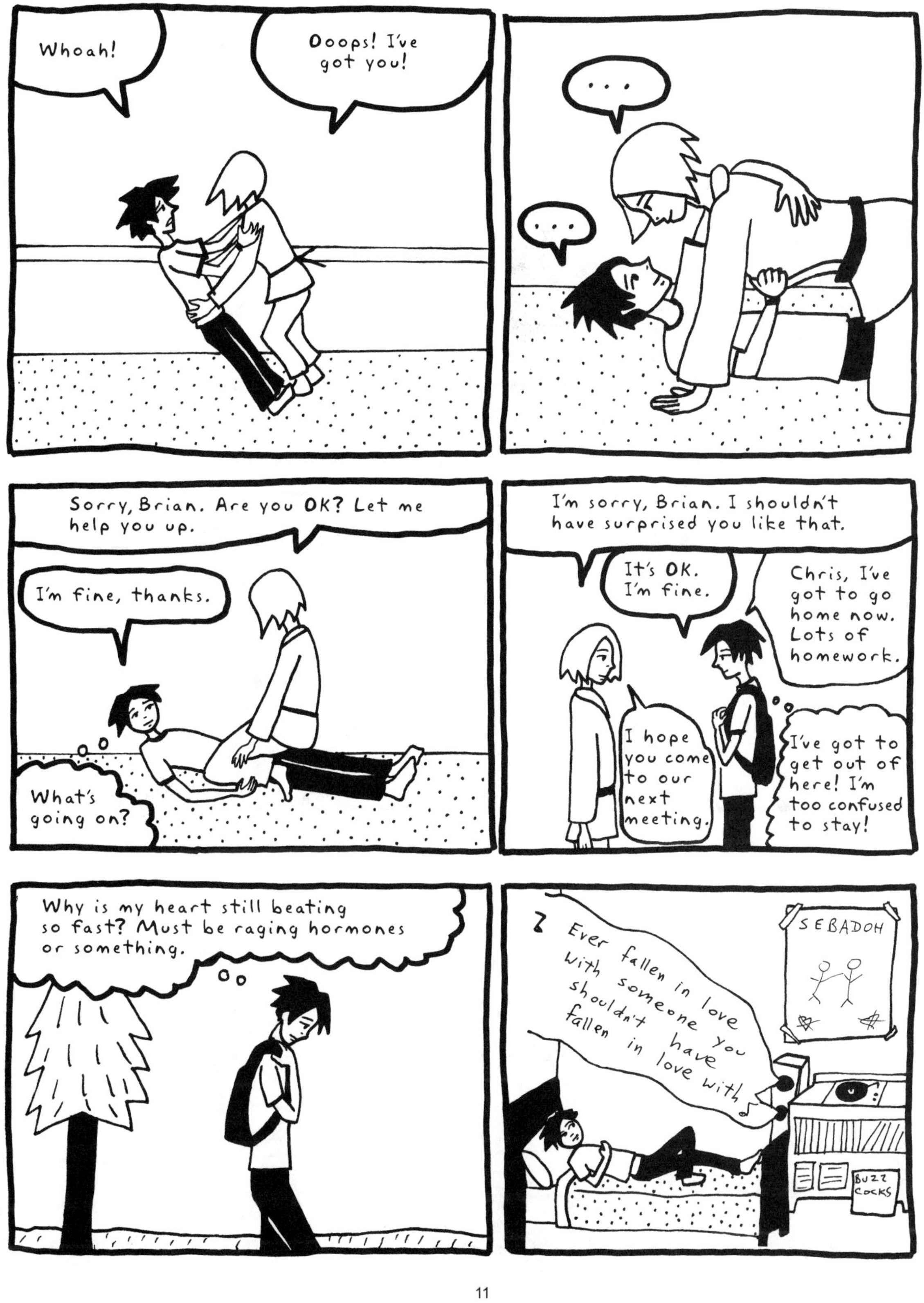
Whoah!
Ooops! I've got you!
...
...
Sorry, Brian. Are you OK? Let me help you up.
I'm fine, thanks.
What's going on?
I'm sorry, Brian. I shouldn't have surprised you like that.
It's OK. I'm fine.
Chris, I've got to go home now. Lots of homework.
I hope you come to our next meeting.
I've got to get out of here! I'm too confused to stay!
Why is my heart still beating so fast? Must be raging hormones or something.
Ever fallen in love with someone you shouldn't have fallen in love with
SEBADOH
BUZZ COCKS

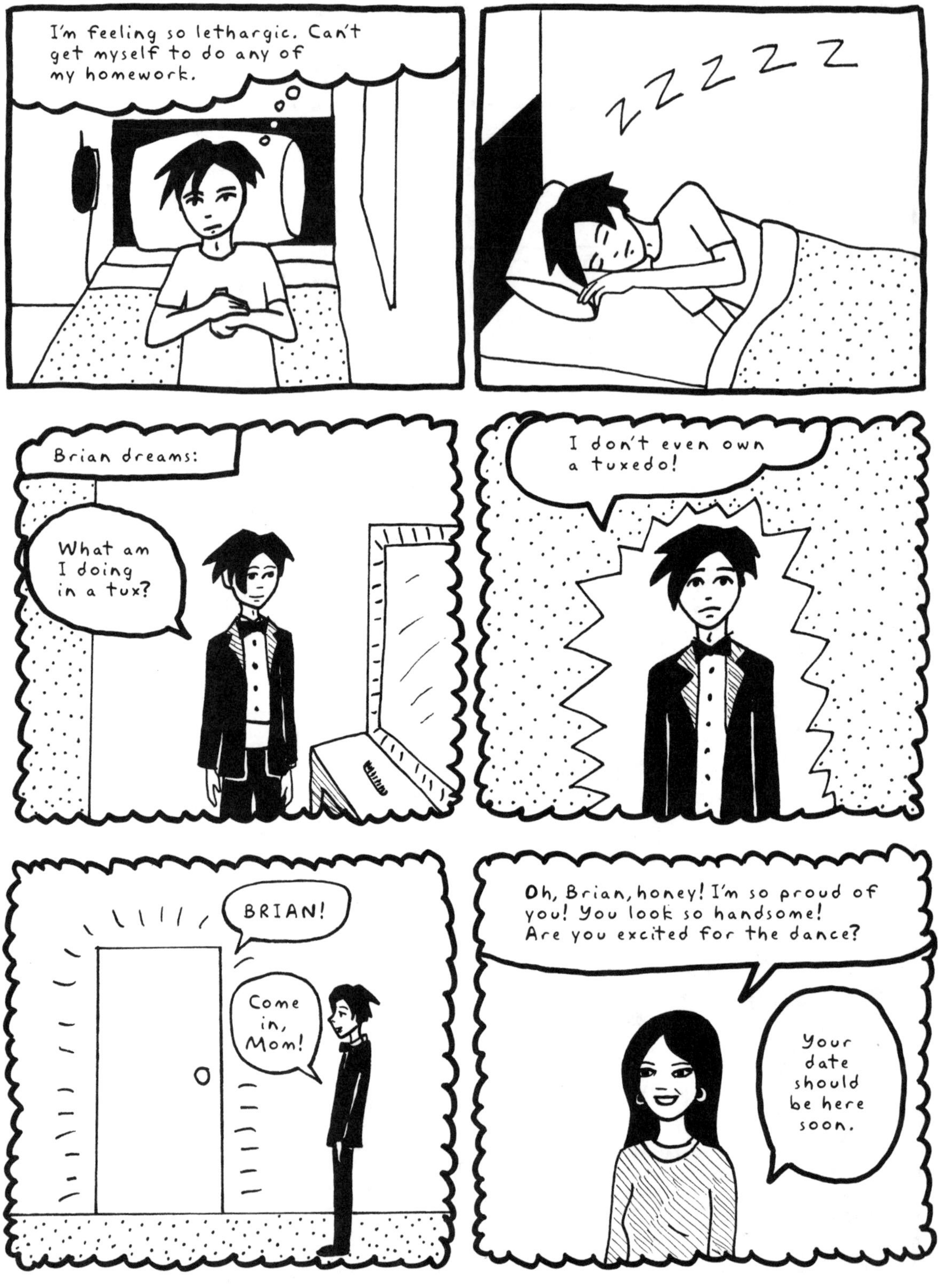
I'm feeling so lethargic. Can't get myself to do any of my homework.
ZZZZZZ
Brian dreams:
What am I doing in a tux?
I don't even own a tuxedo!
BRIAN!
Come in, Mom!
Oh, Brian, honey! I'm so proud of you! You look so handsome! Are you excited for the dance?
Your date should be here soon.

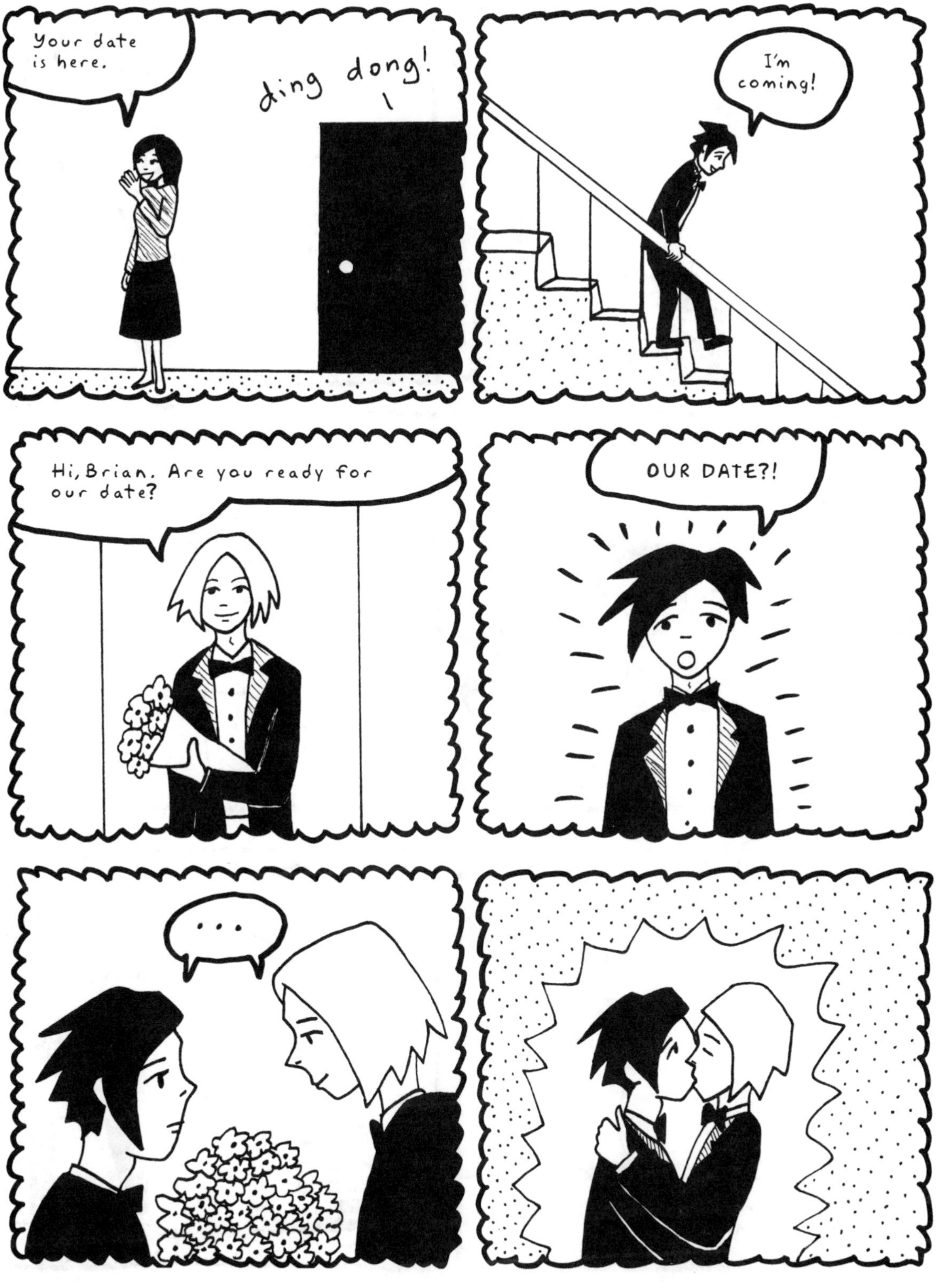
Your date is here.
ding dong!
I'm coming!
Hi, Brian. Are you ready for our date?
OUR DATE?!
...

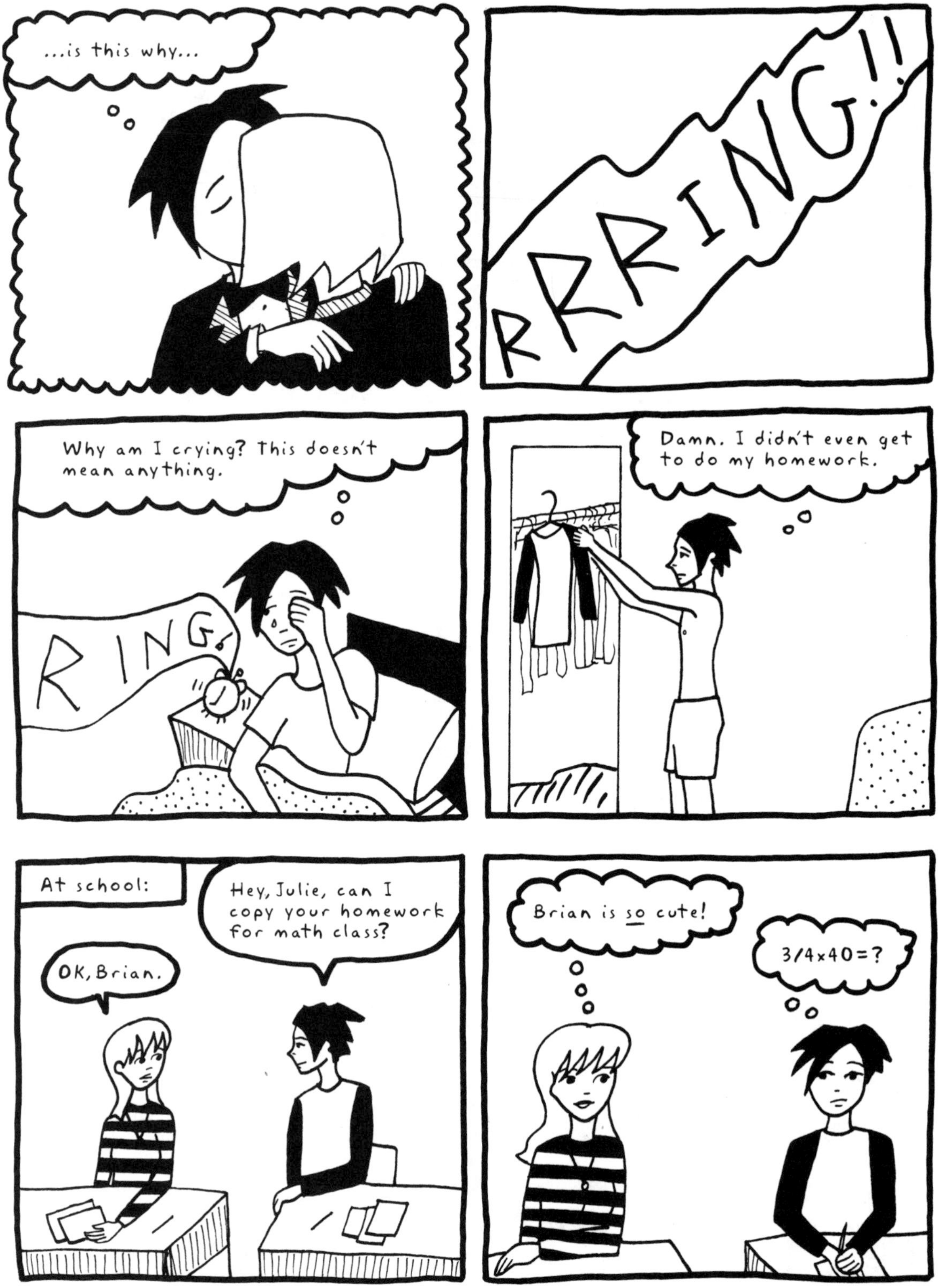
...is this why...
RRRING!!
Why am I crying? This doesn't mean anything.
RING!
Damn. I didn't even get to do my homework.
At school:
Hey, Julie, can I copy your homework for math class?
OK, Brian.
Brian is so cute!
3/4x40=?

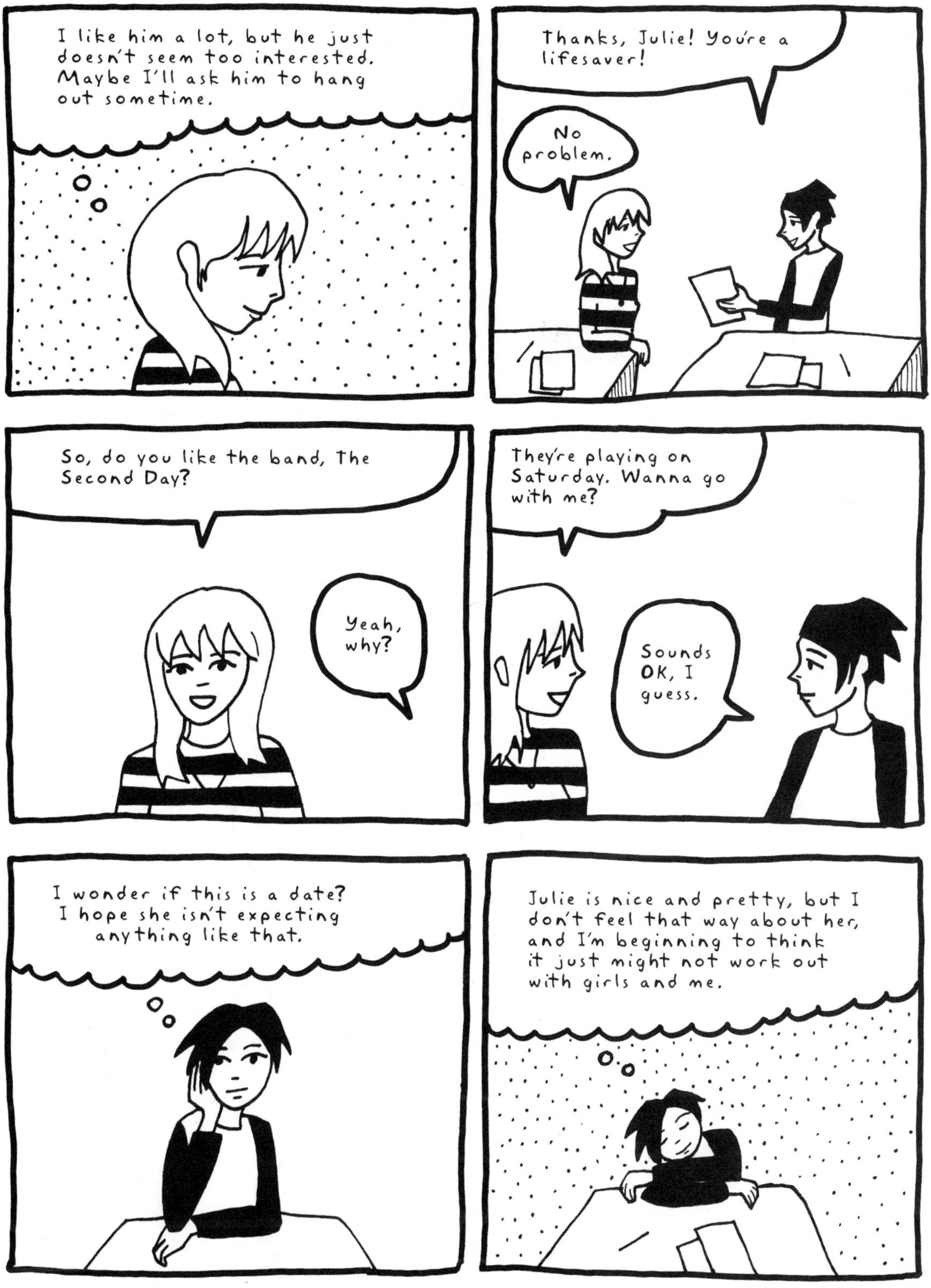
I like him a lot, but he just doesn't seem too interested. Maybe I'll ask him to hang out sometime.
Thanks, Julie! You're a lifesaver!
No problem.
So, do you like the band, The Second Day?
Yeah, why?
They're playing on Saturday. Wanna go with me?
Sounds OK, I guess.
I wonder if this is a date? I hope she isn't expecting anything like that.
Julie is nice and pretty, but I don't feel that way about her, and I'm beginning to think it just might not work out with girls and me.

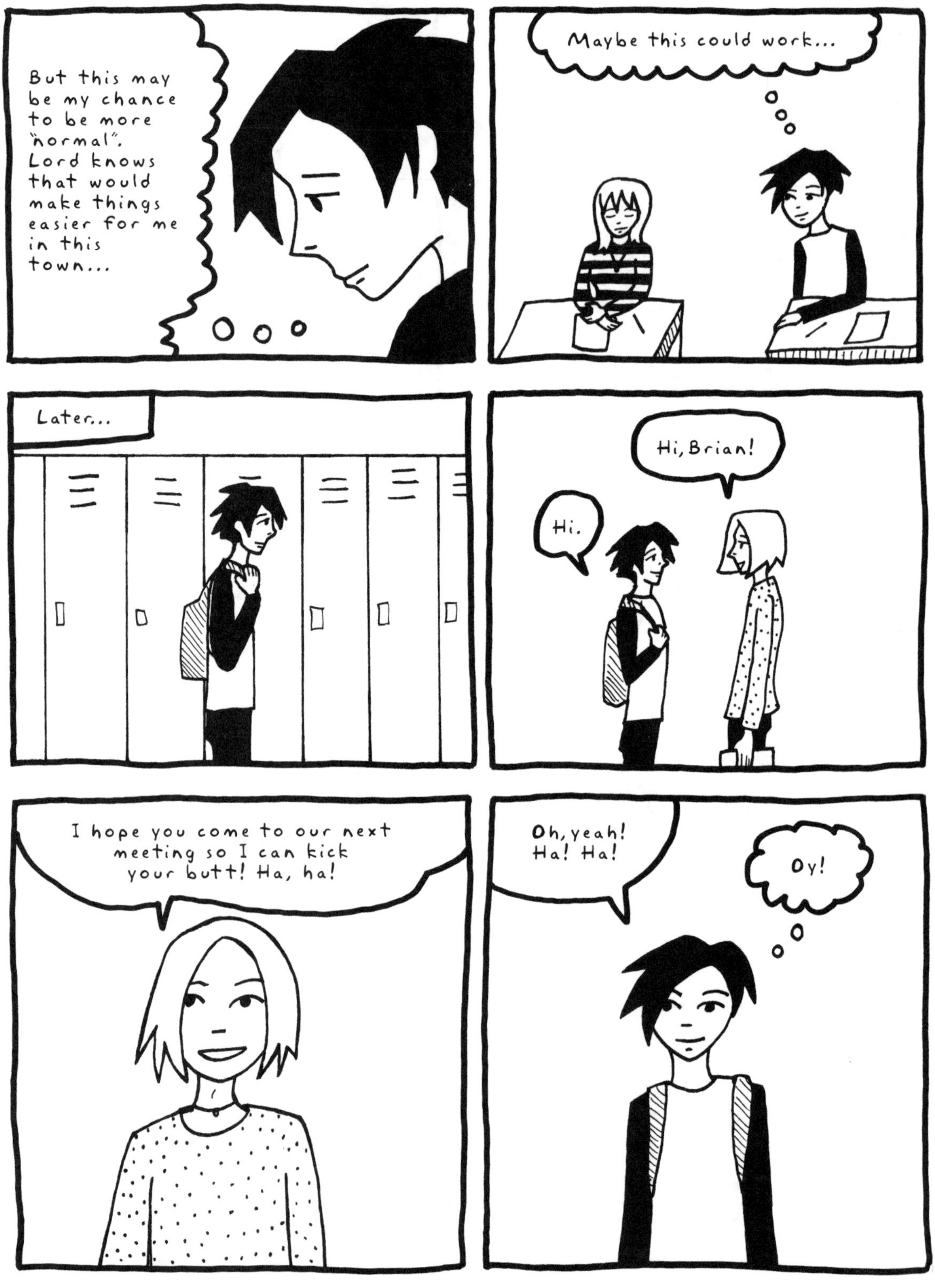
But this may be my chance to be more "normal". Lord knows that would make things easier for me in this town...
Maybe this could work...
Later...
Hi, Brian!
Hi.
I hope you come to our next meeting so I can kick your butt! Ha, ha!
Oh, yeah! Ha! Ha!
Oy!

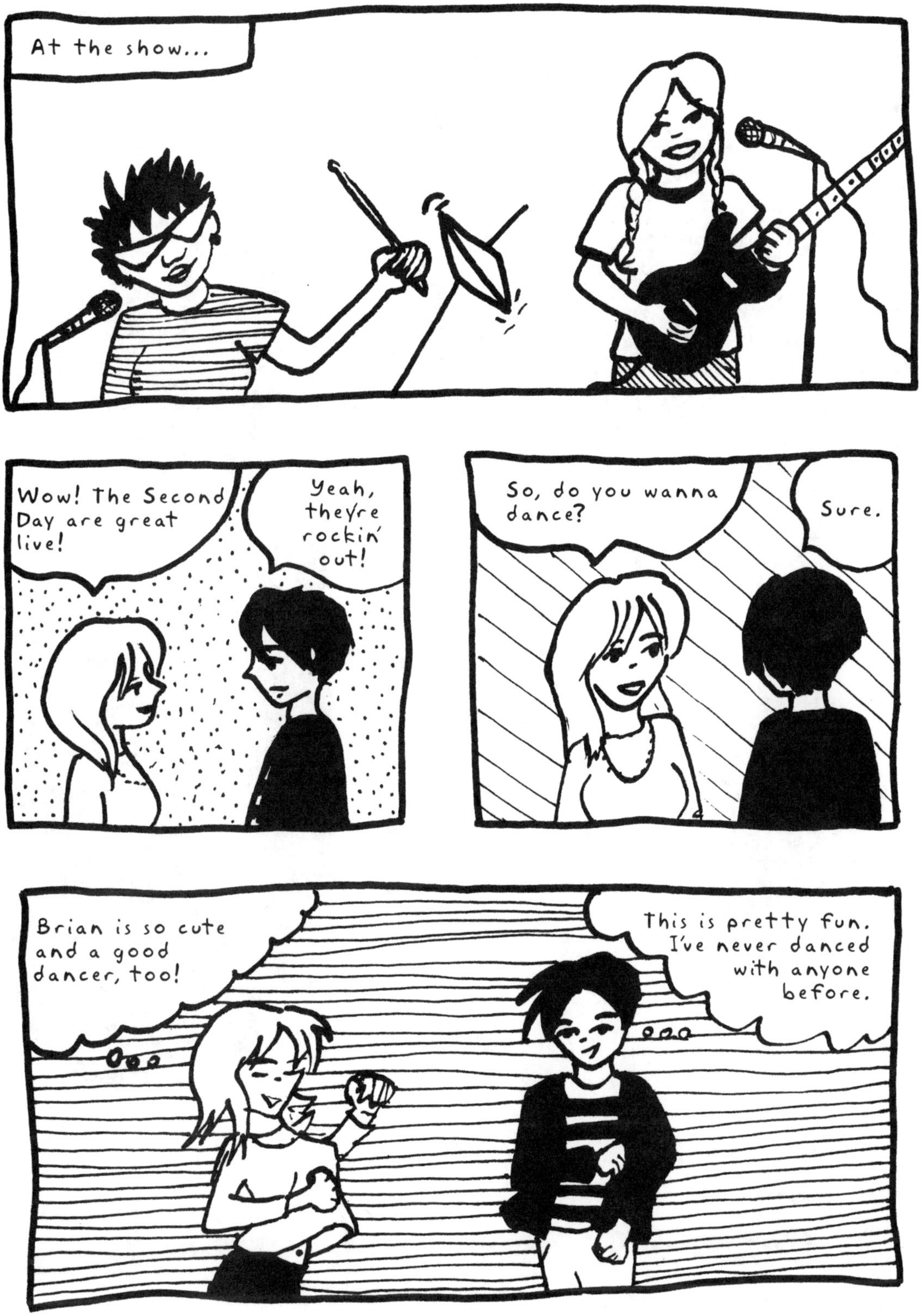
At the show...
Wow! The Second Day are great live!
Yeah, they're rockin' out!
So, do you wanna dance?
Sure.
Brian is so cute and a good dancer, too!
This is pretty fun. I've never danced with anyone before.

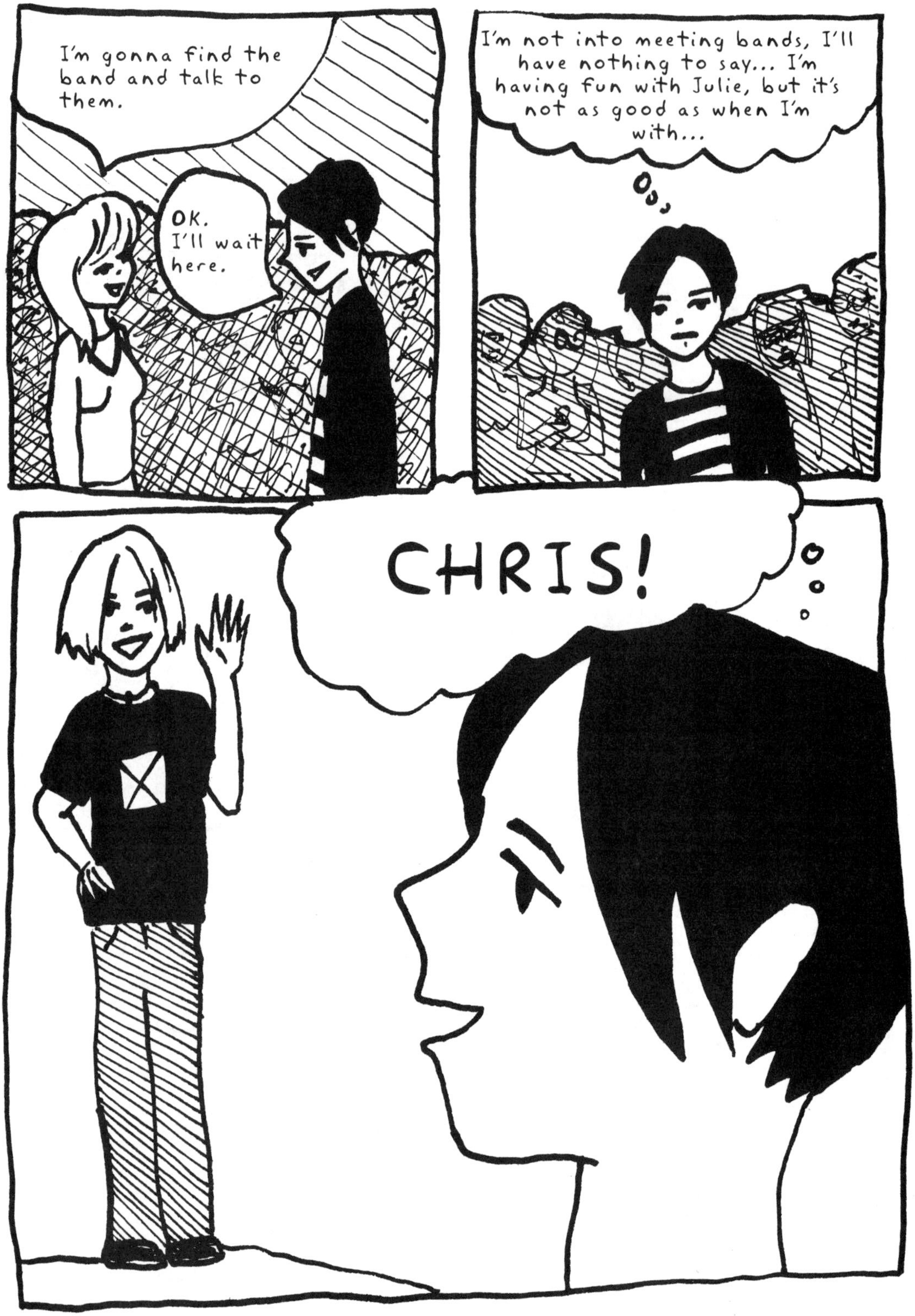

I'm gonna find the band and talk to them.
OK. I'll wait here.
I'm not into meeting bands, I'll have nothing to say... I'm having fun with Julie, but it's not as good as when I'm with...
CHRIS!

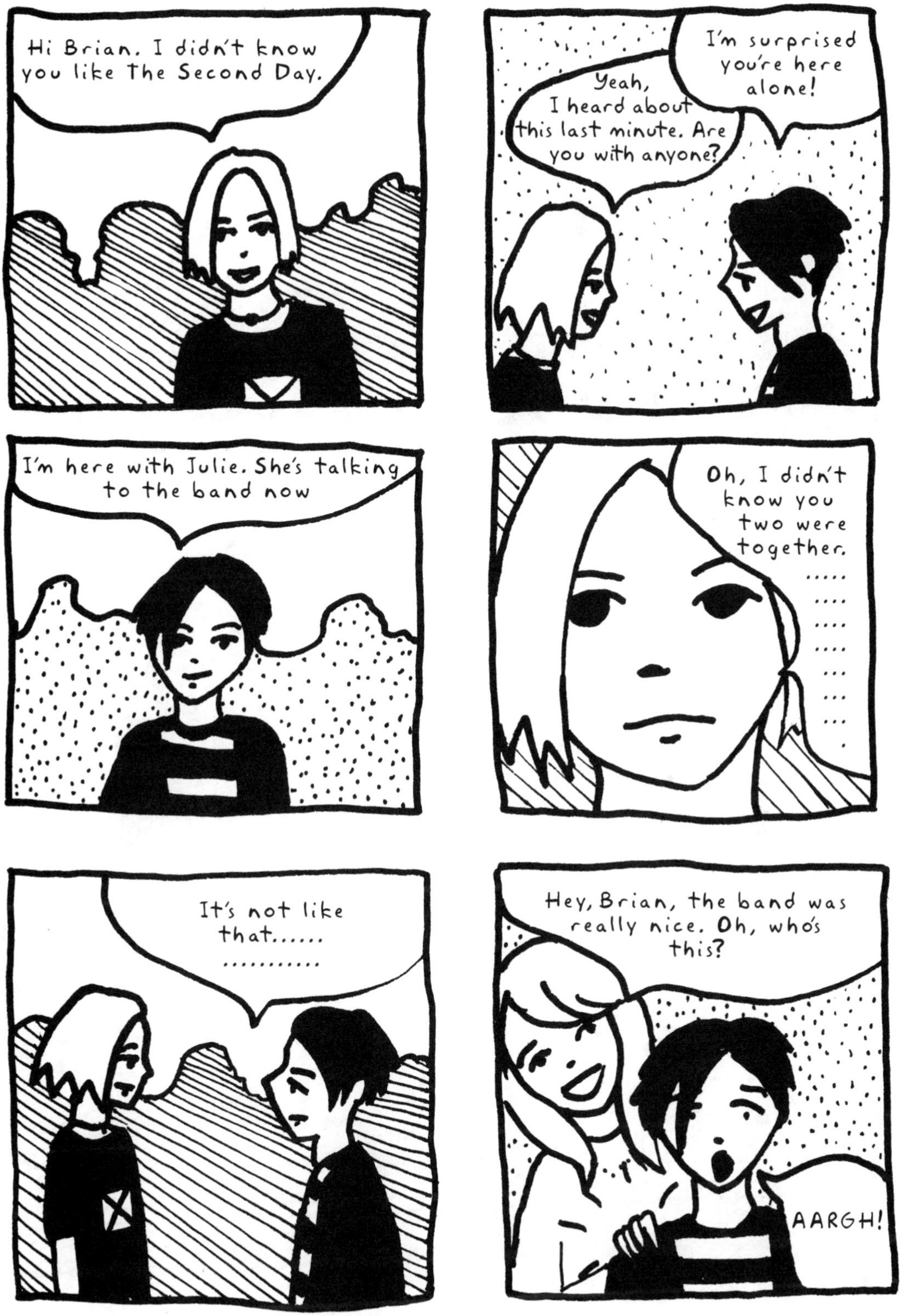
Hi Brian. I didn't know you like The Second Day.
I'm surprised you're here alone!
Yeah, I heard about this last minute. Are you with anyone?
I'm here with Julie. She's talking to the band now
Oh, I didn't know you two were together.
.....
It's not like that......
....
Hey, Brian, the band was really nice. Oh, who's this?
AARGH!

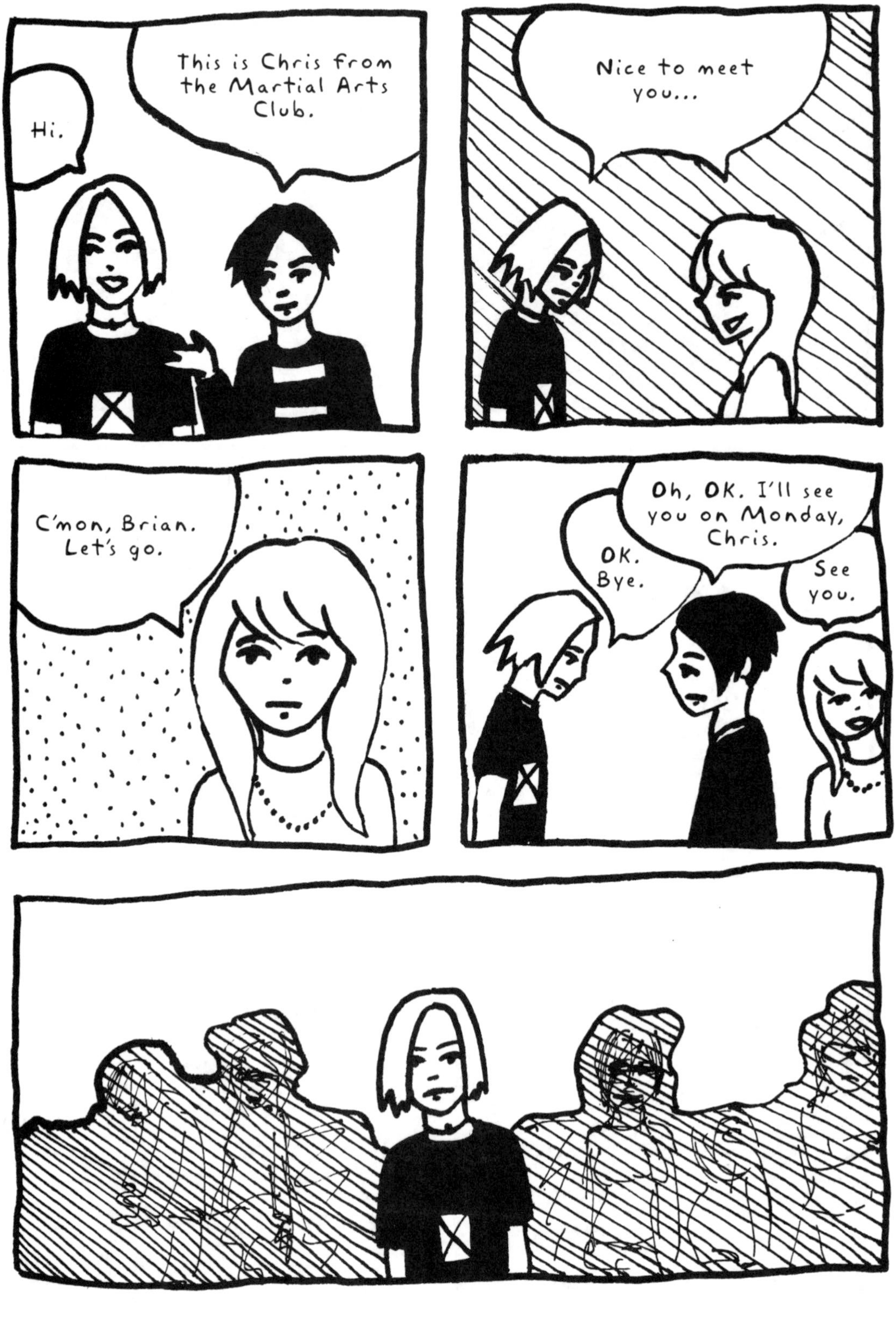
Hi.
This is Chris from the Martial Arts Club.
Nice to meet you...
C'mon, Brian. Let's go.
Oh, OK. I'll see you on Monday, Chris.
OK. Bye.
See you.

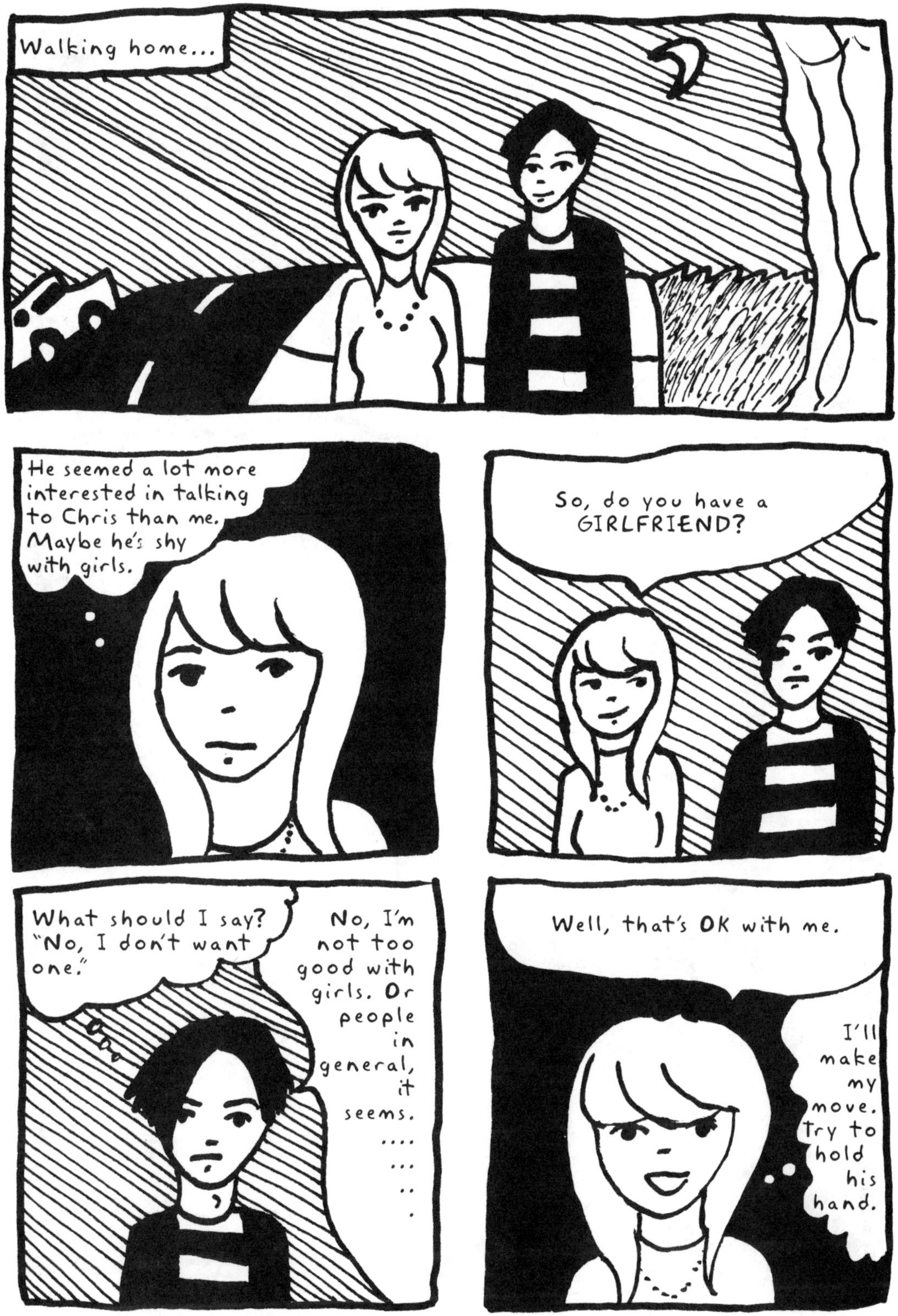
Walking home...
He seemed a lot more interested in talking to Chris than me. Maybe he's shy with girls.
So, do you have a GIRLFRIEND?
What should I say? "No, I don't want one."
No, I'm not too good with girls. Or people in general, it seems.
....
...
..
.
Well, that's OK with me.
I'll make my move. Try to hold his hand.

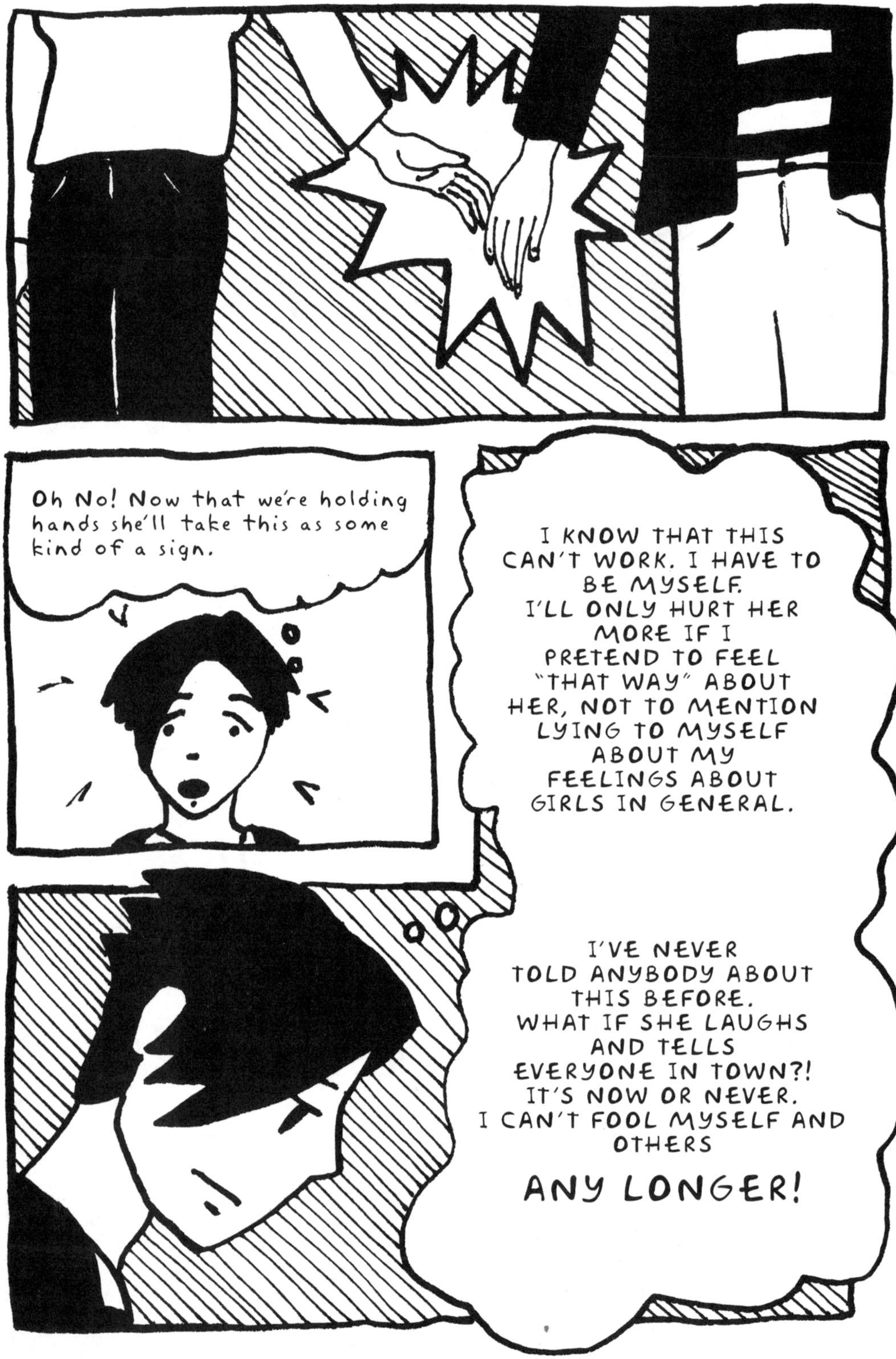

Oh No! Now that we're holding hands she'll take this as some kind of a sign.
I KNOW THAT THIS CAN'T WORK. I HAVE TO BE MYSELF. I'LL ONLY HURT HER MORE IF I PRETEND TO FEEL "THAT WAY" ABOUT HER, NOT TO MENTION LYING TO MYSELF ABOUT MY FEELINGS ABOUT GIRLS IN GENERAL.
I'VE NEVER TOLD ANYBODY ABOUT THIS BEFORE. WHAT IF SHE LAUGHS AND TELLS EVERYONE IN TOWN?! IT'S NOW OR NEVER. I CAN'T FOOL MYSELF AND OTHERS
ANY LONGER!

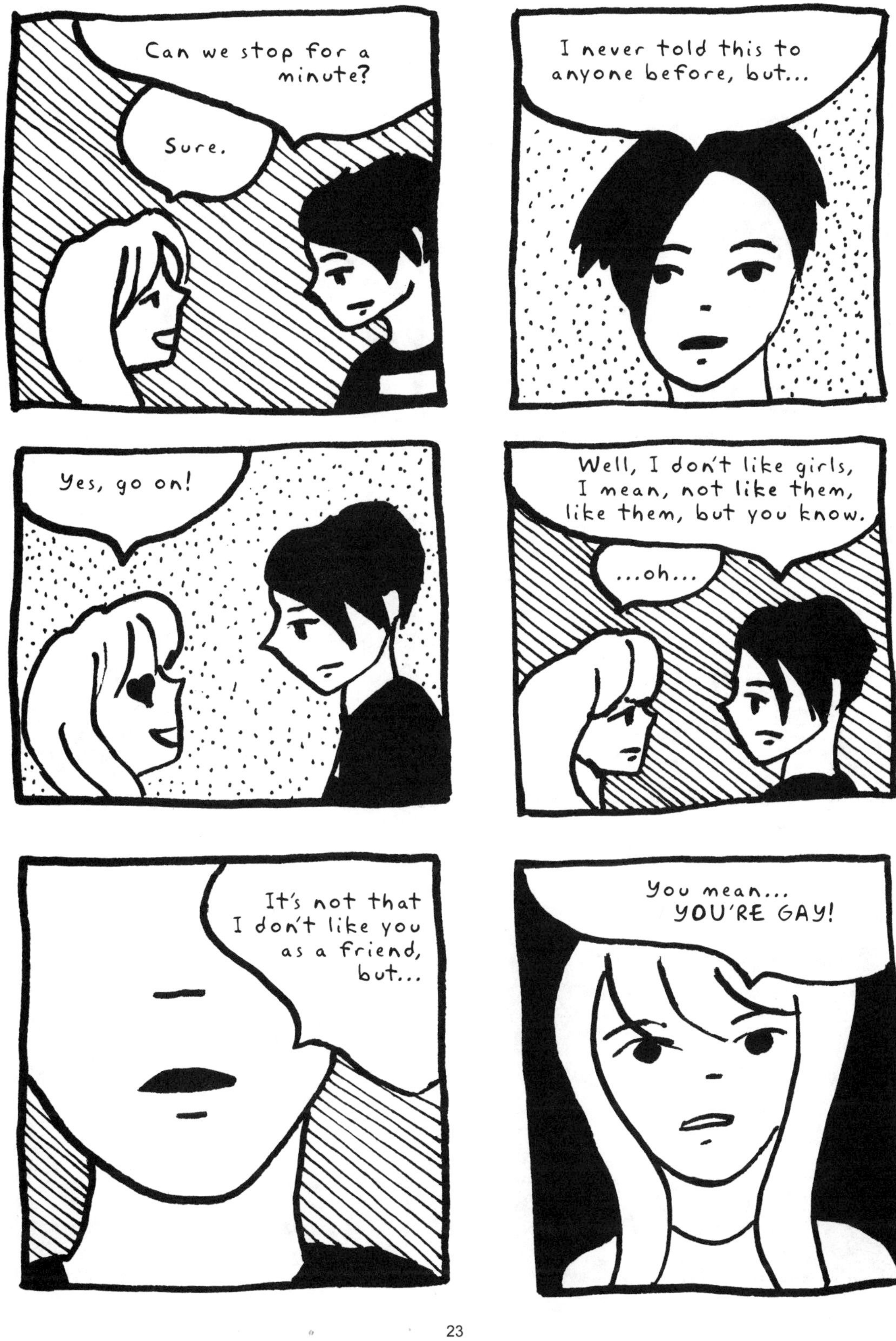

Can we stop for a minute?
Sure.
I never told this to anyone before, but...
Yes, go on!
Well, I don't like girls, I mean, not like them, like them, but you know.
...oh...
It's not that I don't like you as a friend, but...
You mean... YOU'RE GAY!

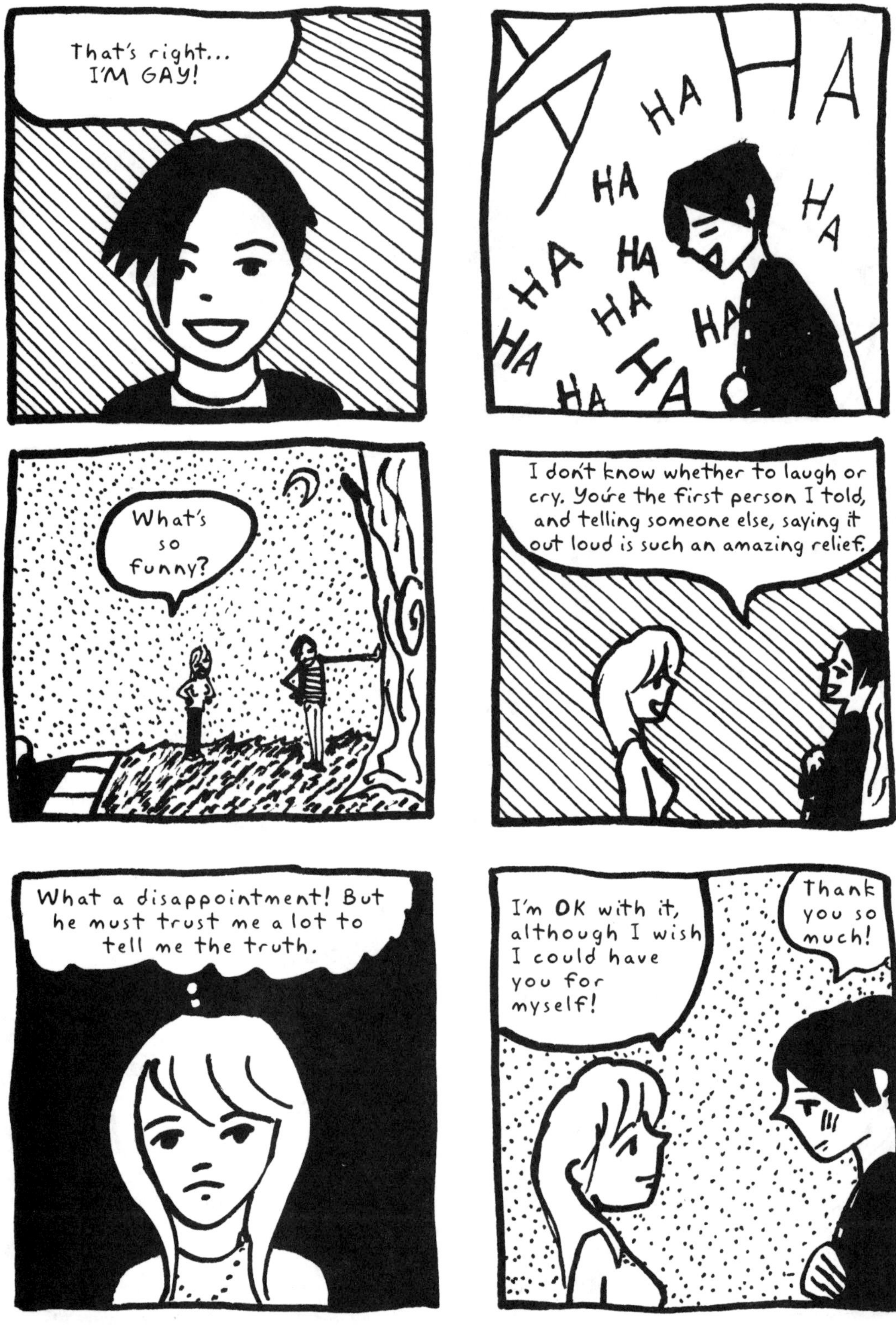
That's right... I'M GAY!
HA HA HA HA HA HA HA HA HA HA HA HA HA
What's so funny?
I don't know whether to laugh or cry. You're the first person I told, and telling someone else, saying it out loud is such an amazing relief.
What a disappointment! But he must trust me a lot to tell me the truth.
I'm OK with it, although I wish I could have you for myself!
Thank you so much!

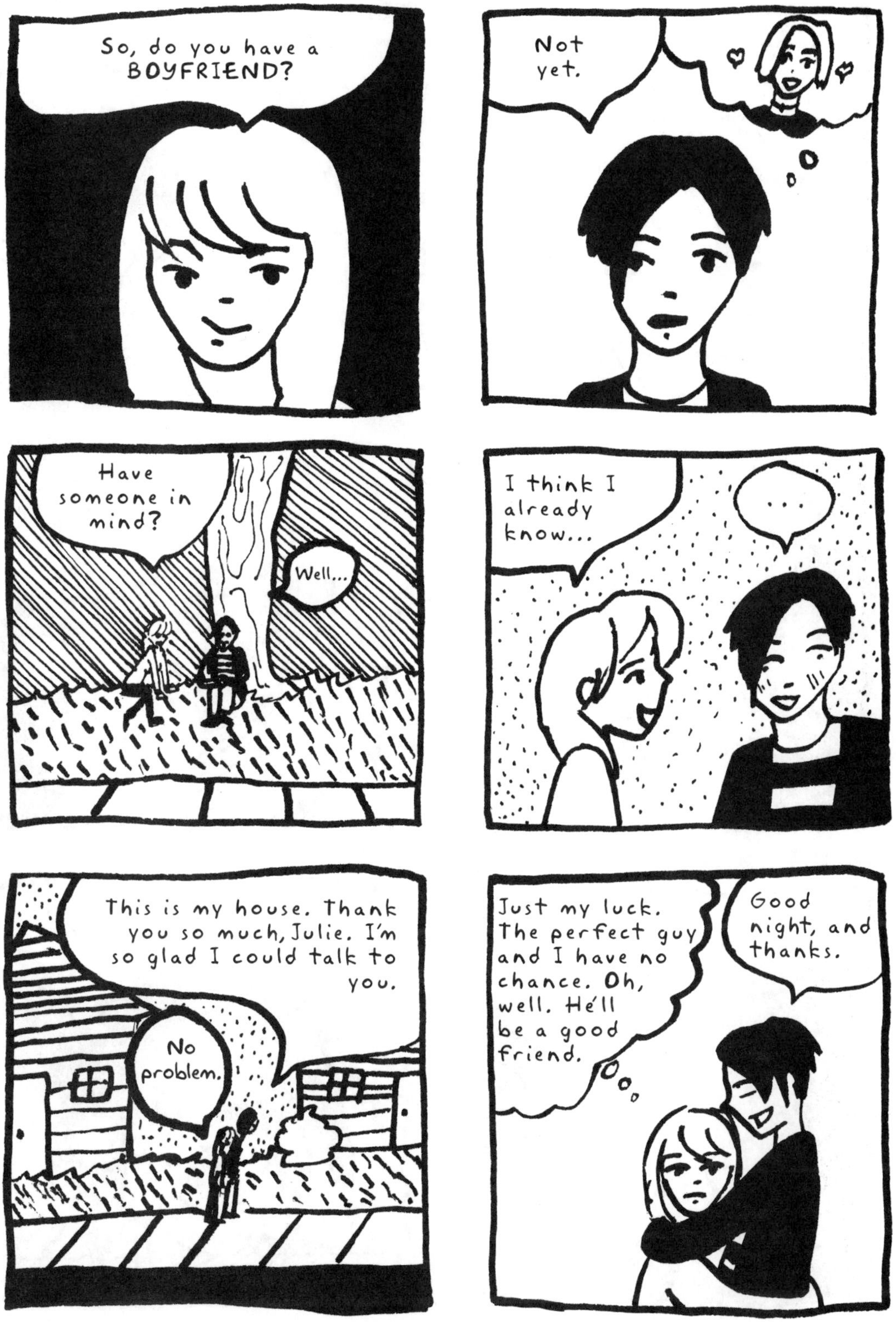
So, do you have a BOYFRIEND?
Not yet.
Have someone in mind?
Well...
I think I already know...
...
This is my house. Thank you so much, Julie. I'm so glad I could talk to you.
No problem.
Just my luck. The perfect guy and I have no chance. Oh, well. He'll be a good friend.
Good night, and thanks.

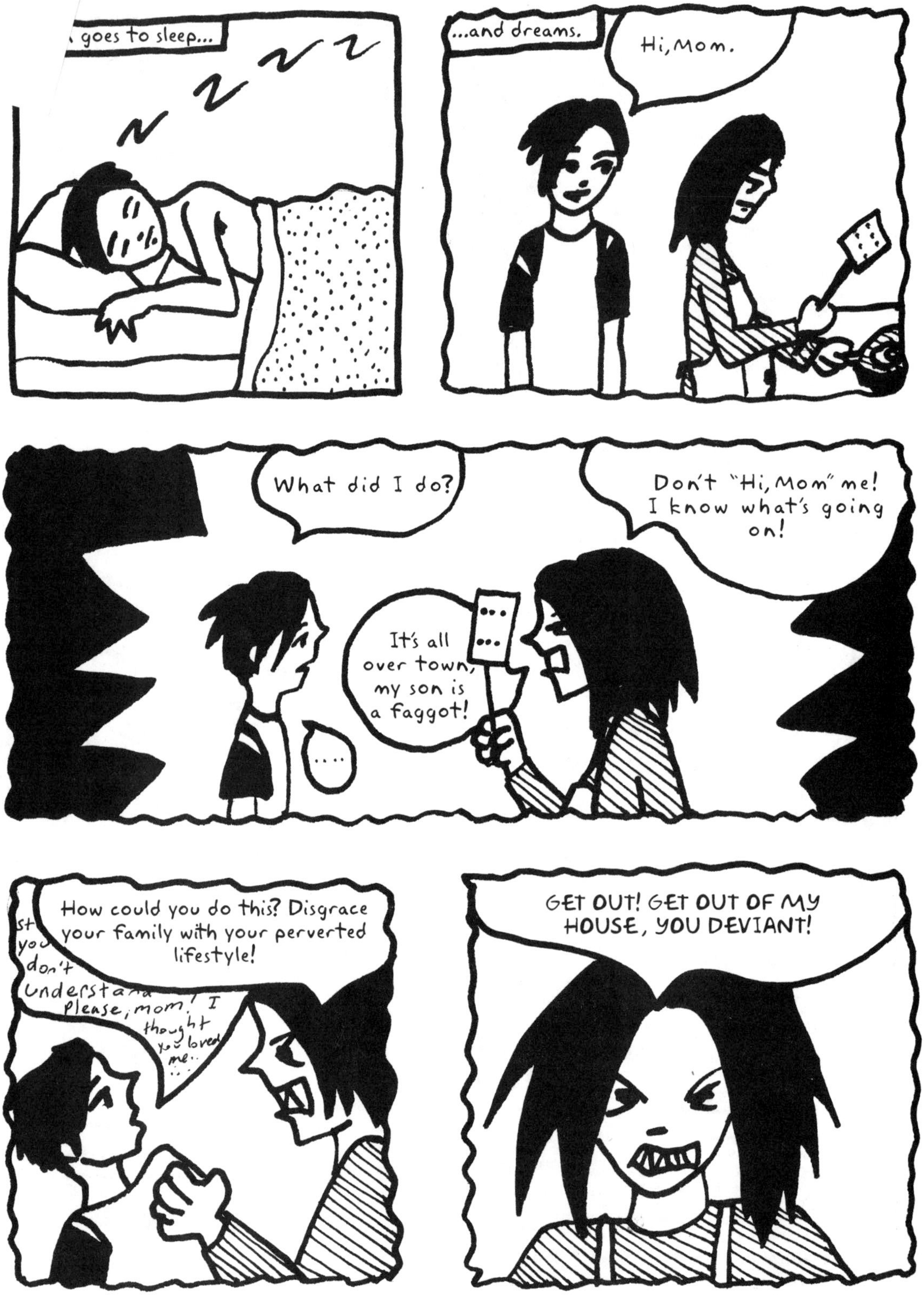

goes to sleep...
ZZZZZ
...and dreams.
Hi, Mom.
What did I do?
Don't "Hi, Mom" me! I know what's going on!
It's all over town, my son is a faggot!
....
How could you do this? Disgrace your family with your perverted lifestyle!
st you don't understa
Please, mom! I thought you loved me...
GET OUT! GET OUT OF MY HOUSE, YOU DEVIANT!

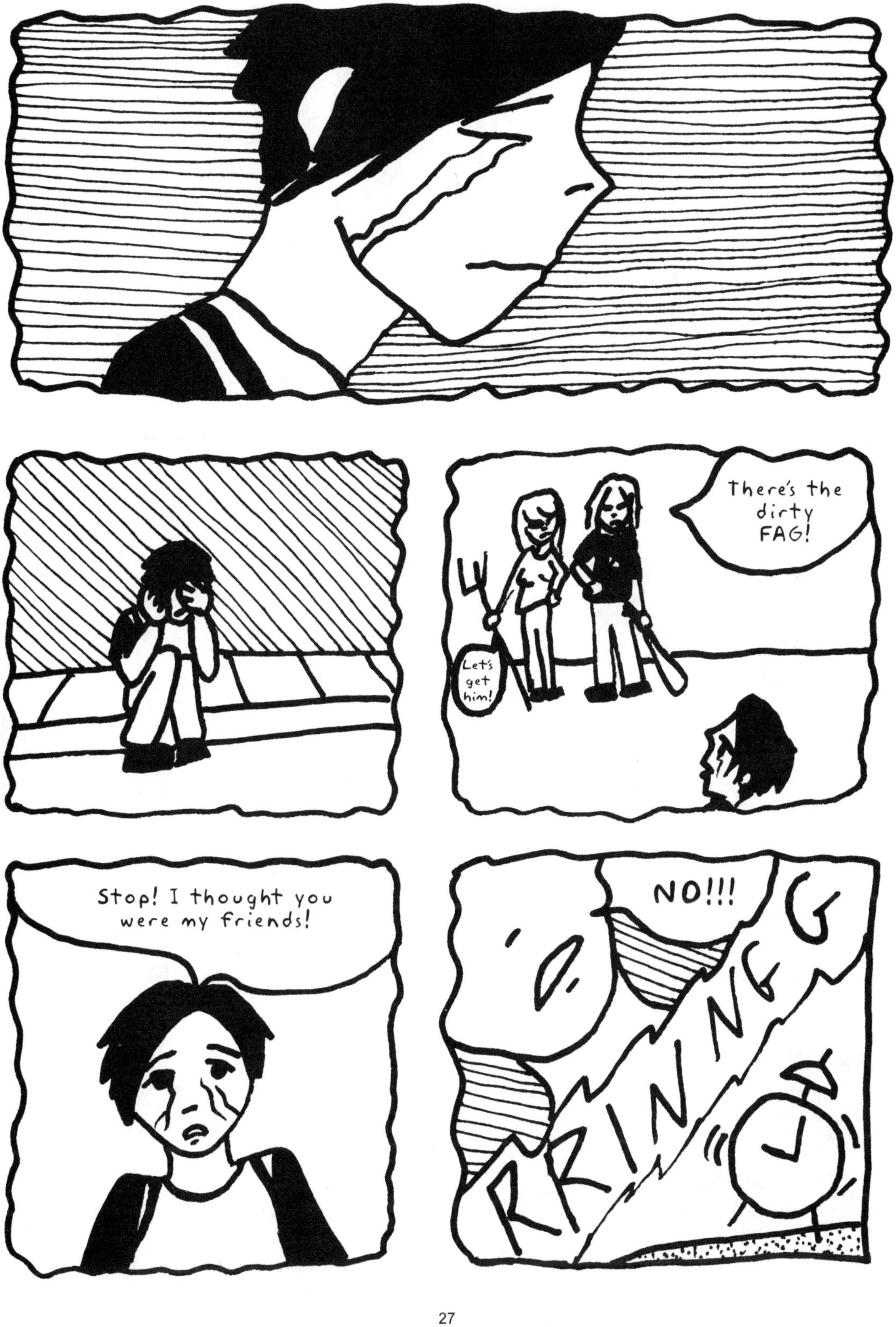
There's the dirty FAG!
Let's get him!
Stop! I thought you were my friends!
NO!!!
RRINNGG

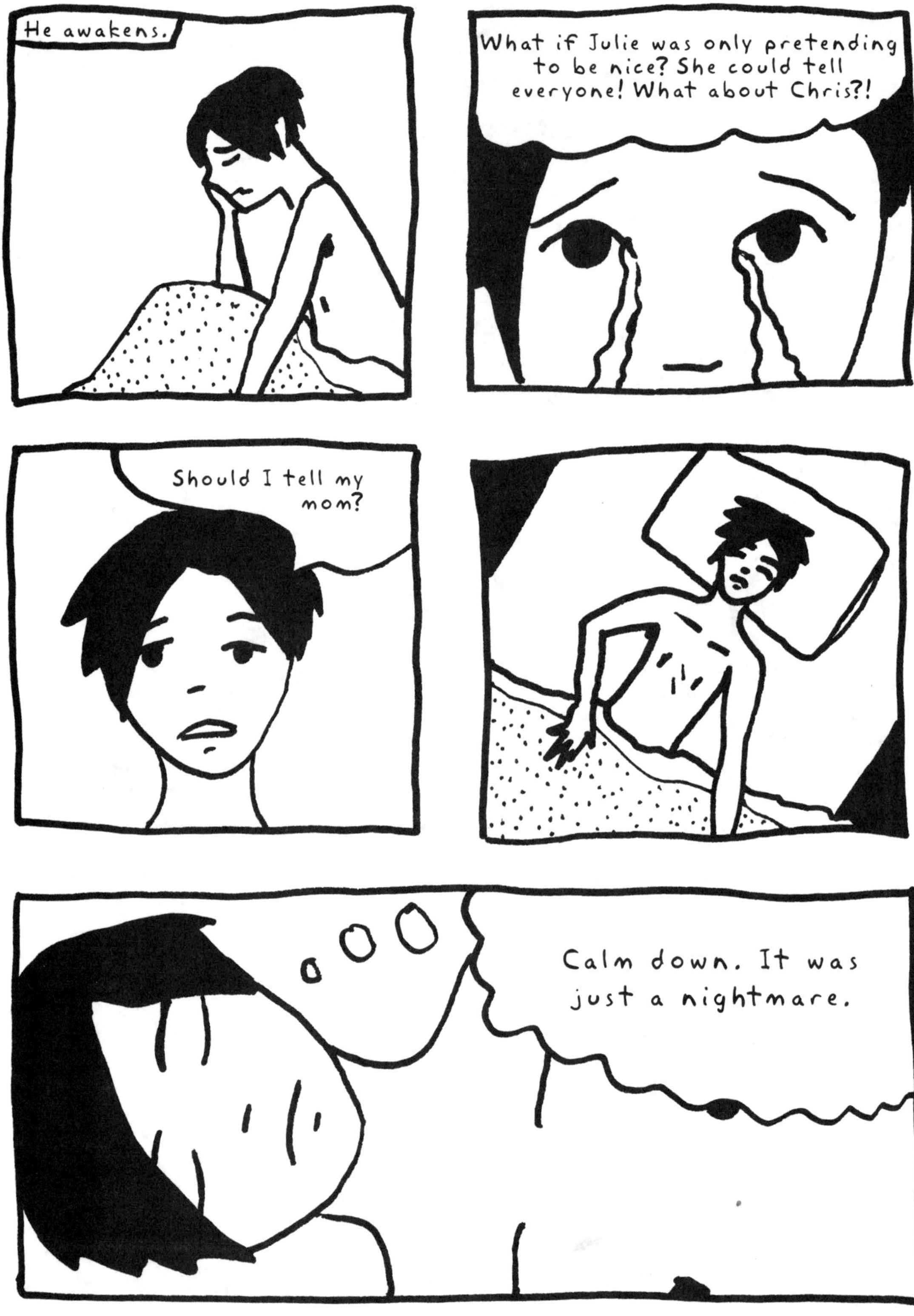
He awakens.
What if Julie was only pretending to be nice? She could tell everyone! What about Chris?!
Should I tell my mom?
Calm down. It was just a nightmare.

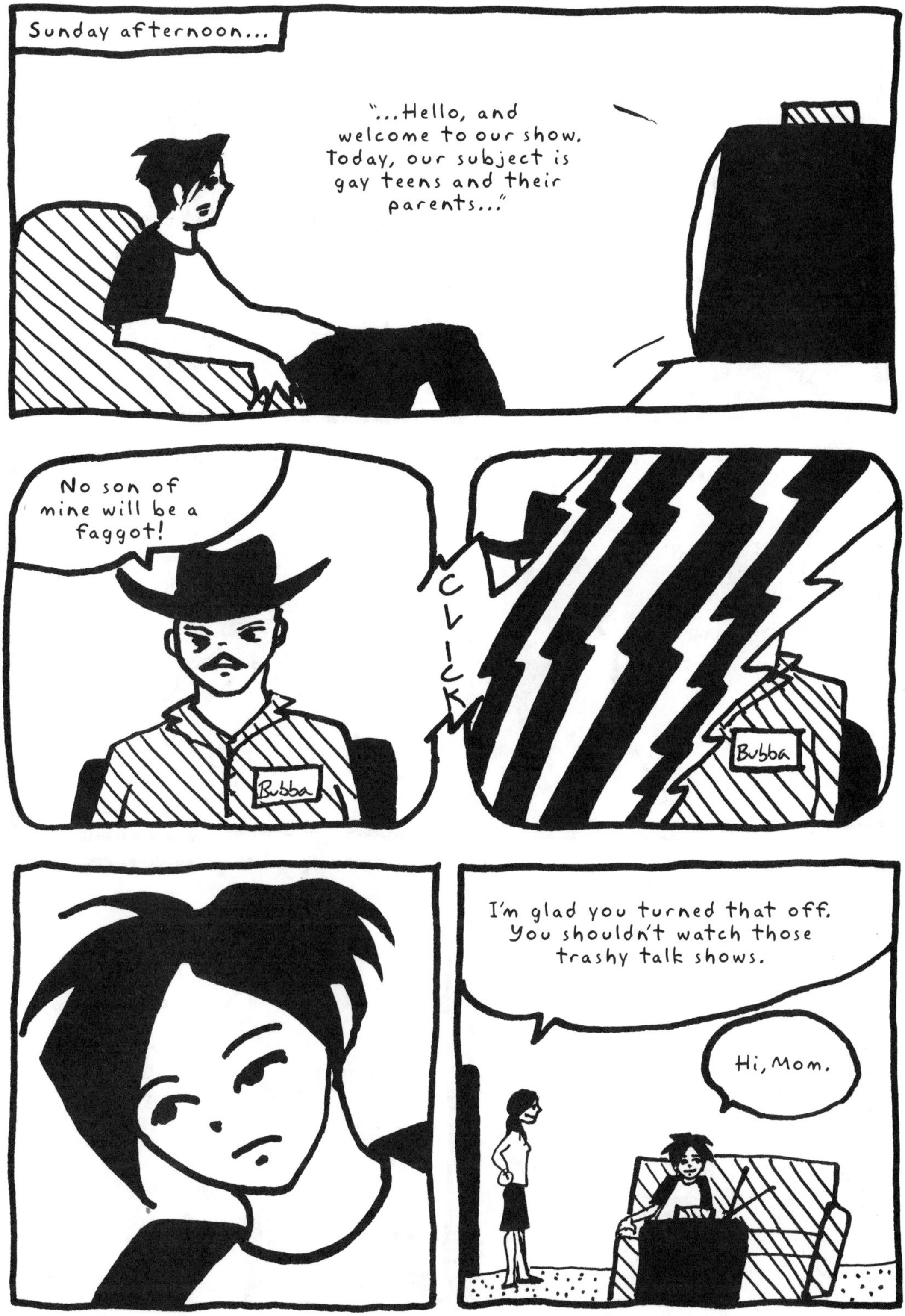
Sunday afternoon...
"...Hello, and welcome to our show. Today, our subject is gay teens and their parents..."
No son of mine will be a faggot!
Bubba
CLICK
Bubba
I'm glad you turned that off. You shouldn't watch those trashy talk shows.
Hi, Mom.

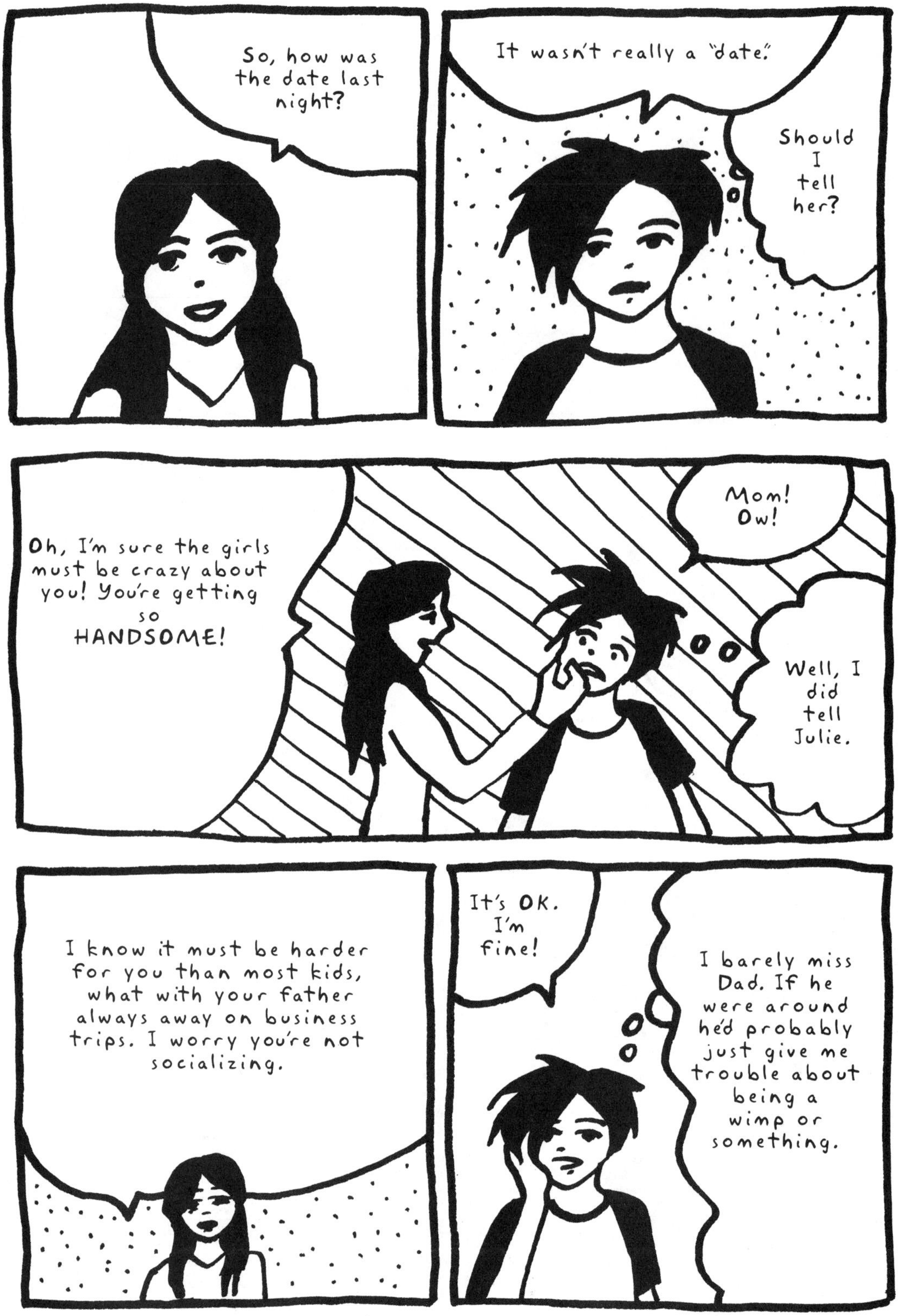
So, how was the date last night?
It wasn't really a "date."
Should I tell her?
Oh, I'm sure the girls must be crazy about you! You're getting so HANDSOME!
Mom! Ow!
Well, I did tell Julie.
I know it must be harder for you than most kids, what with your father always away on business trips. I worry you're not socializing.
It's OK. I'm fine!
I barely miss Dad. If he were around he'd probably just give me trouble about being a wimp or something.

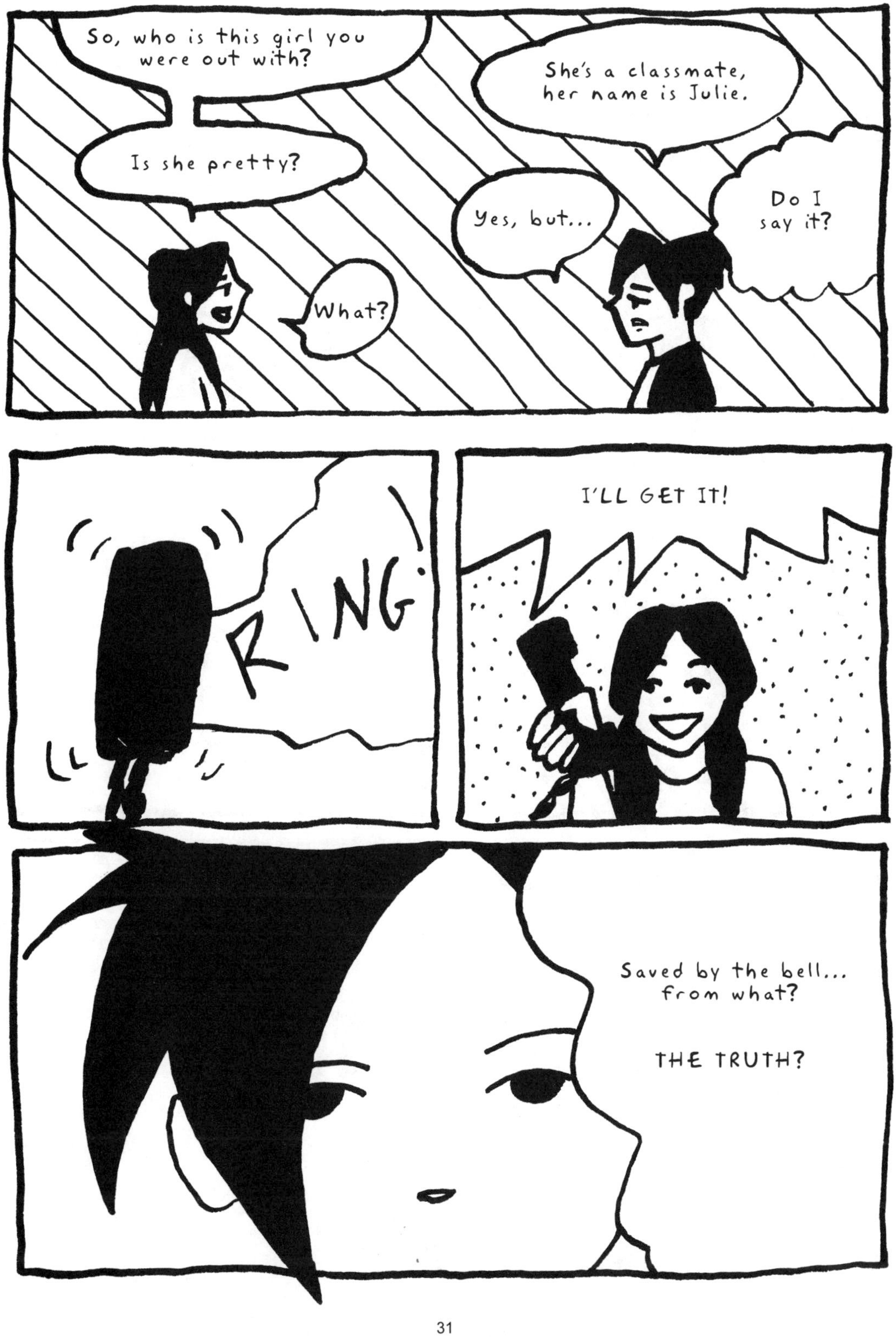
So, who is this girl you were out with?
Is she pretty?
She's a classmate, her name is Julie.
What?
Yes, but...
Do I say it?
RING!
I'LL GET IT!
Saved by the bell... from what?
THE TRUTH?

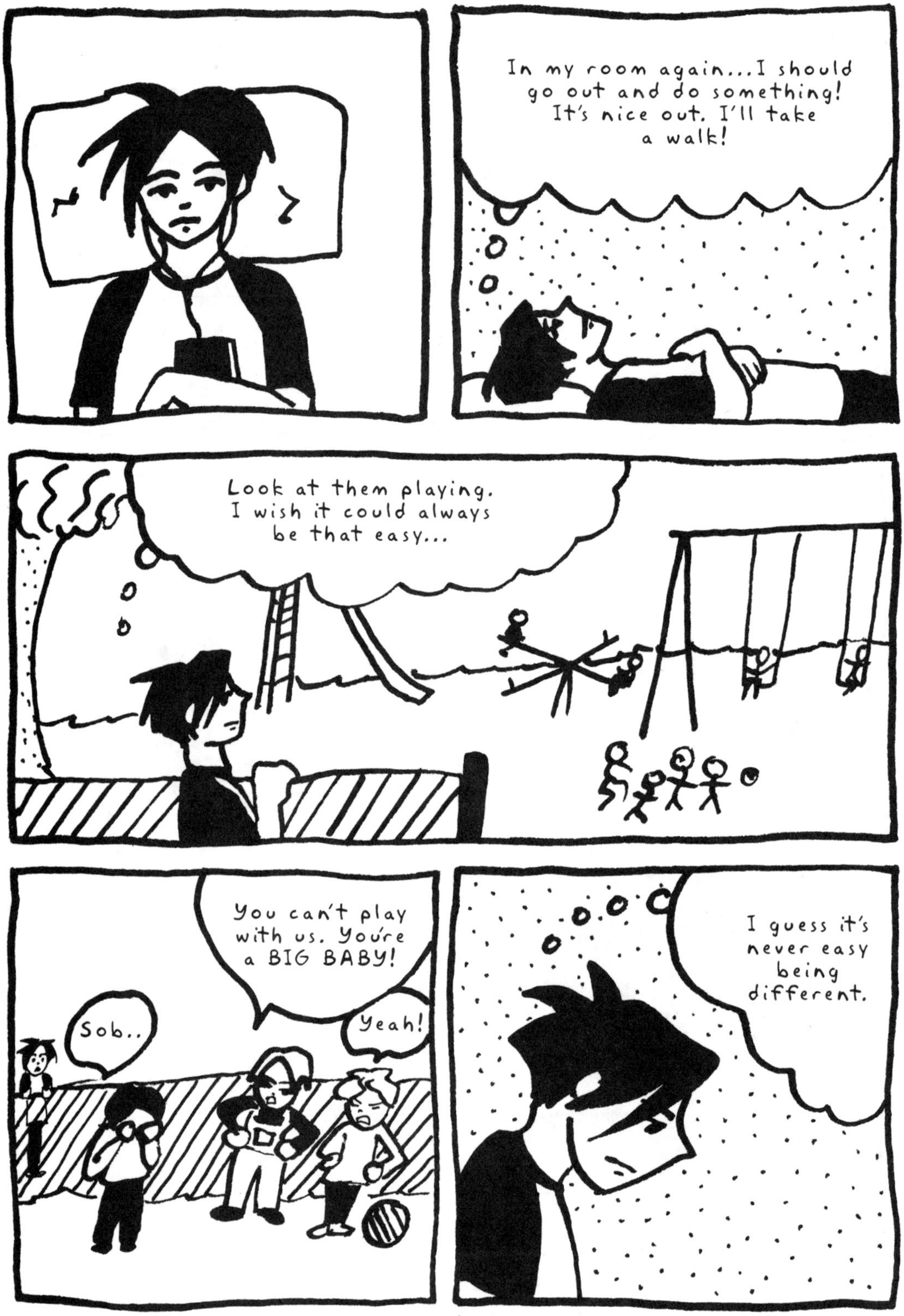
In my room again...I should go out and do something! It's nice out. I'll take a walk!
Look at them playing. I wish it could always be that easy...
You can't play with us. You're a BIG BABY!
Sob..
Yeah!
I guess it's never easy being different.

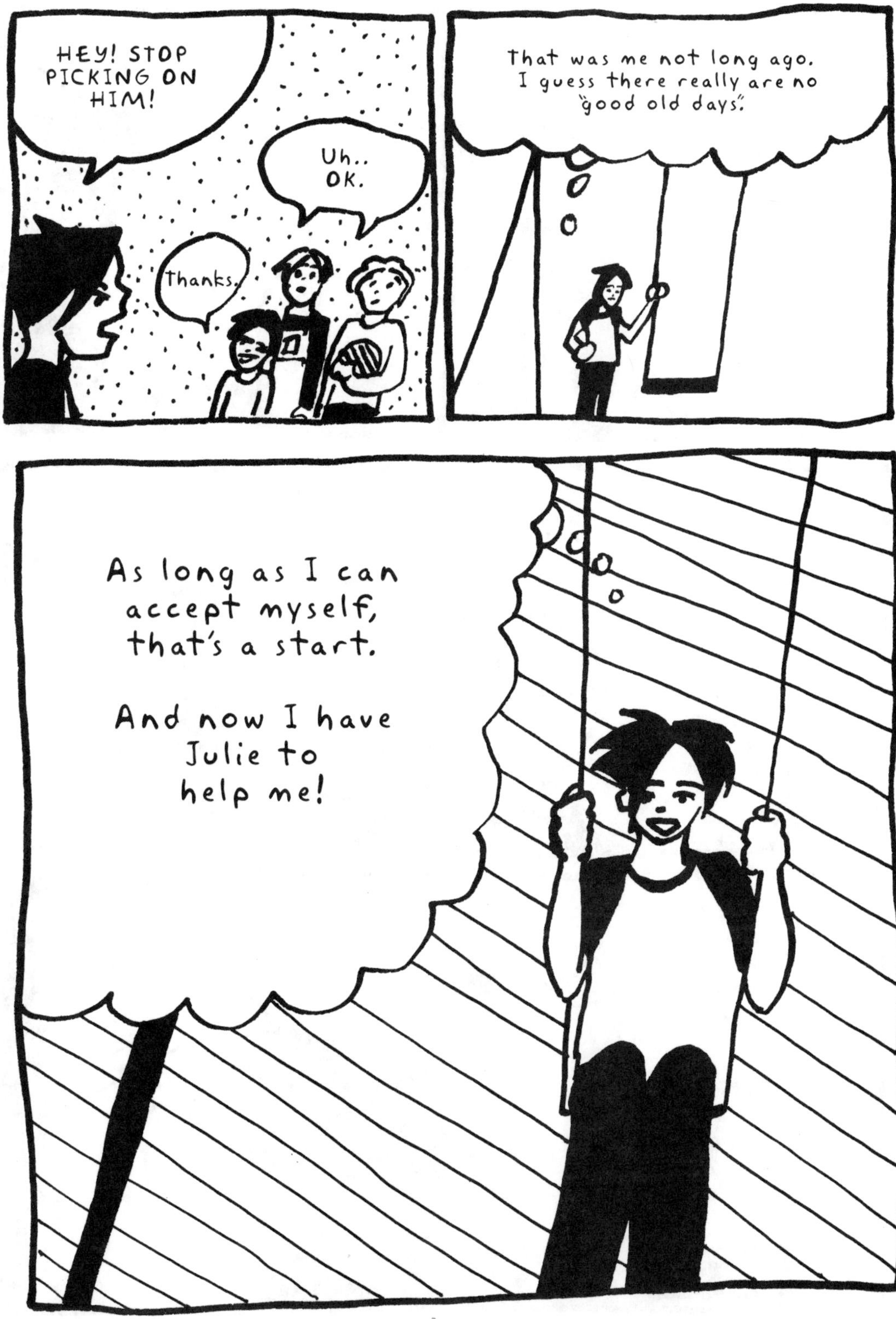
HEY! STOP PICKING ON HIM!
Uh.. OK.
Thanks.
That was me not long ago. I guess there really are no "good old days."
As long as I can accept myself, that's a start.
And now I have Julie to help me!

At school on Monday...
Hey, Julie!
Hey, Brian! How's it going?
Oh, fine. Thanks for being so understanding Saturday night...
It's no trouble! So what are you doing after school?
Martial Arts Club.
Say "Hi" to Chris for me, OK?
-wink!
Julie...
After class...
I'm early again... don't want to seem anxious...
Oh, well. Here goes...

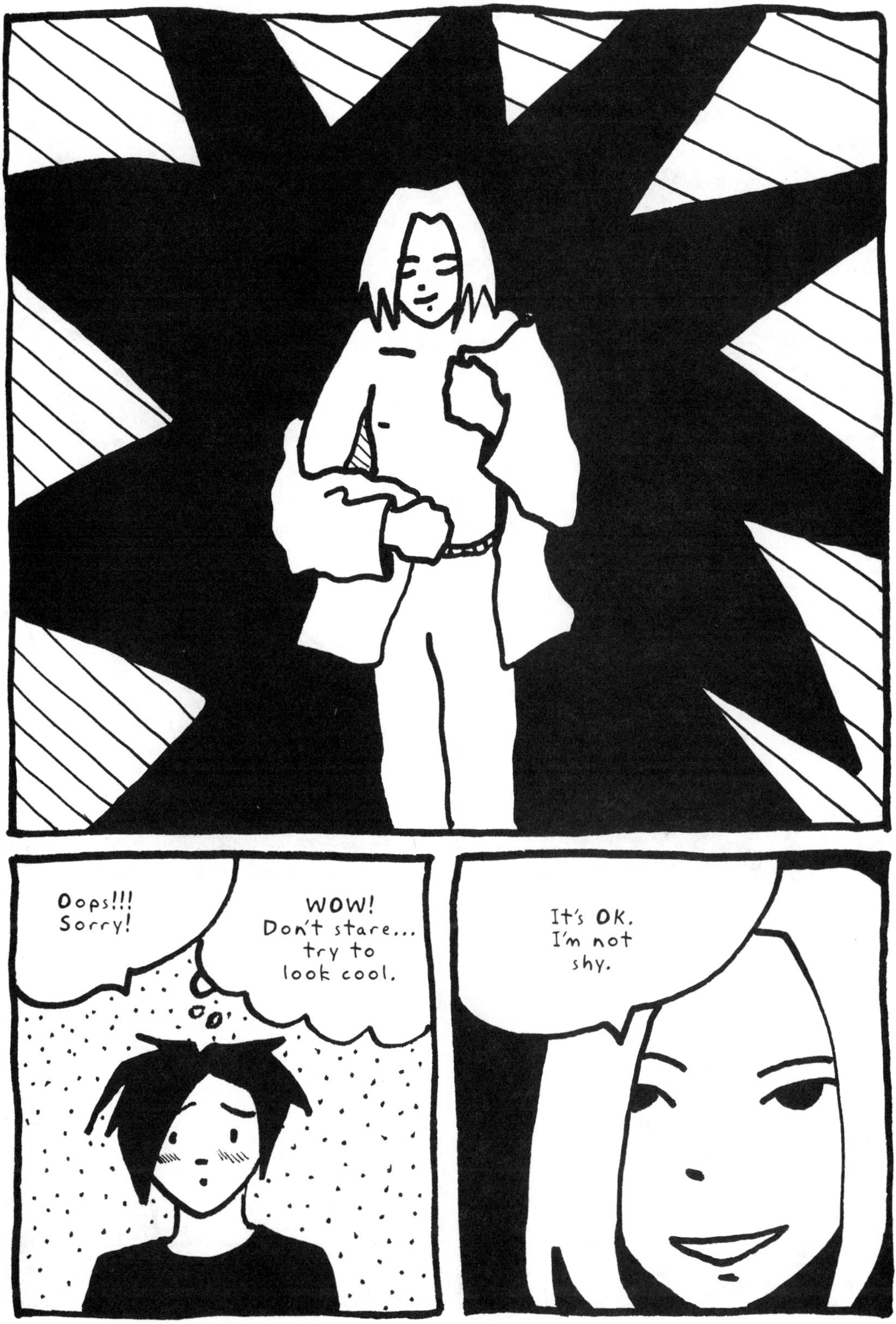
Oops!!! Sorry!
WOW! Don't stare... try to look cool.
It's OK. I'm not shy.

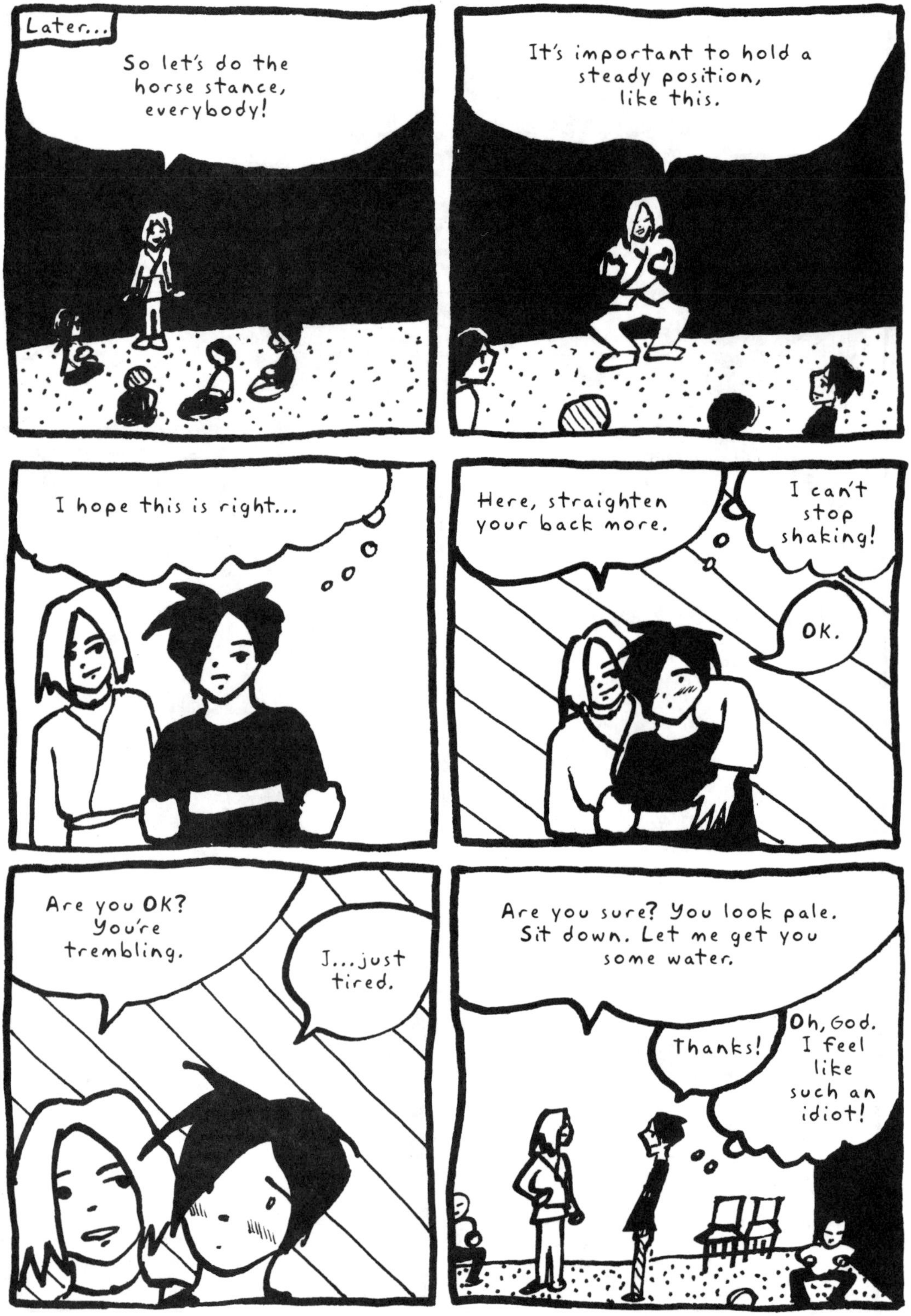
Later...
So let's do the horse stance, everybody!
It's important to hold a steady position, like this.
I hope this is right...
Here, straighten your back more.
I can't stop shaking!
OK.
Are you OK? You're trembling.
I...just tired.
Are you sure? You look pale. Sit down. Let me get you some water.
Thanks!
Oh, God. I feel like such an idiot!

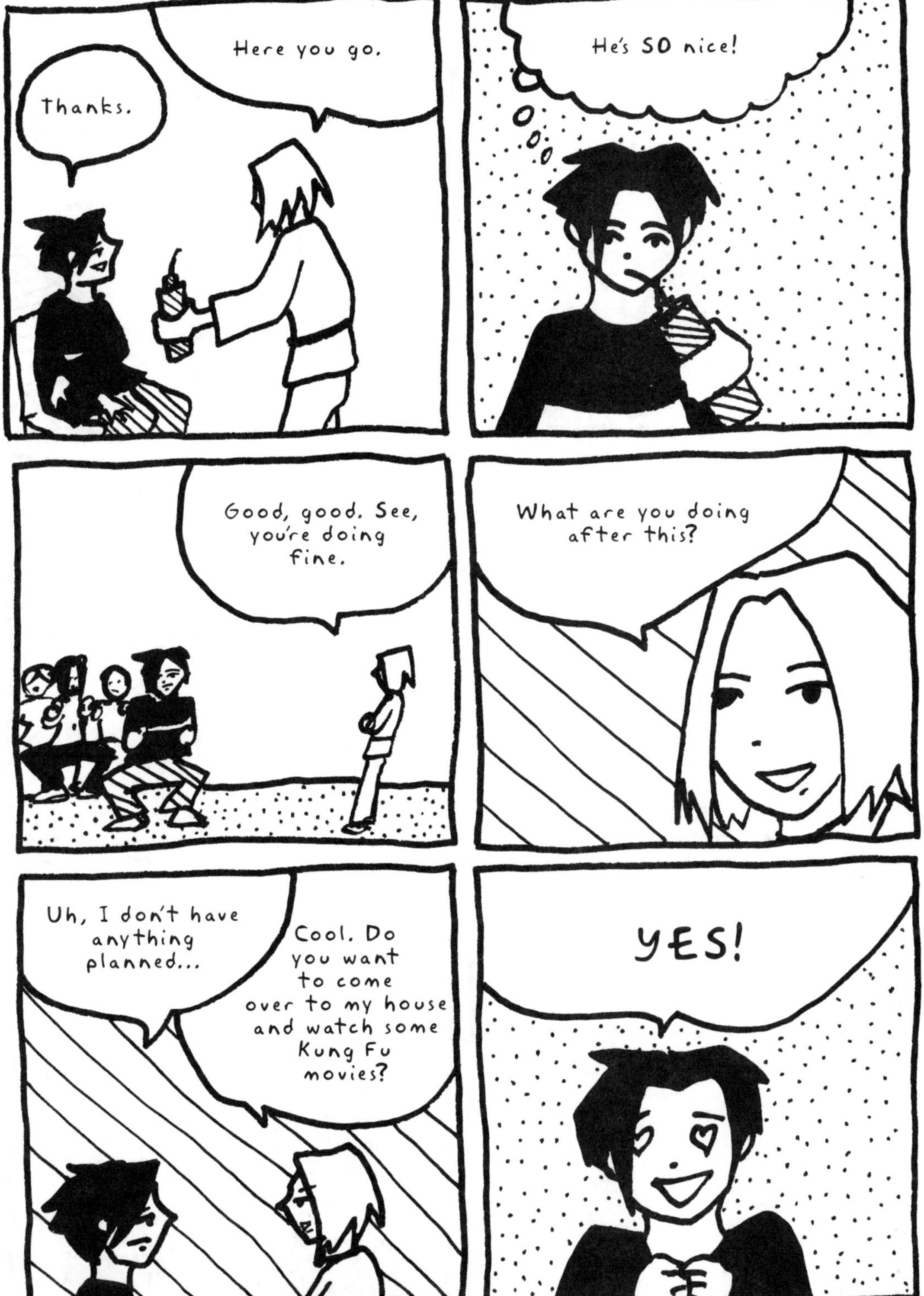
Here you go.
Thanks.
He's SO nice!
Good, good. See, you're doing fine.
What are you doing after this?
Uh, I don't have anything planned...
Cool. Do you want to come over to my house and watch some Kung Fu movies?
YES!

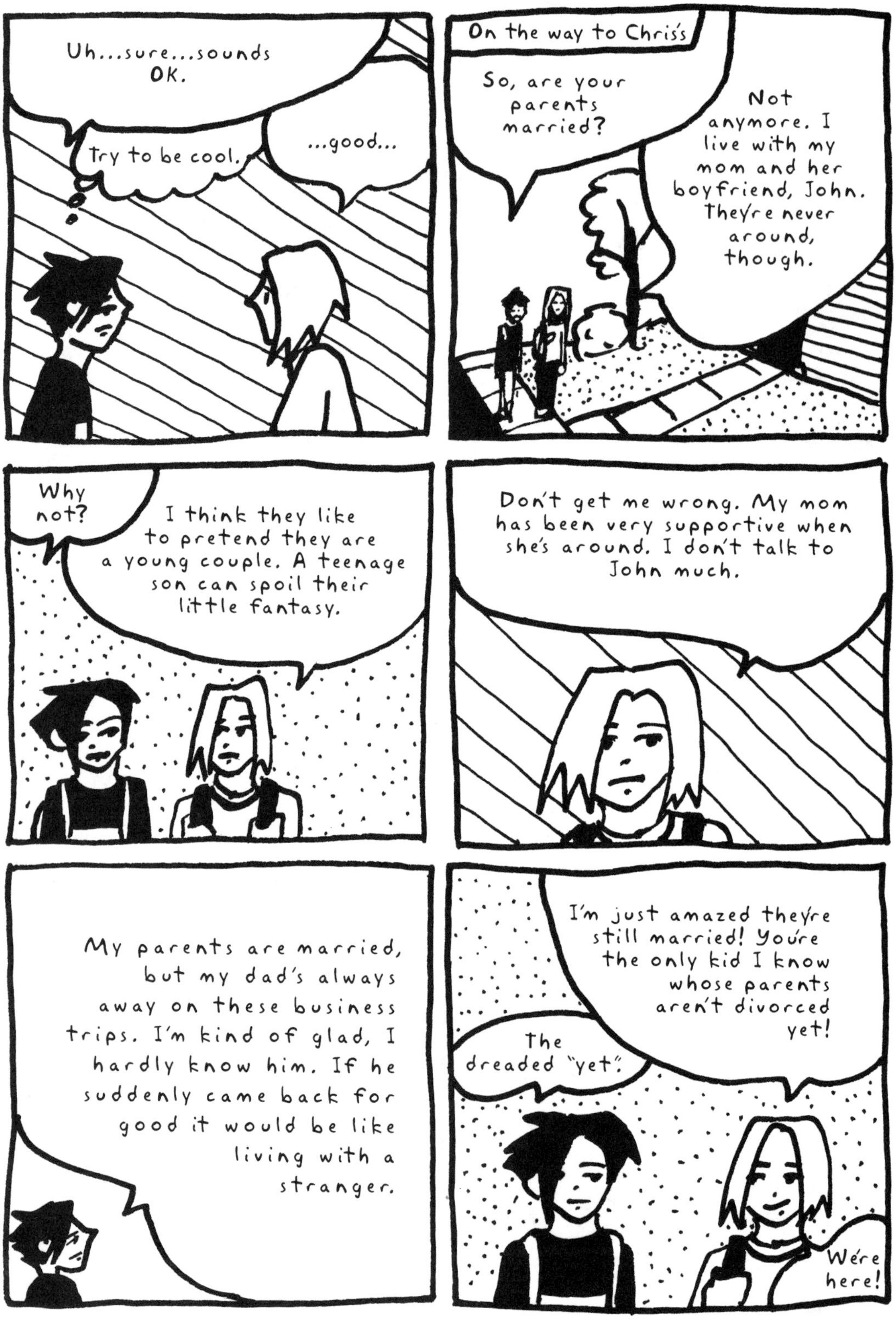
Uh...sure...sounds OK.
Try to be cool.
...good...
On the way to Chris's
So, are your parents married?
Not anymore. I live with my mom and her boyfriend, John. They're never around, though.
Why not?
I think they like to pretend they are a young couple. A teenage son can spoil their little fantasy.
Don't get me wrong. My mom has been very supportive when she's around. I don't talk to John much.
My parents are married, but my dad's always away on these business trips. I'm kind of glad, I hardly know him. If he suddenly came back for good it would be like living with a stranger.
I'm just amazed they're still married! You're the only kid I know whose parents aren't divorced yet!
The dreaded "yet".
We're here!

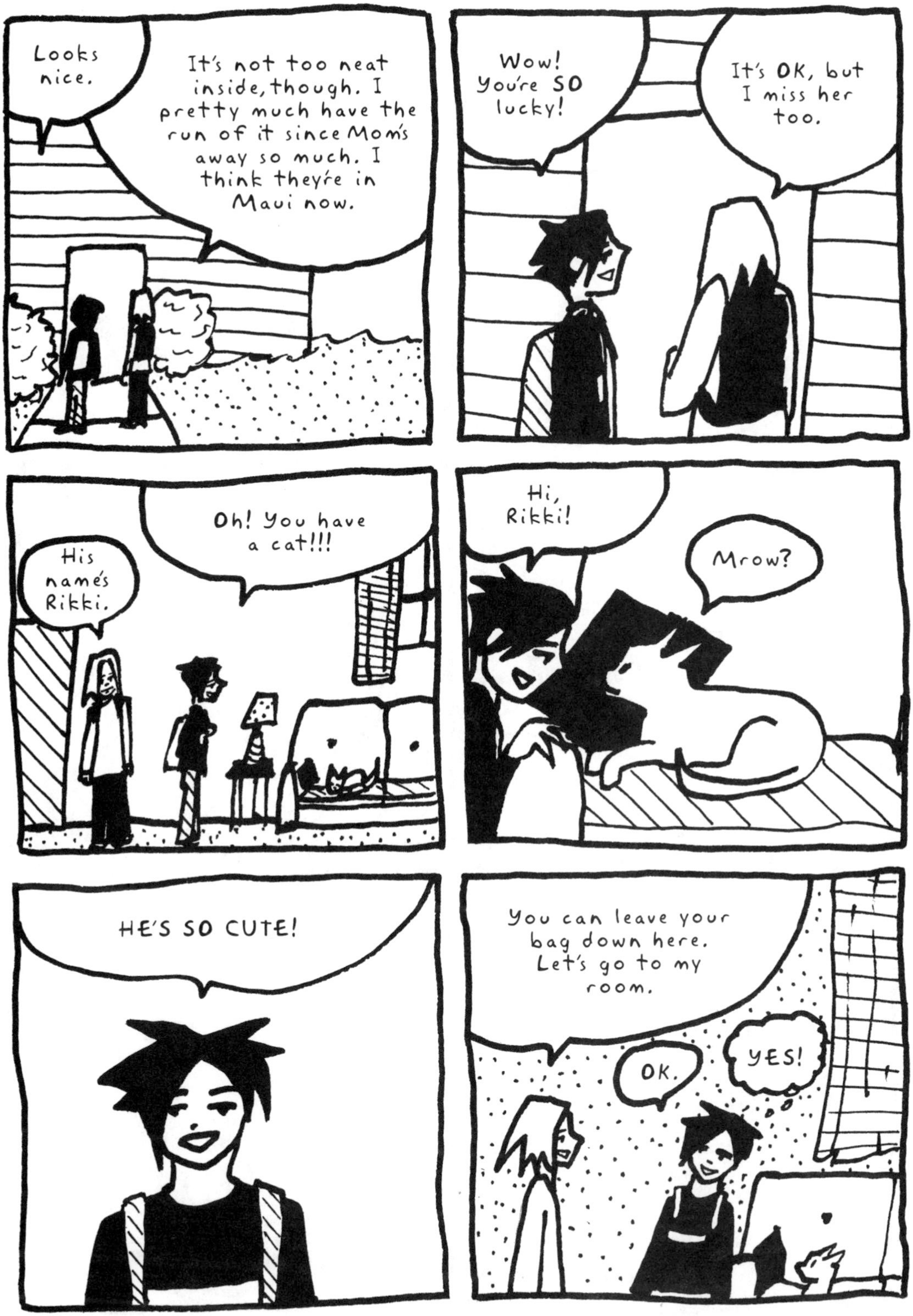
Looks nice.
It's not too neat inside, though. I pretty much have the run of it since Mom's away so much. I think they're in Maui now.
Wow! You're SO lucky!
It's OK, but I miss her too.
Oh! You have a cat!!!
His name's Rikki.
Hi, Rikki!
Mrow?
HE'S SO CUTE!
You can leave your bag down here. Let's go to my room.
OK.
YES!

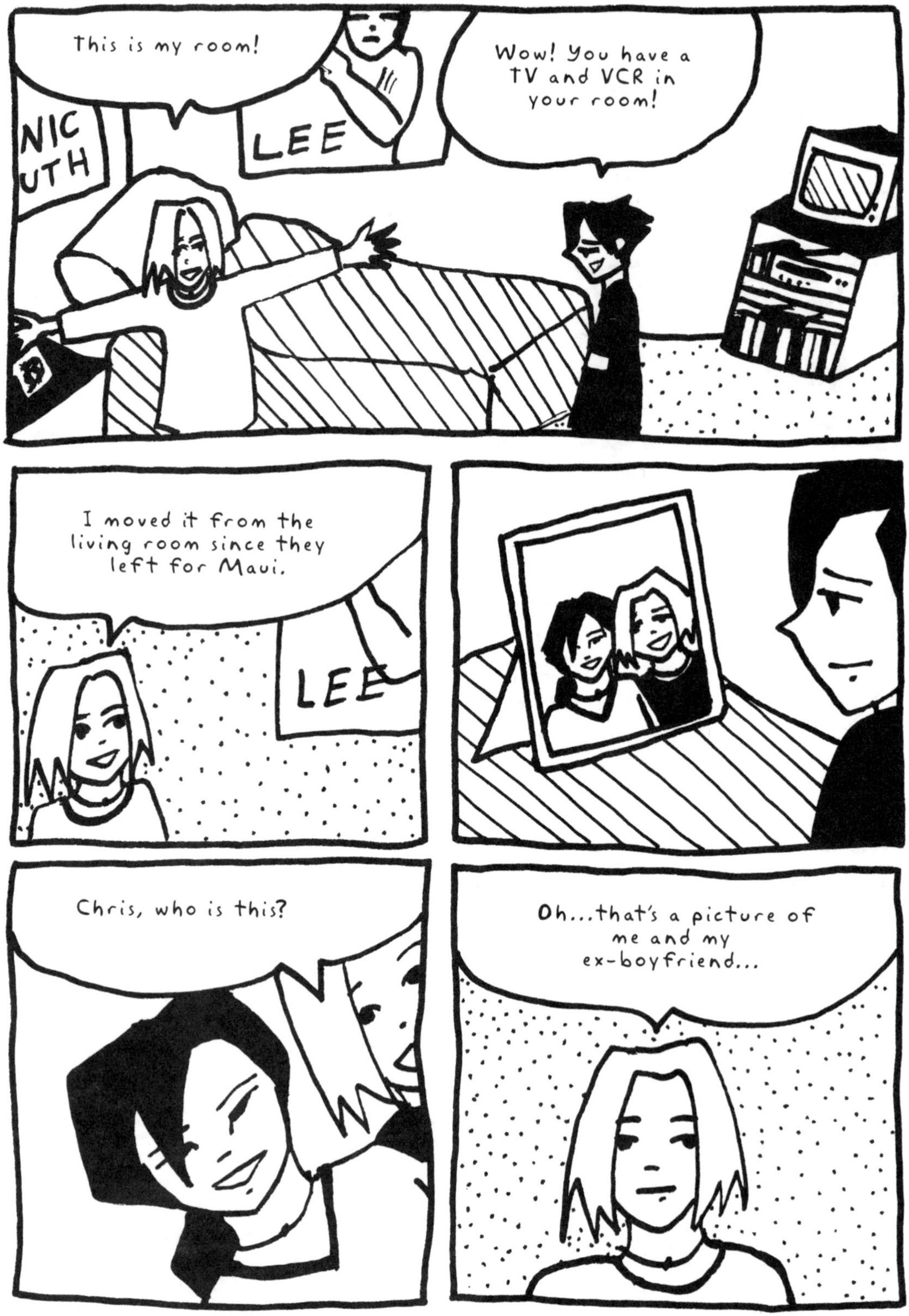
This is my room!
NIC
UTH
LEE
Wow! You have a TV and VCR in your room!
I moved it from the living room since they left for Maui.
LEE
Chris, who is this?
Oh...that's a picture of me and my ex-boyfriend...

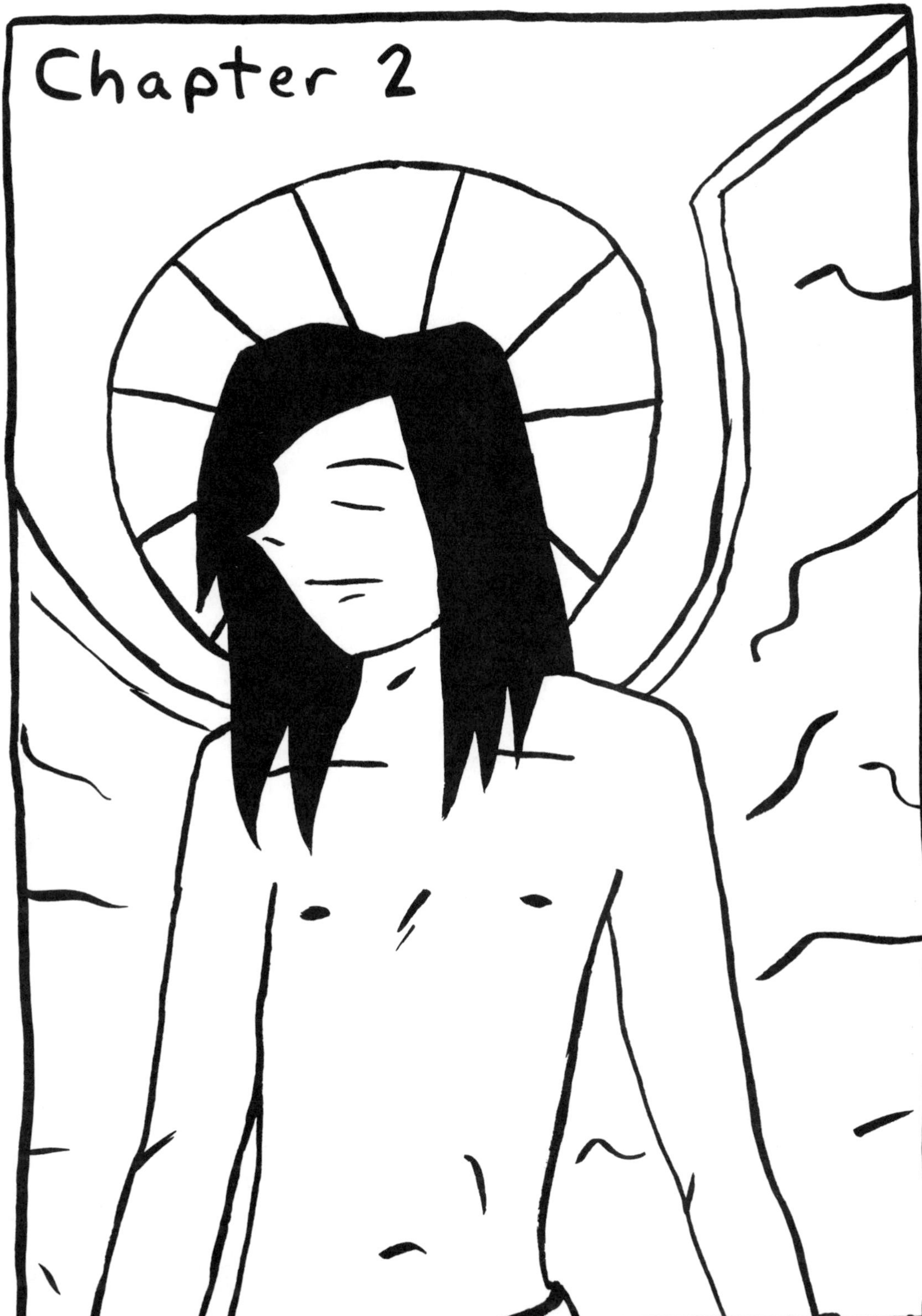
Chapter 2

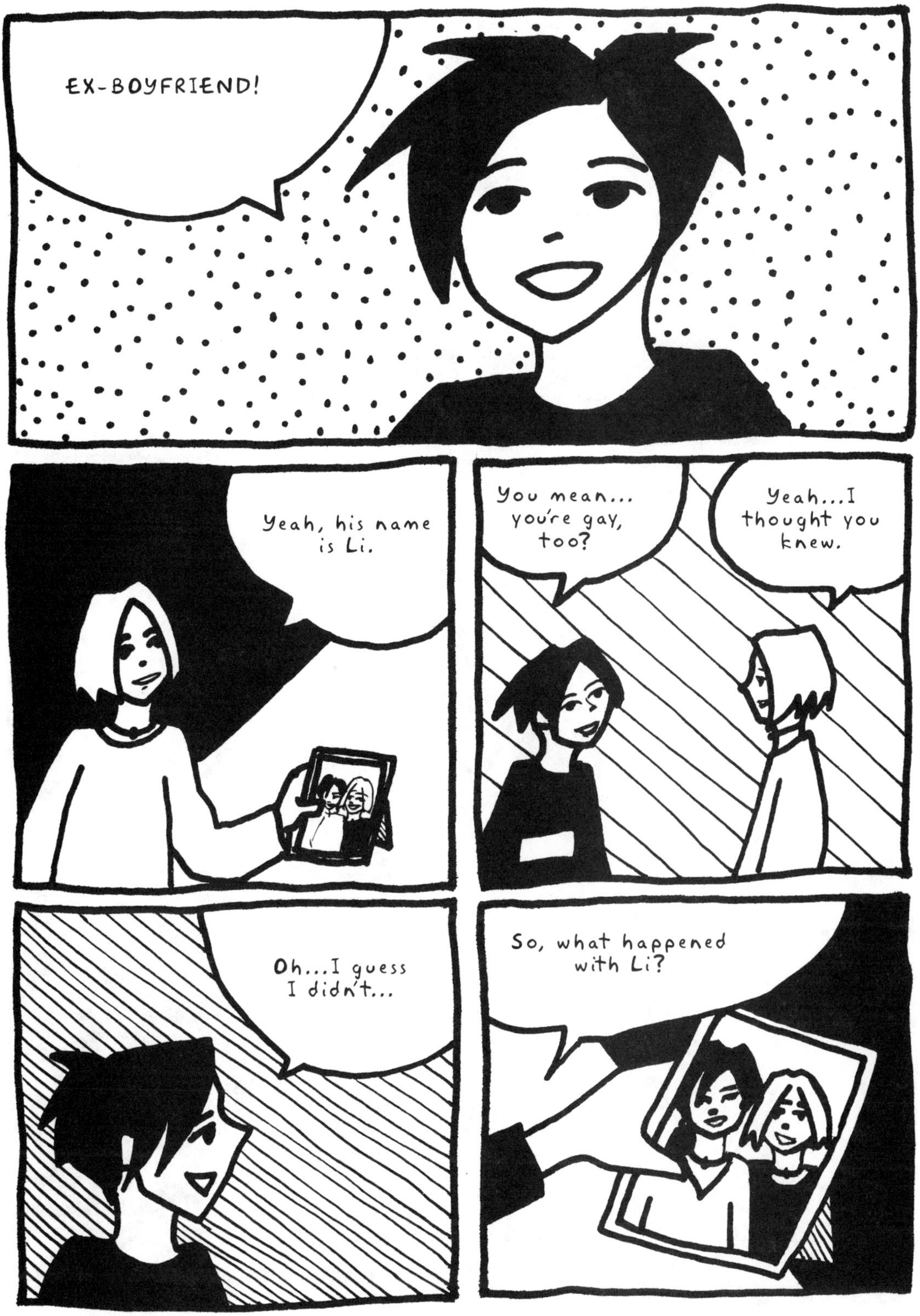
EX-BOYFRIEND!
Yeah, his name is Li.
You mean... you're gay, too?
Yeah...I thought you knew.
Oh...I guess I didn't...
So, what happened with Li?

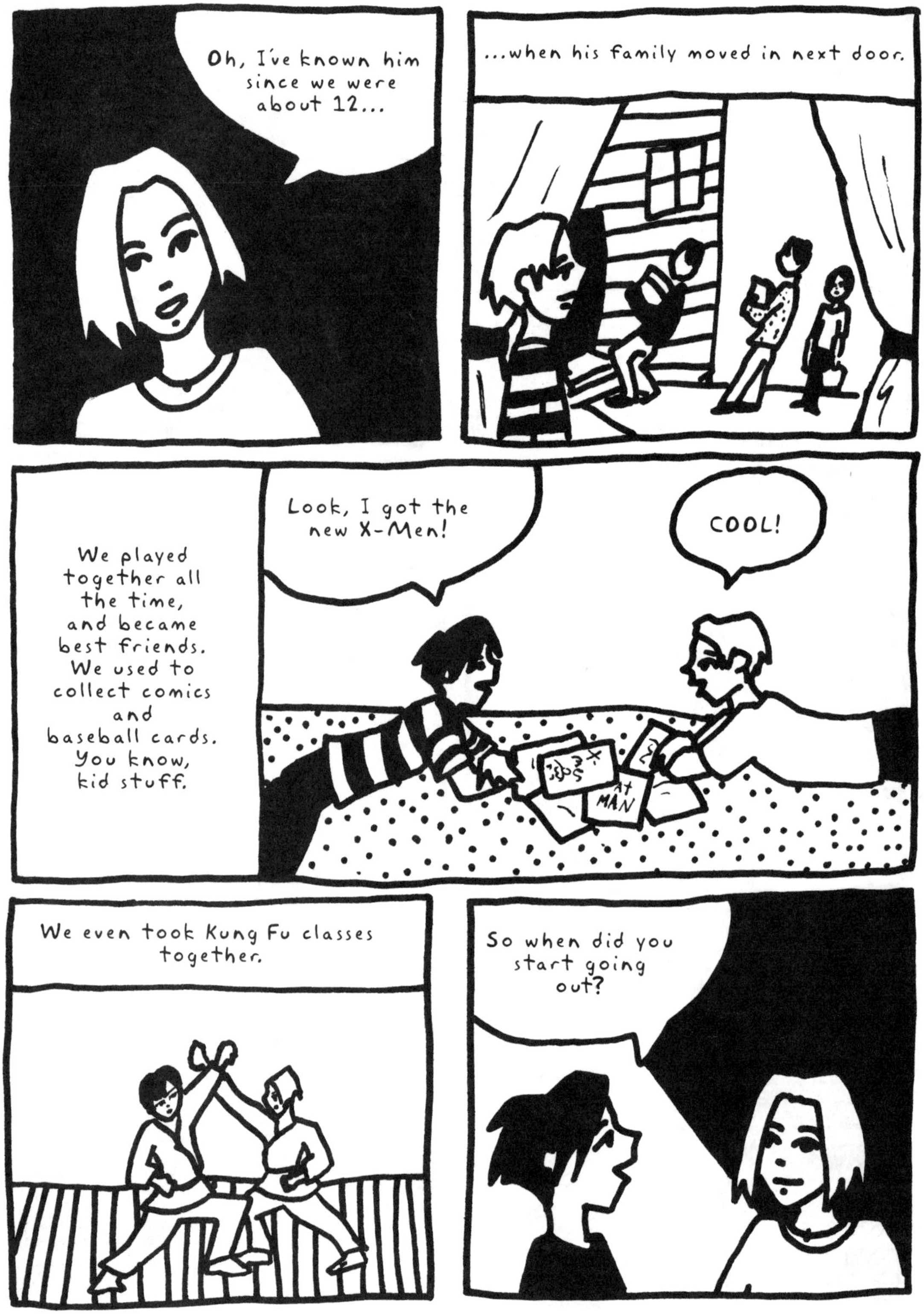
Oh, I've known him since we were about 12...
...when his family moved in next door.
We played together all the time, and became best friends. We used to collect comics and baseball cards. You know, kid stuff.
Look, I got the new X-Men!
COOL!
We even took Kung Fu classes together.
So when did you start going out?

It wasn't until we were 15 that our relationship took a new direction.

Up until then we were just friends and we both were suppressing our deeper feelings for each other.

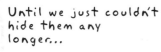

Until we just couldn't hide them any longer...

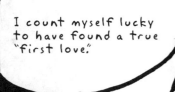

I count myself lucky to have found a true "first love."

But what about your parents? Did they know?

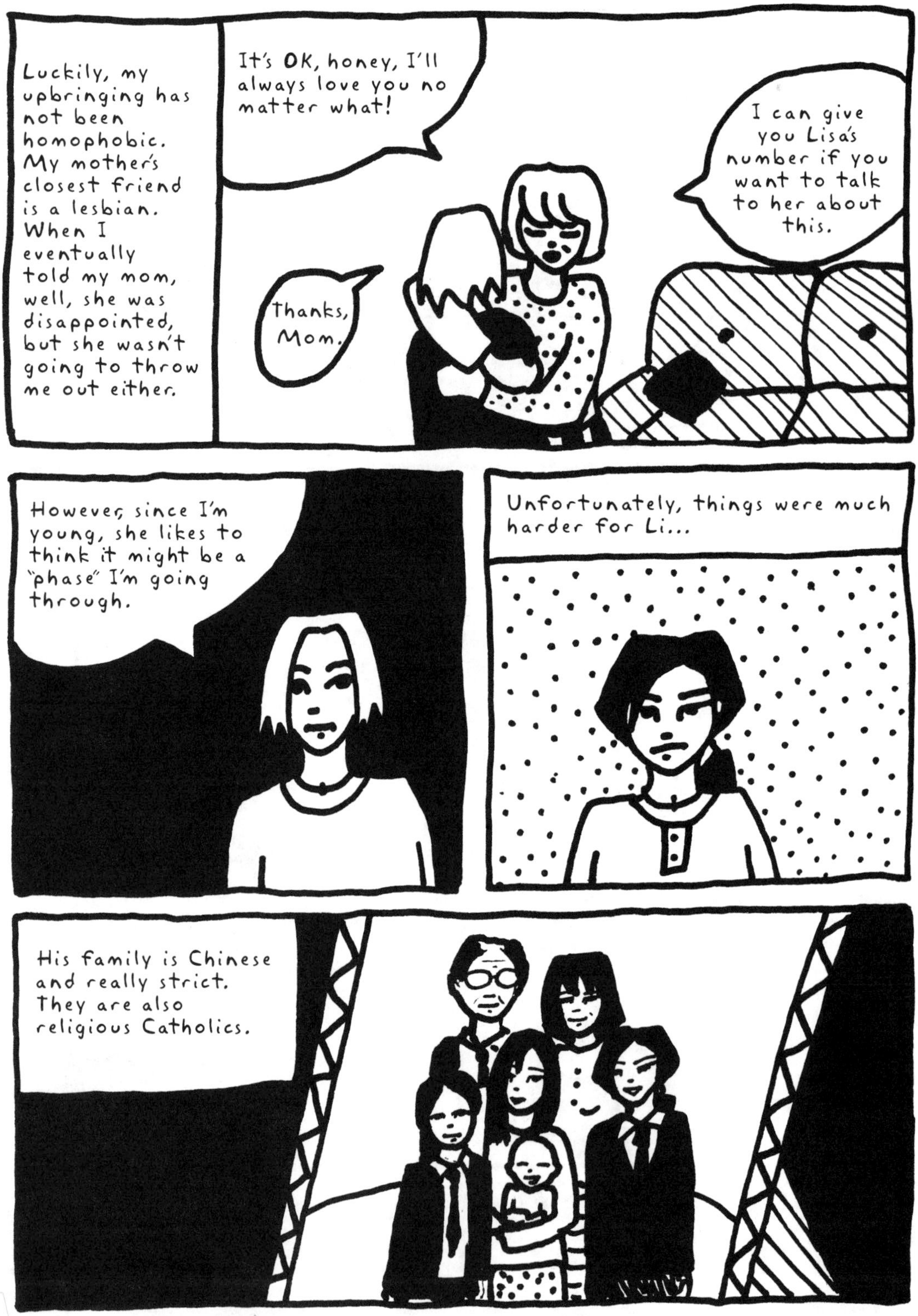
Luckily, my upbringing has not been homophobic. My mother's closest friend is a lesbian. When I eventually told my mom, well, she was disappointed, but she wasn't going to throw me out either.
It's OK, honey, I'll always love you no matter what!
Thanks, Mom.
I can give you Lisa's number if you want to talk to her about this.
However, since I'm young, she likes to think it might be a "phase" I'm going through.
Unfortunately, things were much harder for Li...
His family is Chinese and really strict. They are also religious Catholics.

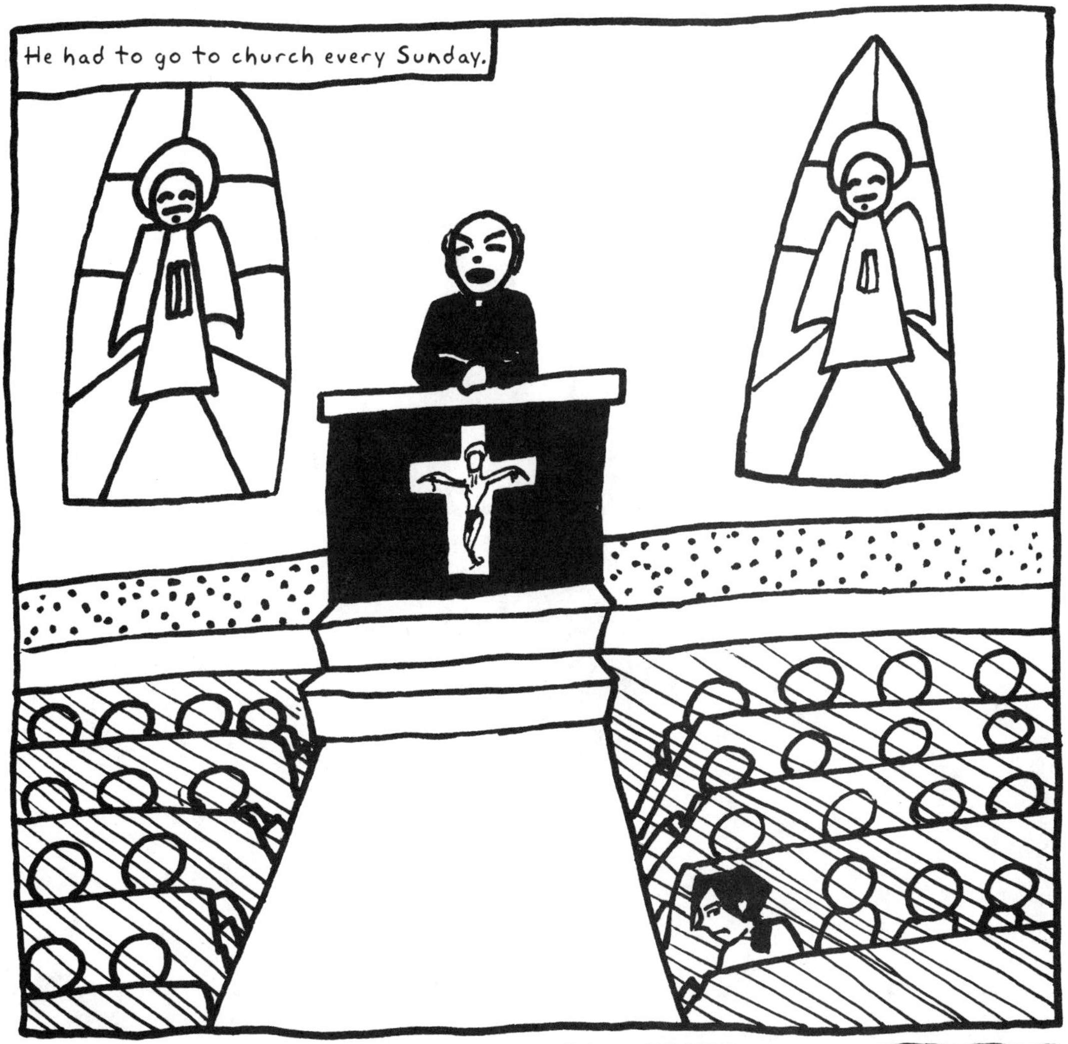
He had to go to church every Sunday.

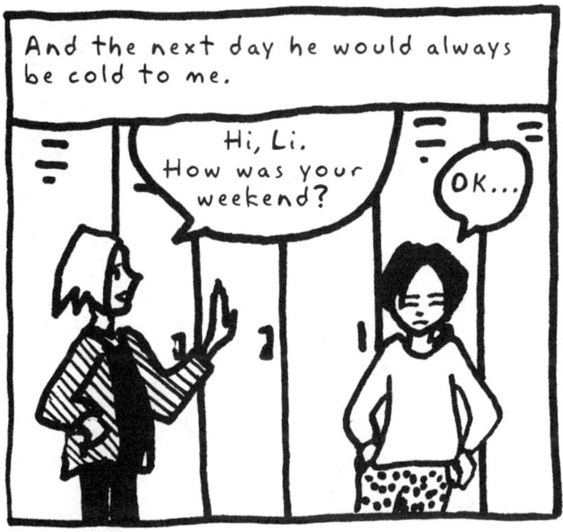
And the next day he would always be cold to me.
Hi, Li.
How was your weekend?
OK...

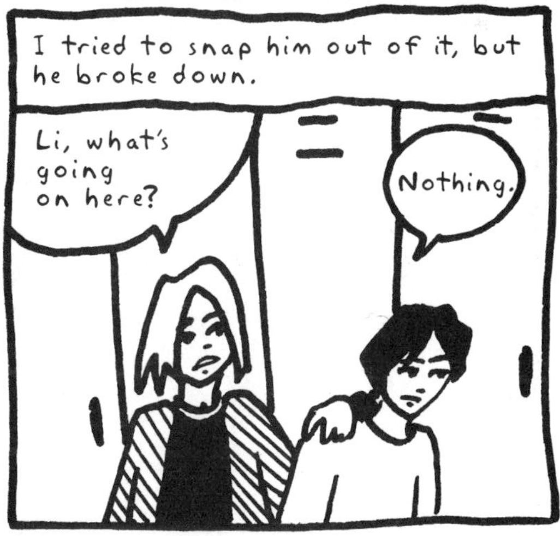
I tried to snap him out of it, but he broke down.
Li, what's going on here?
Nothing.

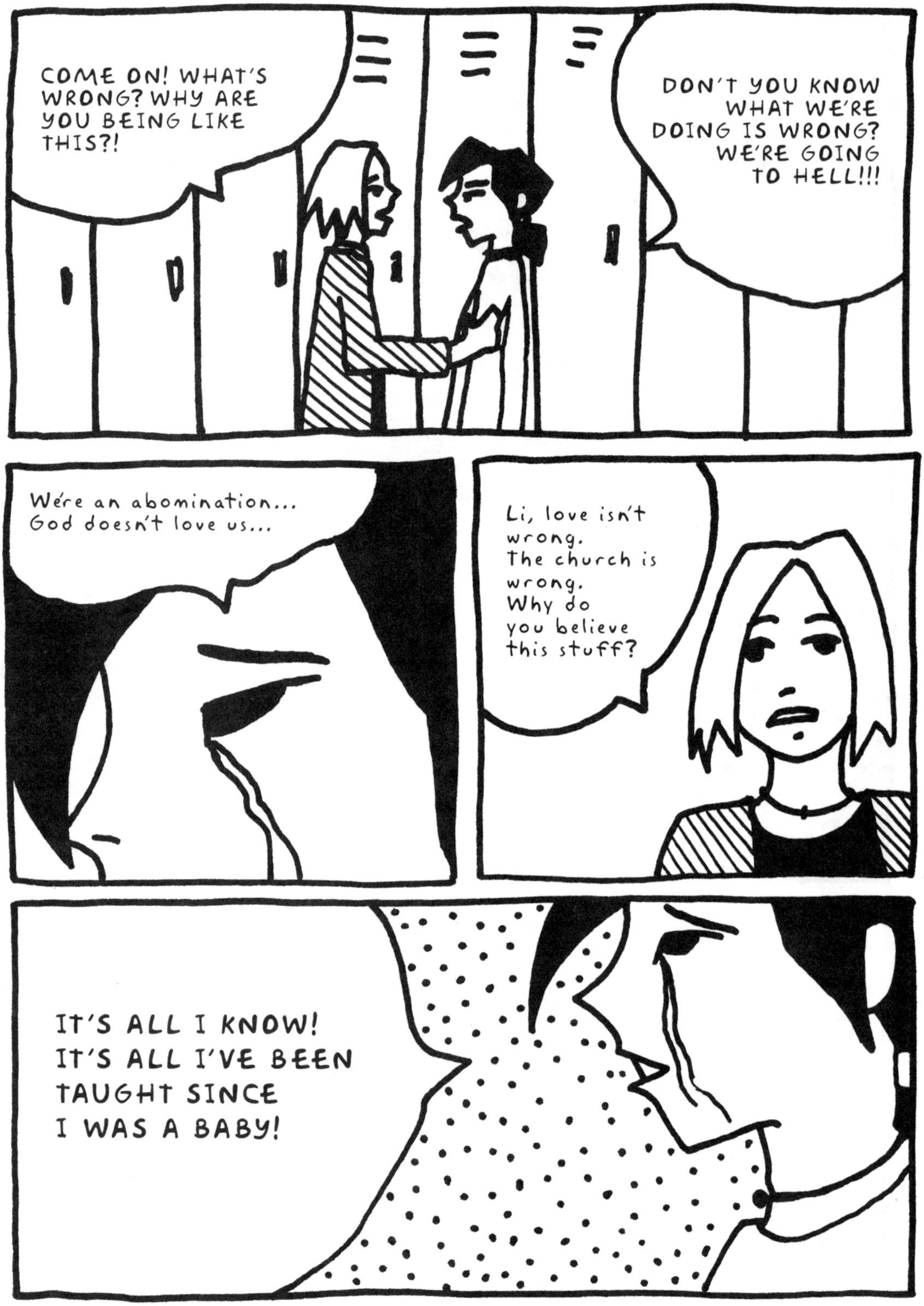
COME ON! WHAT'S WRONG? WHY ARE YOU BEING LIKE THIS?!
DON'T YOU KNOW WHAT WE'RE DOING IS WRONG? WE'RE GOING TO HELL!!!
We're an abomination... God doesn't love us...
Li, love isn't wrong. The church is wrong. Why do you believe this stuff?
IT'S ALL I KNOW! IT'S ALL I'VE BEEN TAUGHT SINCE I WAS A BABY!

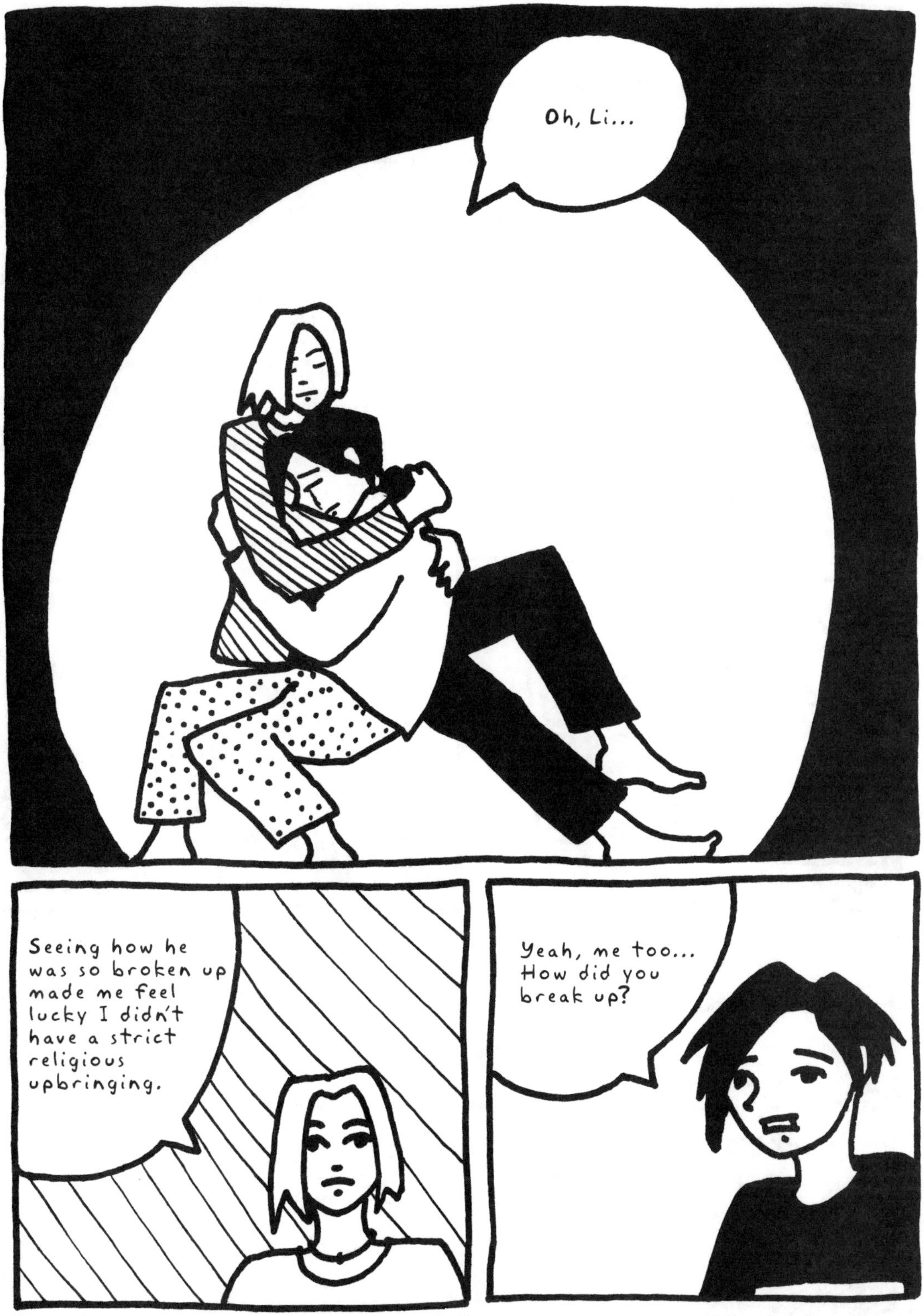
Oh, Li...
Seeing how he was so broken up made me feel lucky I didn't have a strict religious upbringing.
Yeah, me too... How did you break up?

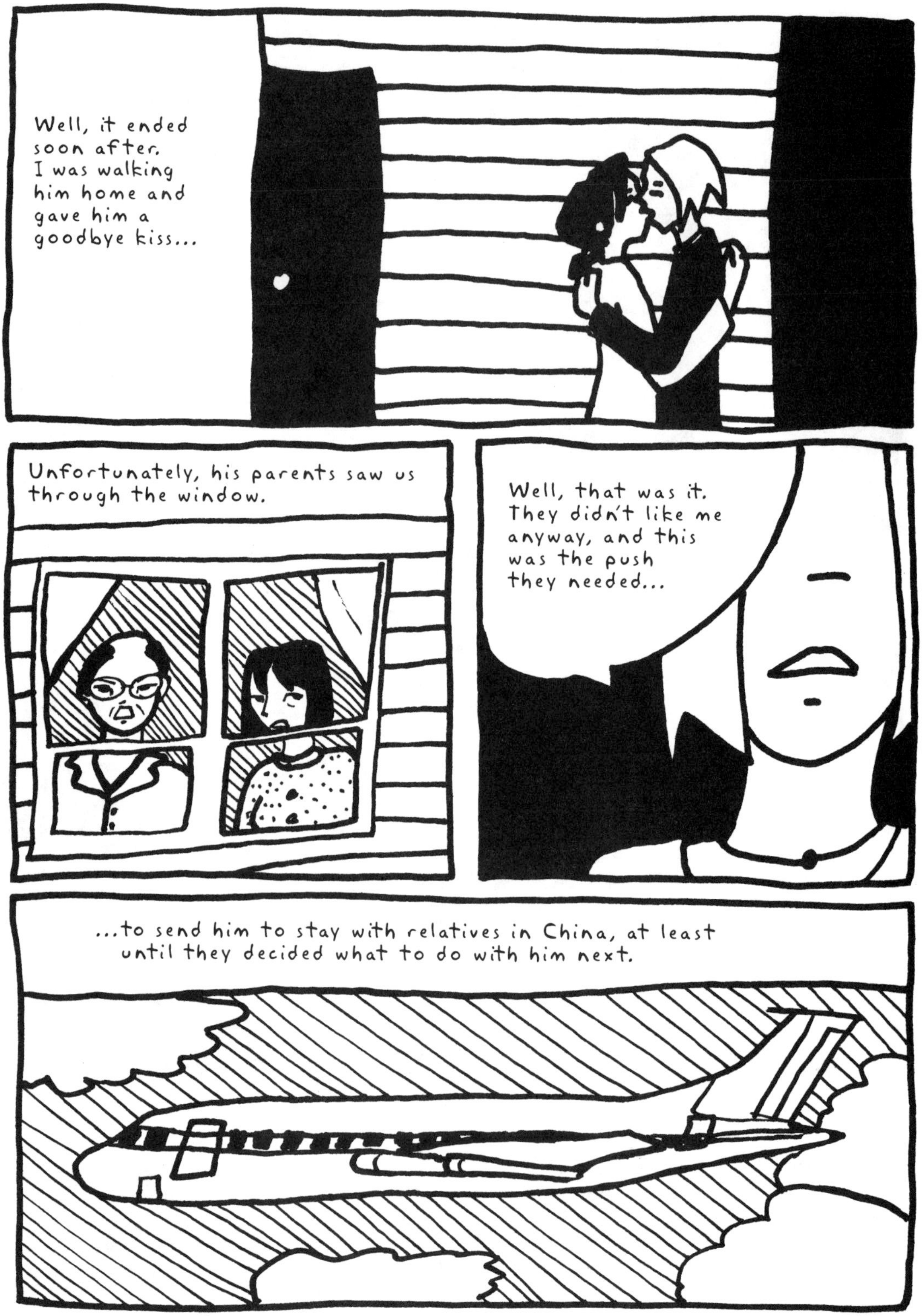
Well, it ended soon after. I was walking him home and gave him a goodbye kiss...
Unfortunately, his parents saw us through the window.
Well, that was it. They didn't like me anyway, and this was the push they needed...
...to send him to stay with relatives in China, at least until they decided what to do with him next.

That was three months ago...
Are you OK? How can I help?
I'm fine...let's watch a video. You pick. OK?
"Drunken Master"! That looks good!
GOOD CHOICE! Oh! It's really funny! Let's watch it!

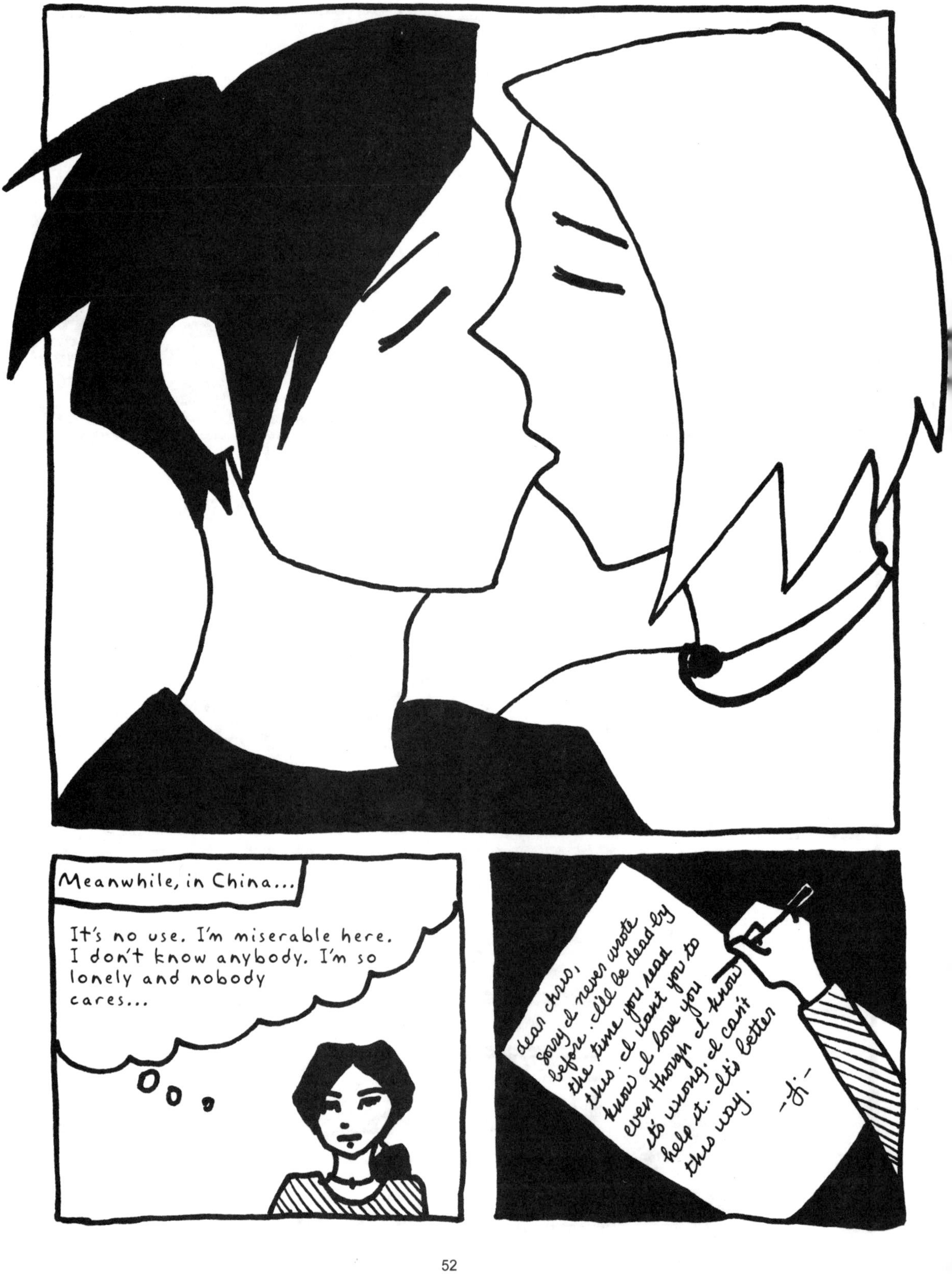

Meanwhile, in China...
It's no use. I'm miserable here. I don't know anybody. I'm so lonely and nobody cares...
dear chris,
sorry I never wrote
before. I'll be dead by
the time you read
this. I want you to
know I love you
even though I know
it's wrong. I can't
help it. It's better
this way.
-Li-

So I sent it.
That's it,
then...

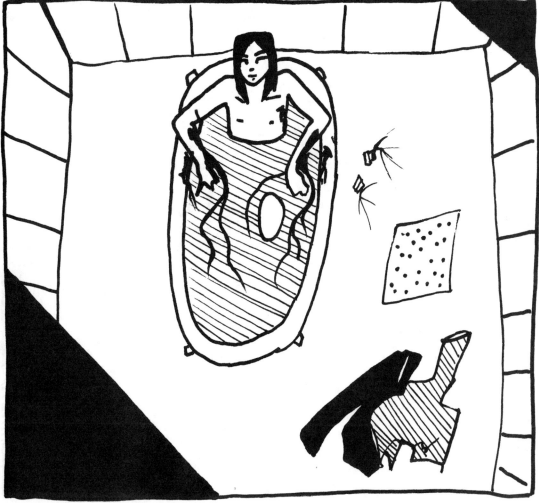

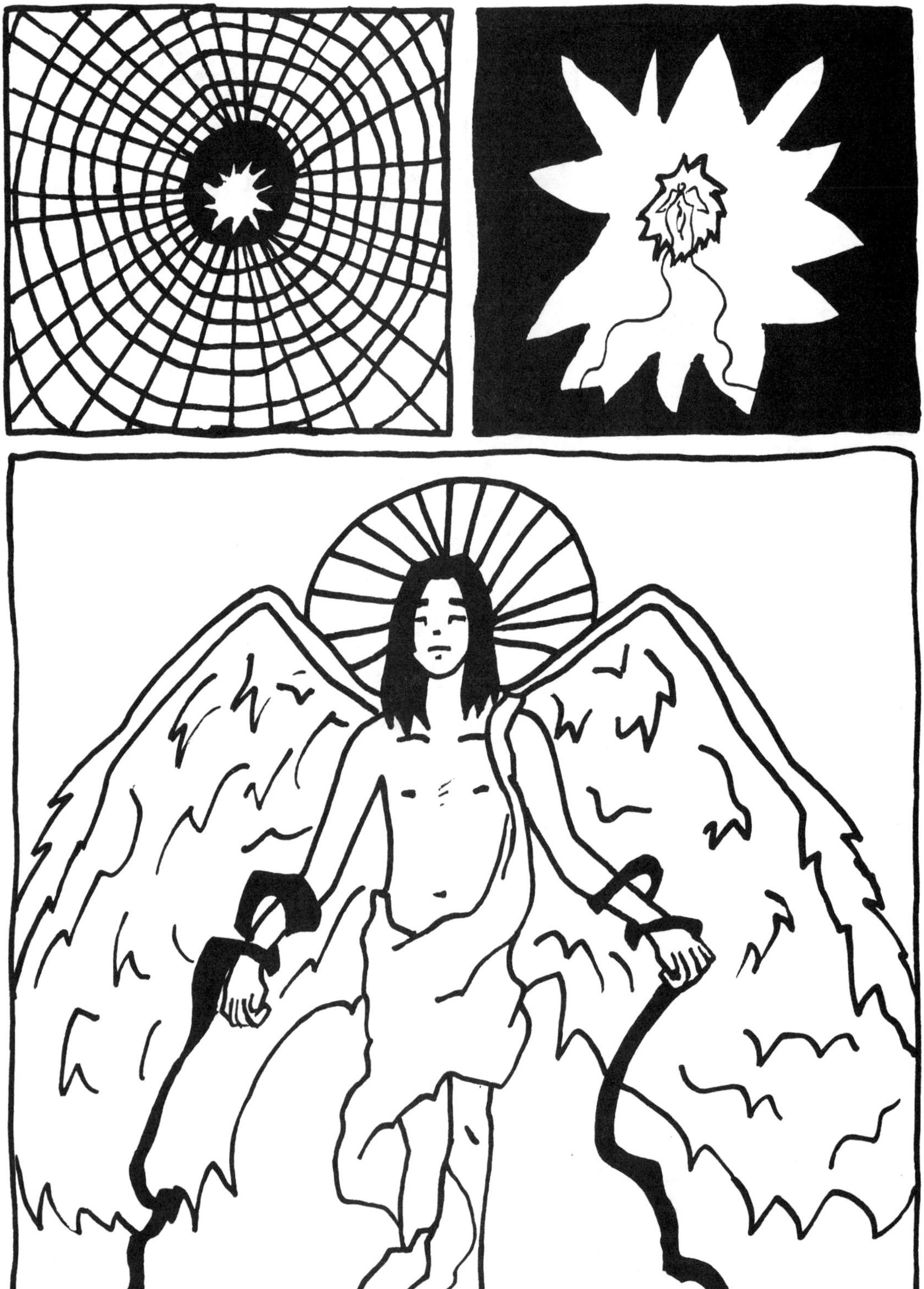

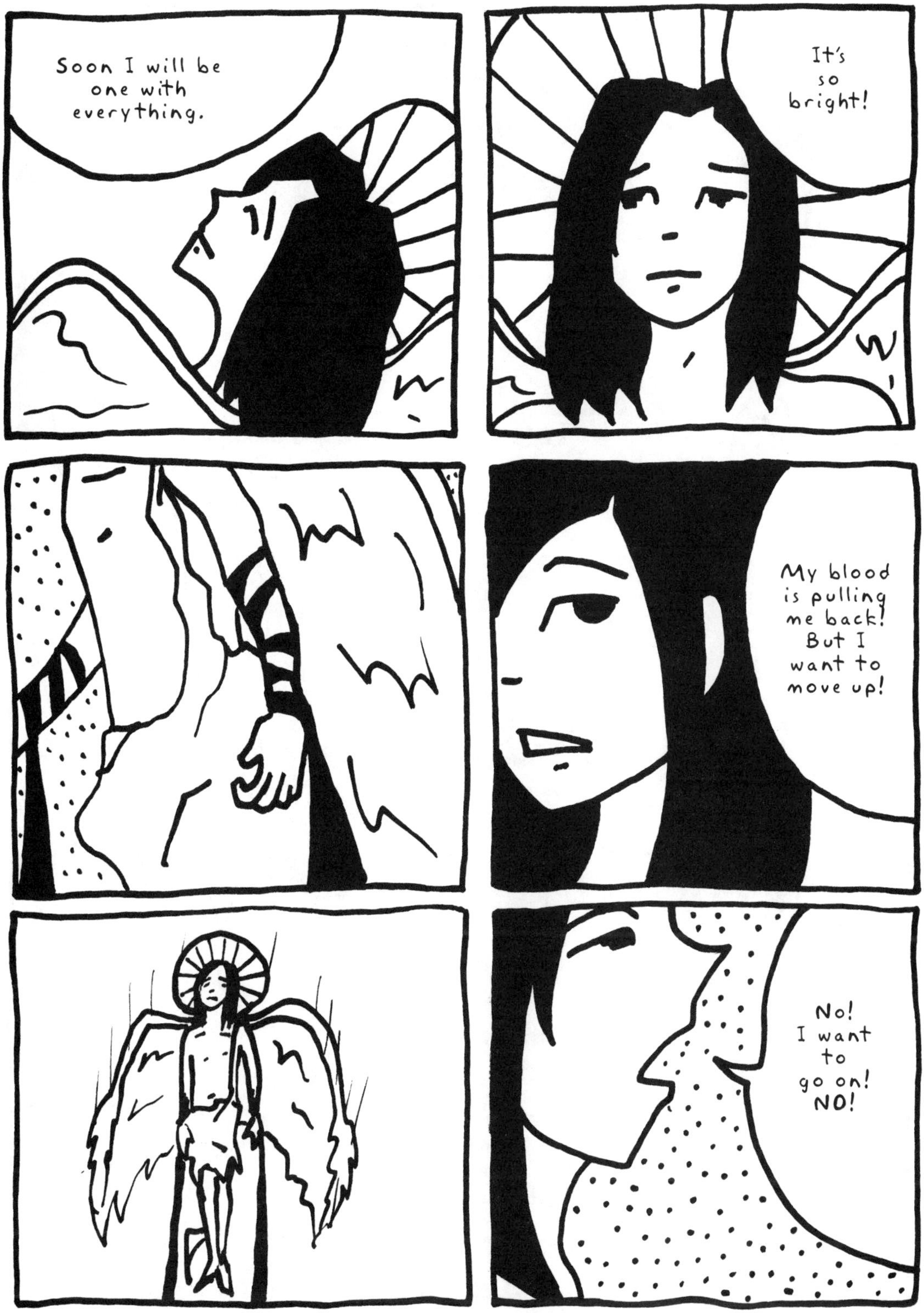
Soon I will be one with everything.
It's so bright!
My blood is pulling me back! But I want to move up!
No! I want to go on! NO!

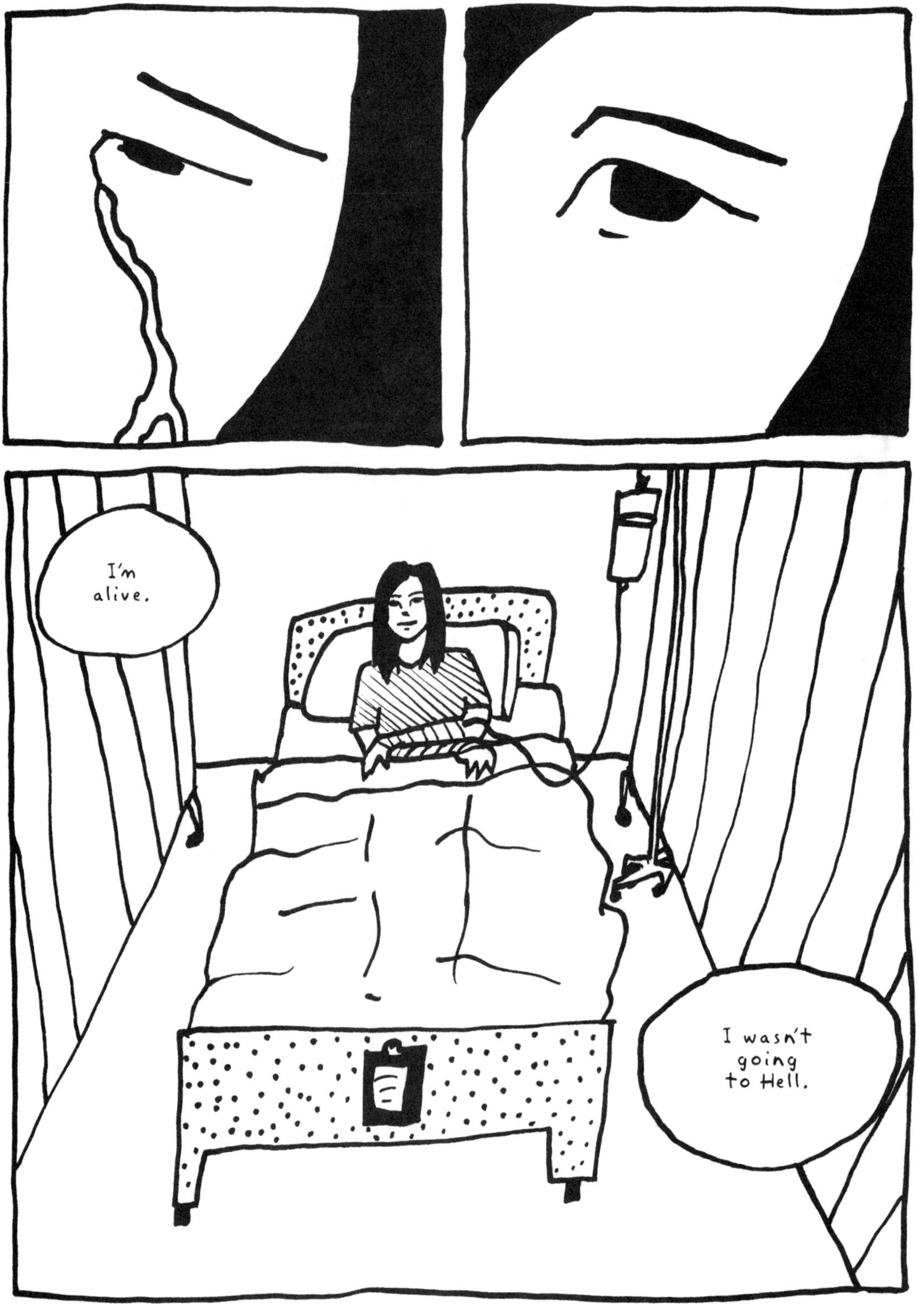
I'm alive.
I wasn't going to Hell.

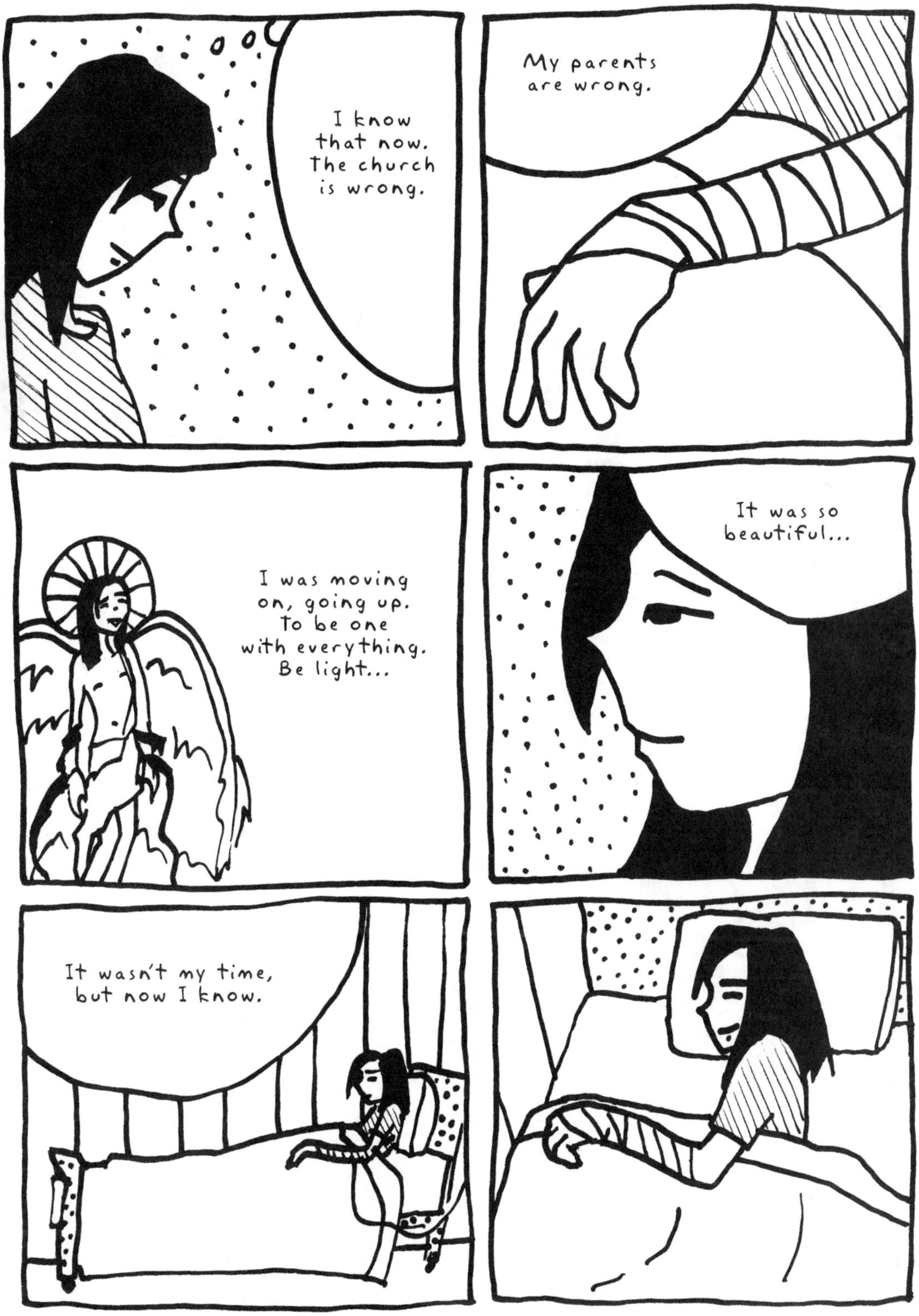
I know that now. The church is wrong.
My parents are wrong.
I was moving on, going up. To be one with everything. Be light...
It was so beautiful...
It wasn't my time, but now I know.

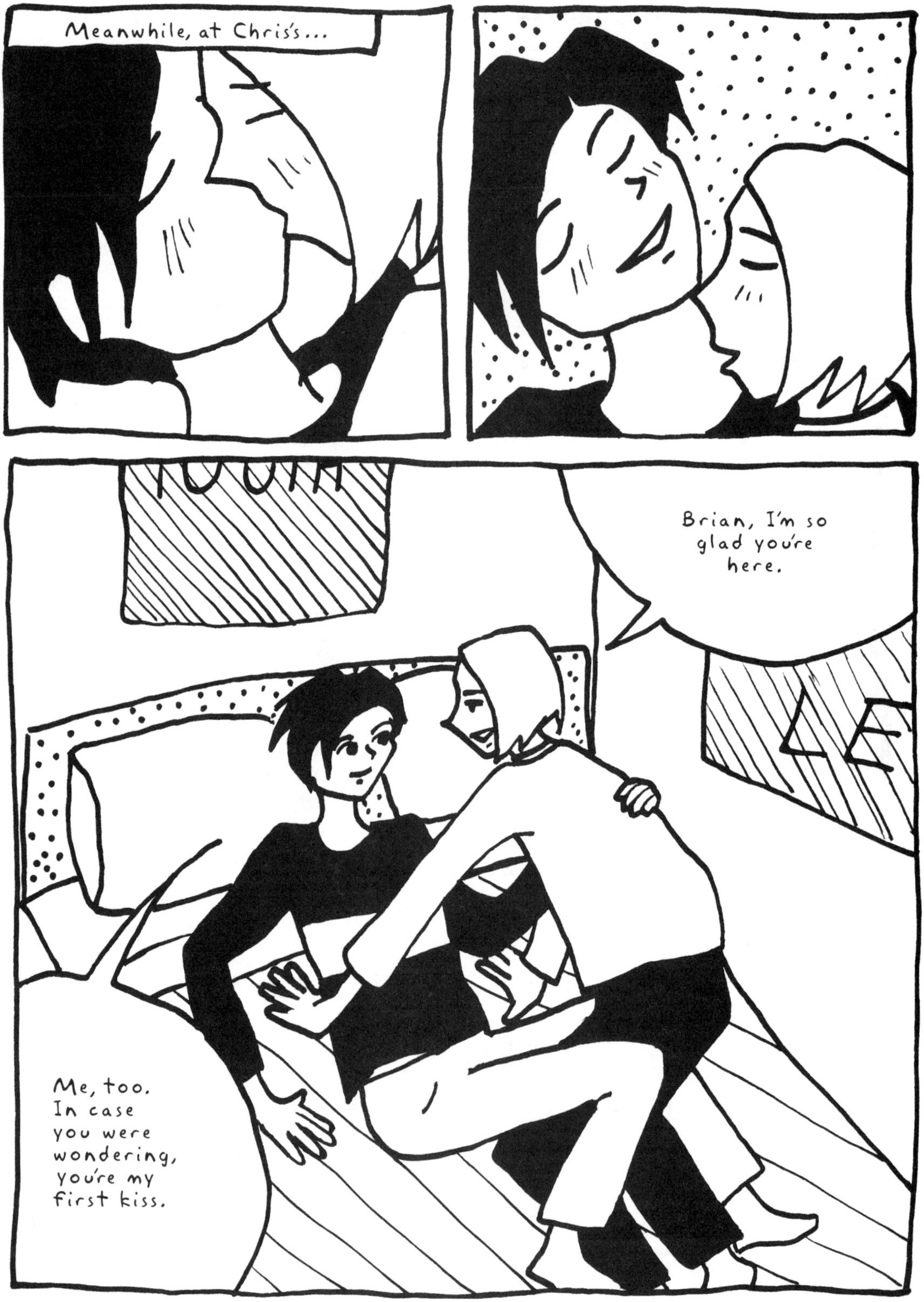
Meanwhile, at Chris's...
Brian, I'm so glad you're here.
Me, too. In case you were wondering, you're my first kiss.

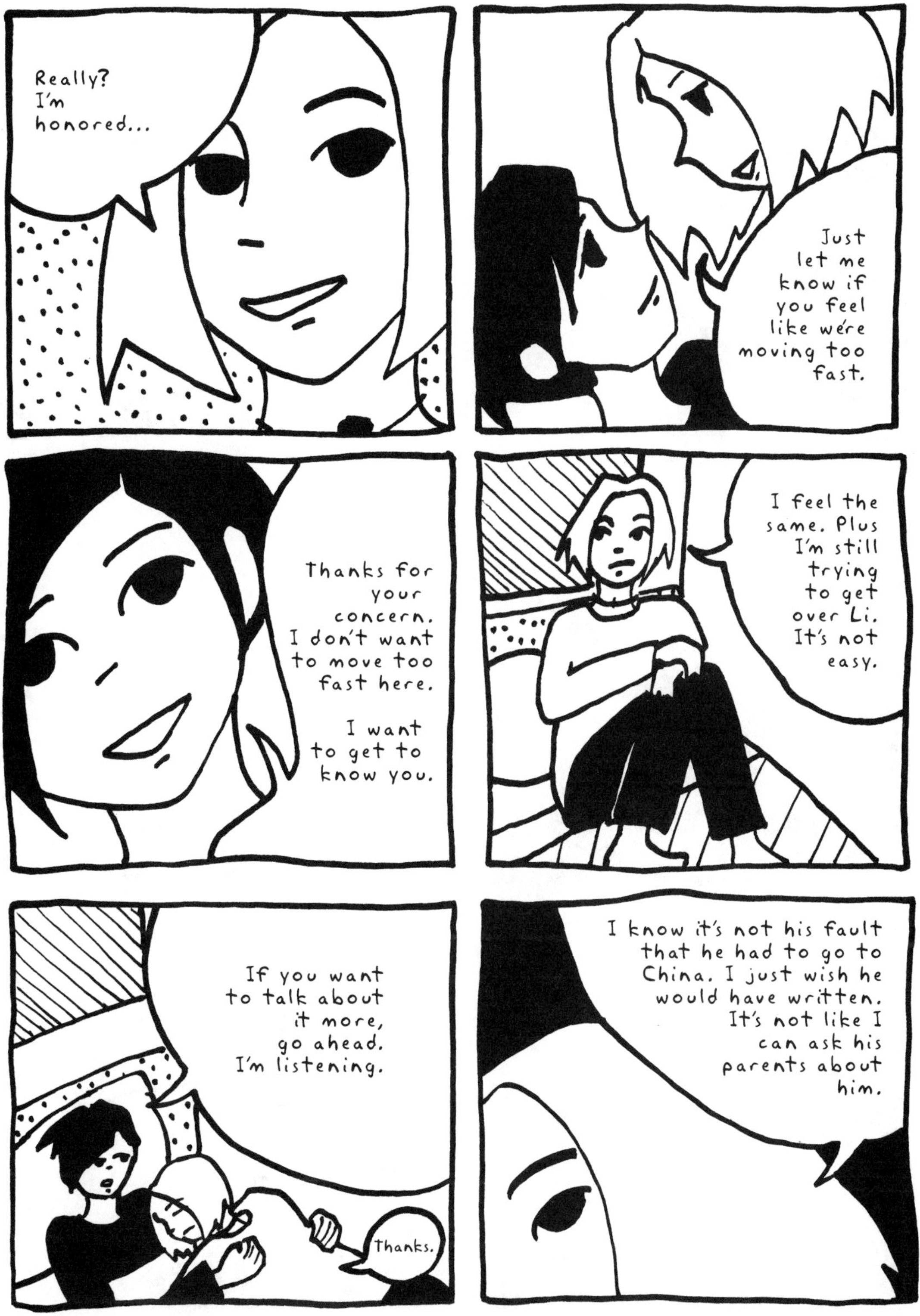

Really? I'm honored...
Just let me know if you feel like we're moving too fast.
Thanks for your concern. I don't want to move too fast here.
I want to get to know you.
I feel the same. Plus I'm still trying to get over Li. It's not easy.
If you want to talk about it more, go ahead. I'm listening.
Thanks.
I know it's not his fault that he had to go to China. I just wish he would have written. It's not like I can ask his parents about him.

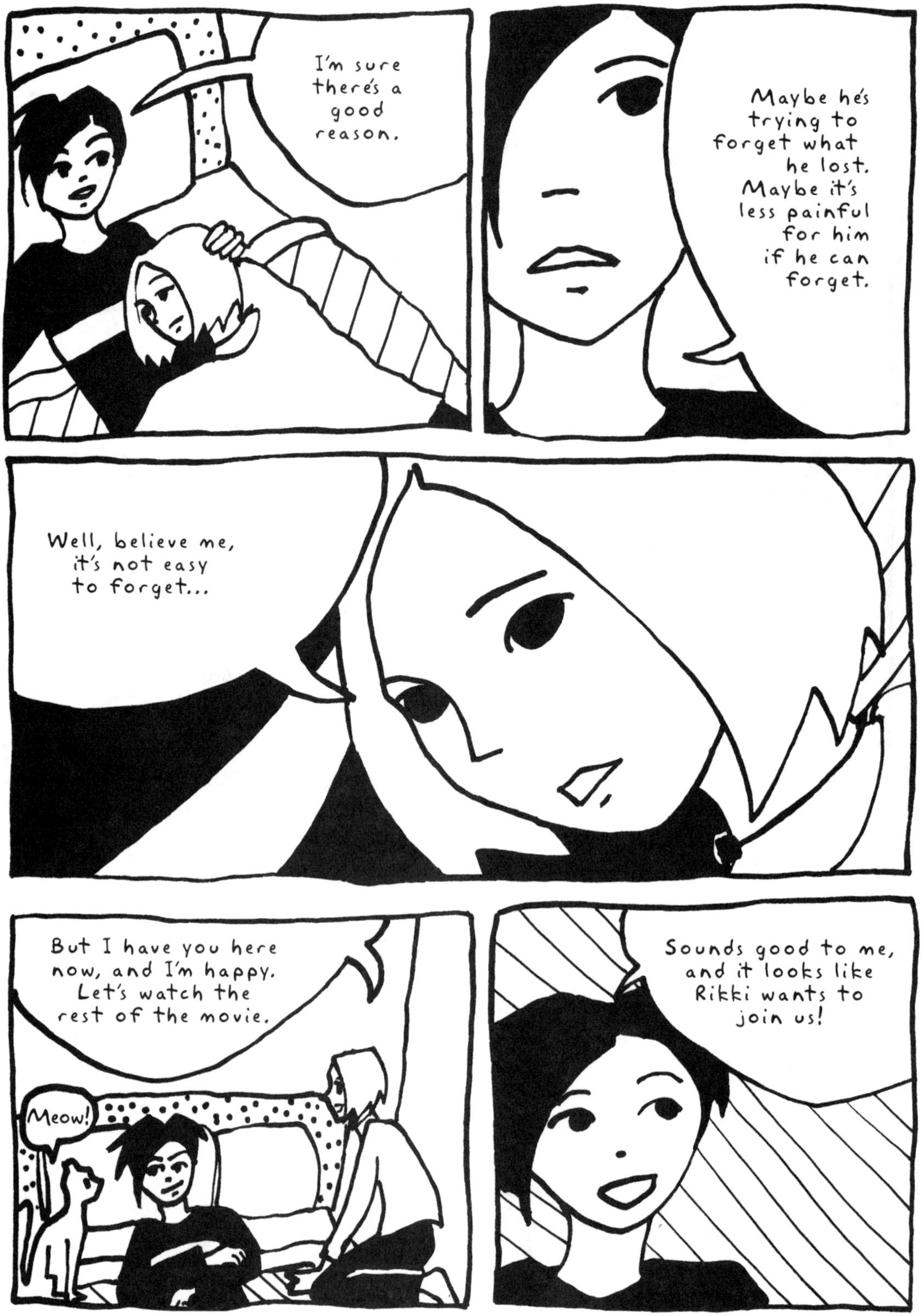

I'm sure there's a good reason.
Maybe he's trying to forget what he lost. Maybe it's less painful for him if he can forget.
Well, believe me, it's not easy to forget...
But I have you here now, and I'm happy. Let's watch the rest of the movie.
Meow!
Sounds good to me, and it looks like Rikki wants to join us!

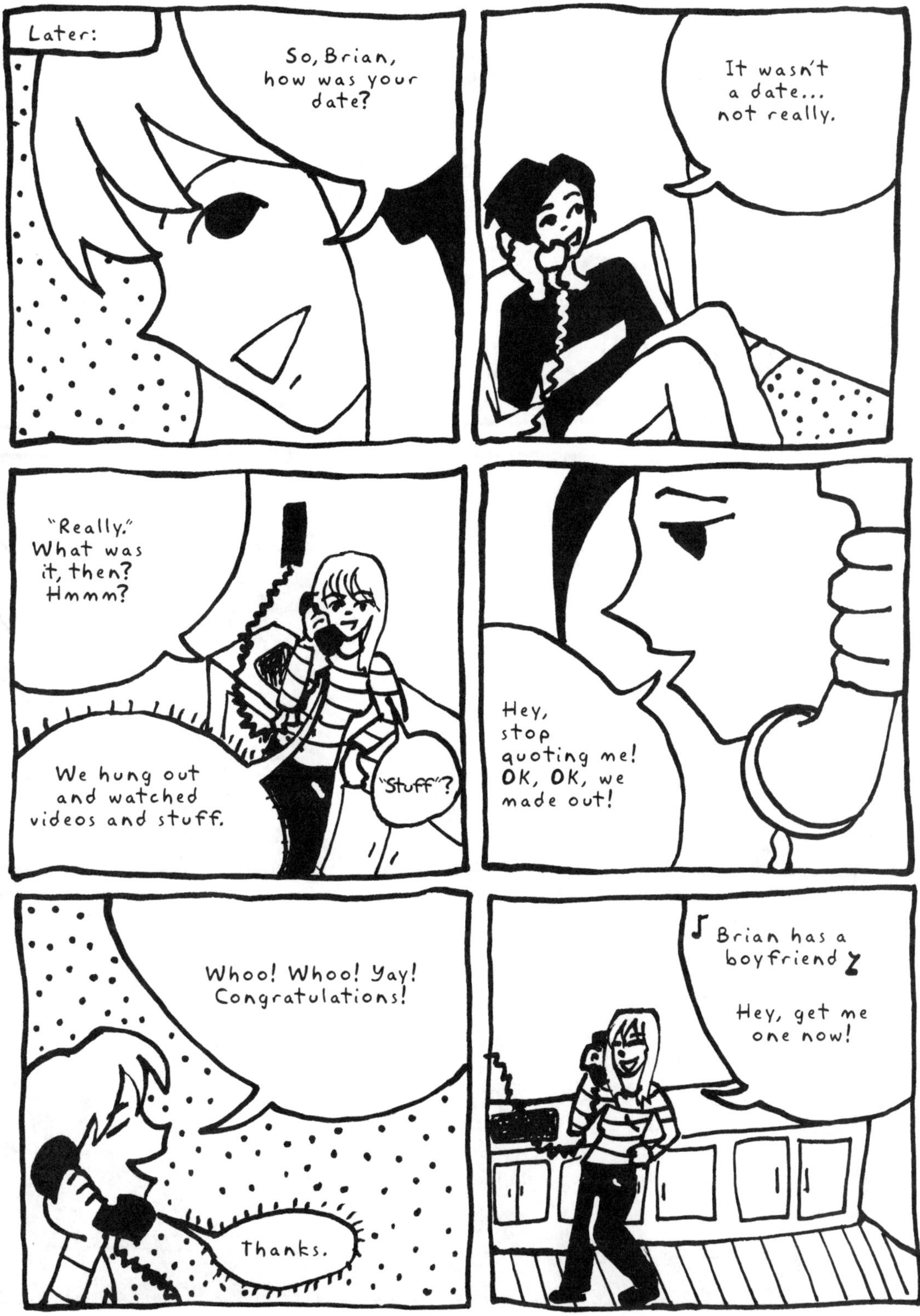
Later:
So, Brian, how was your date?
It wasn't a date... not really.
"Really." What was it, then? Hmmm?
We hung out and watched videos and stuff.
"Stuff"?
Hey, stop quoting me! OK, OK, we made out!
Whoo! Whoo! Yay! Congratulations!
Thanks.
Brian has a boyfriend
Hey, get me one now!

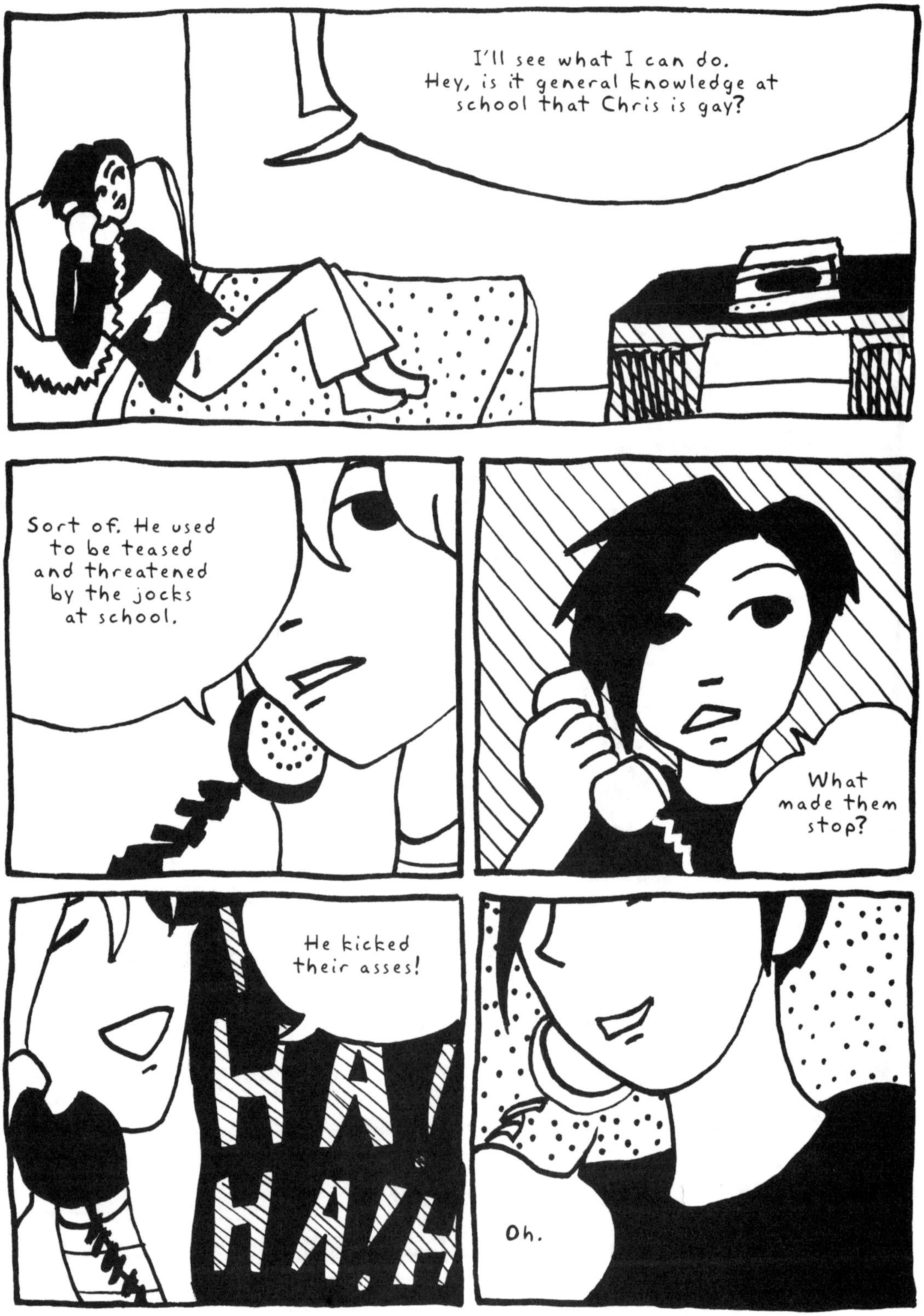
I'll see what I can do. Hey, is it general knowledge at school that Chris is gay?
Sort of. He used to be teased and threatened by the jocks at school.
What made them stop?
He kicked their asses!
HA! HA! HA!H
Oh.

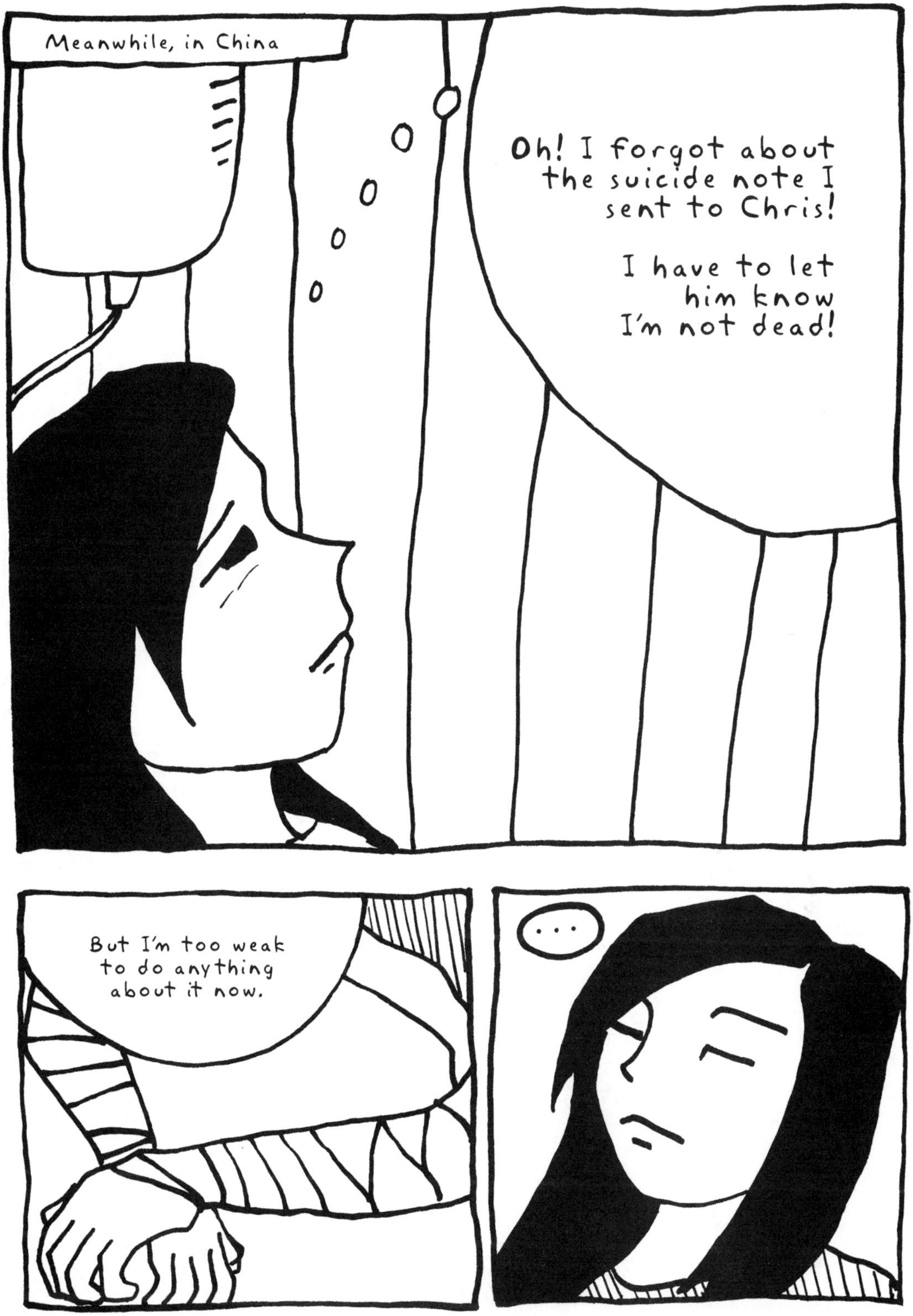

Meanwhile, in China
Oh! I forgot about the suicide note I sent to Chris!
I have to let him know I'm not dead!
But I'm too weak to do anything about it now.
...

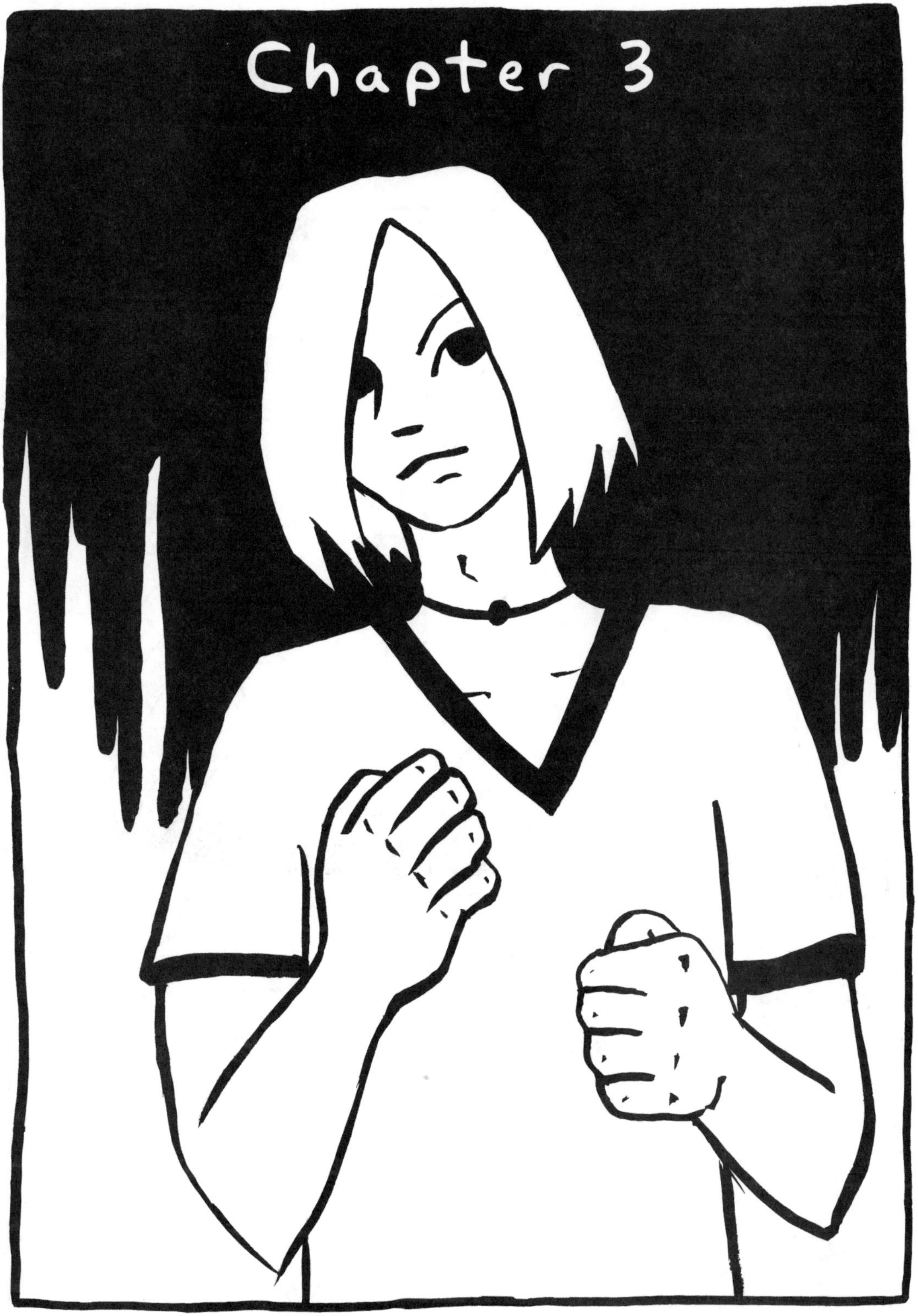
Chapter 3

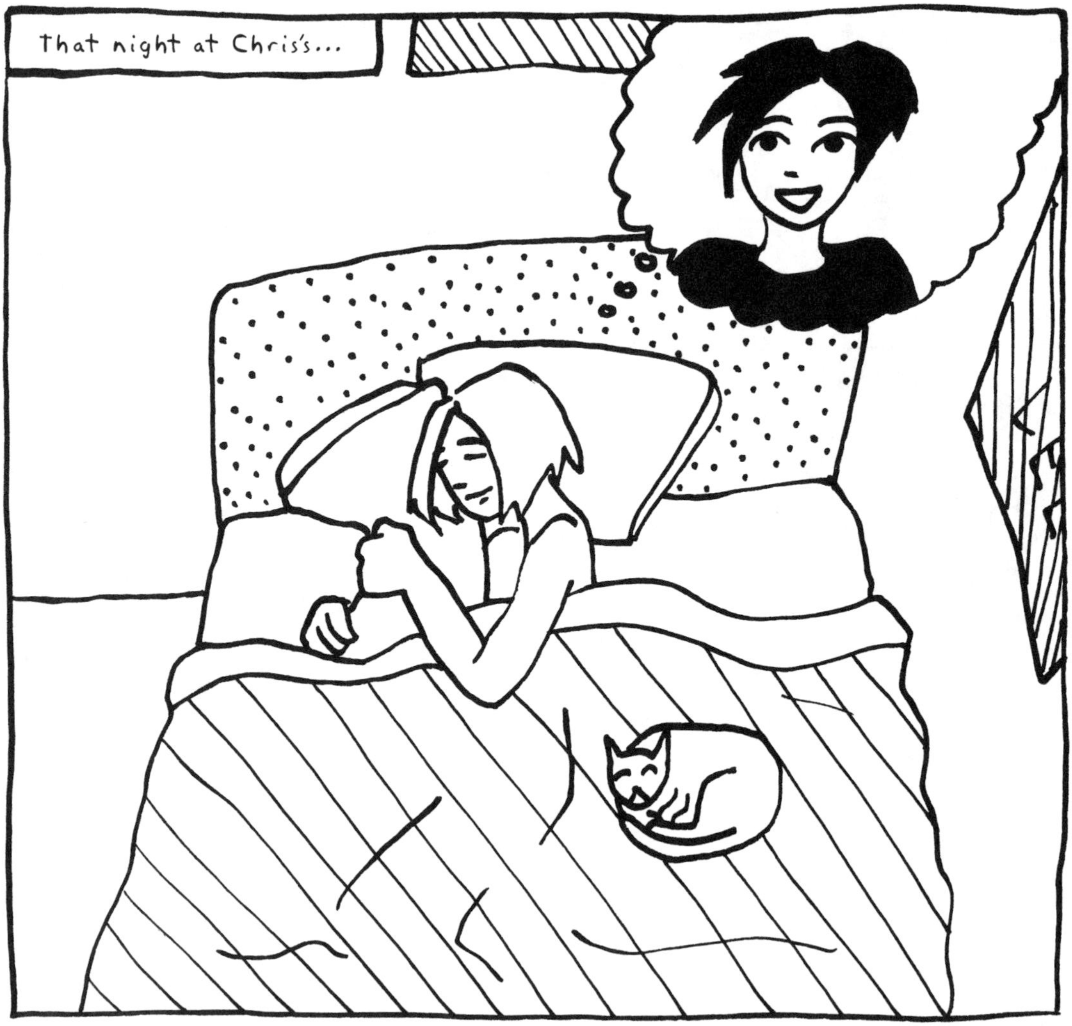
That night at Chris's...

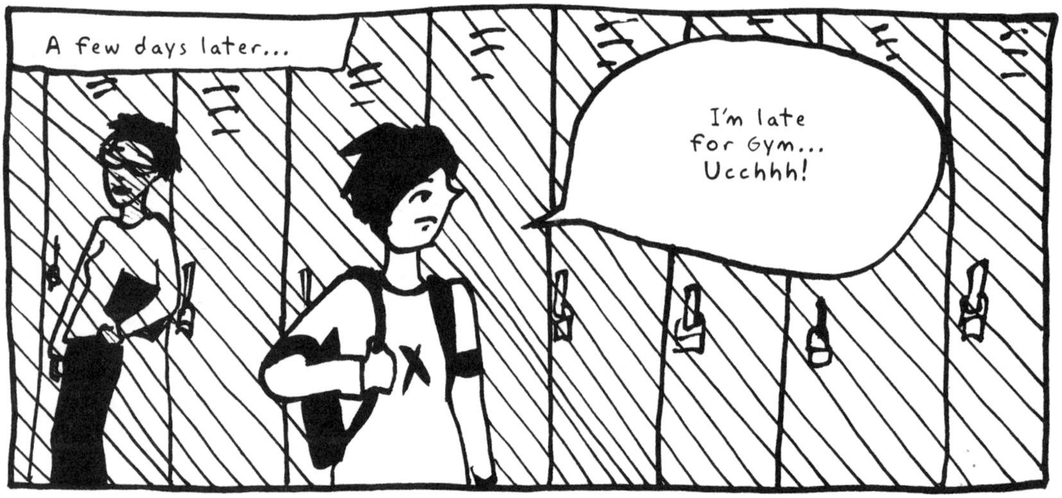
A few days later...
I'm late for Gym... Ucchhh!

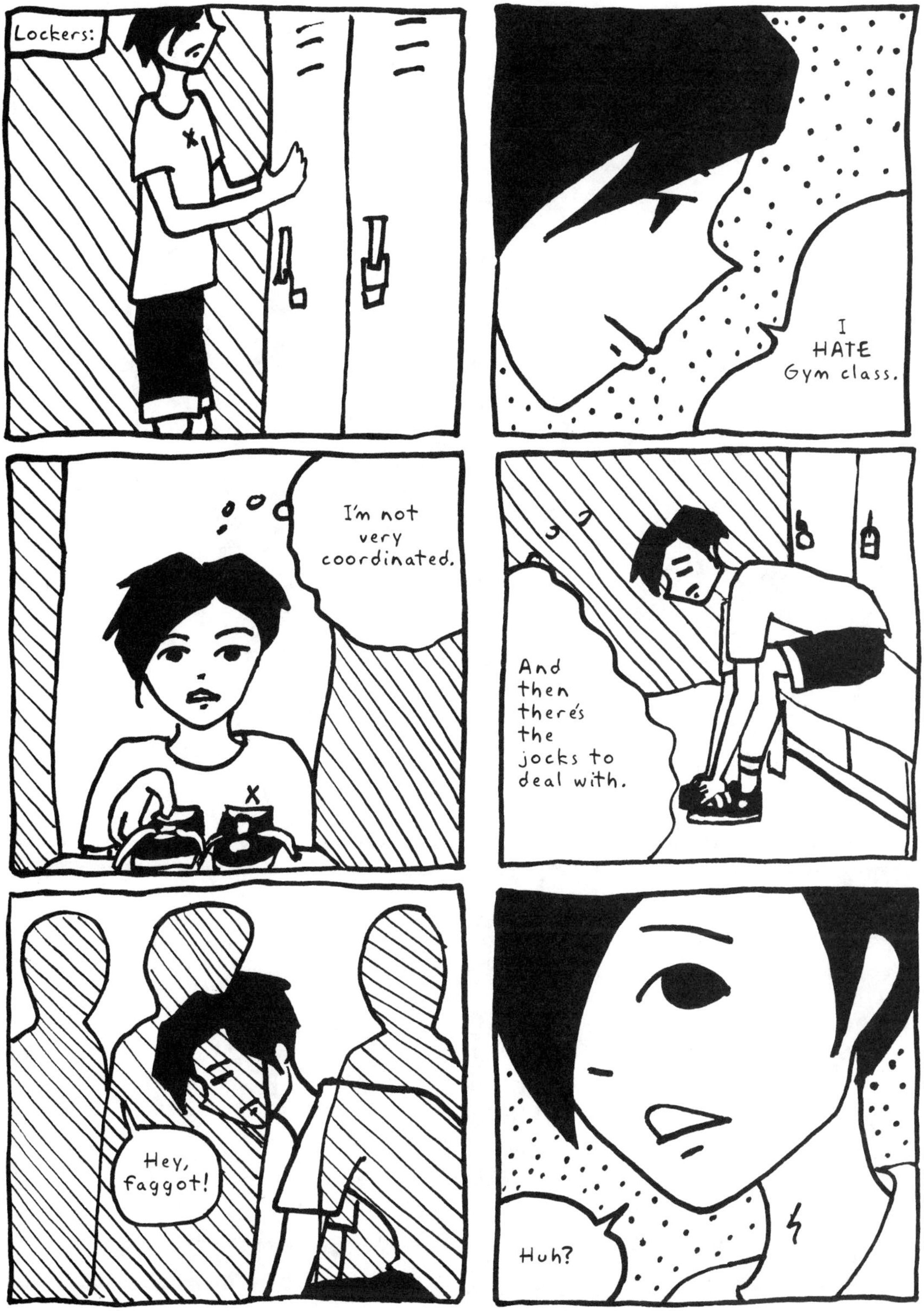
Lockers:
I HATE Gym class.
I'm not very coordinated.
And then there's the jocks to deal with.
Hey, faggot!
Huh?

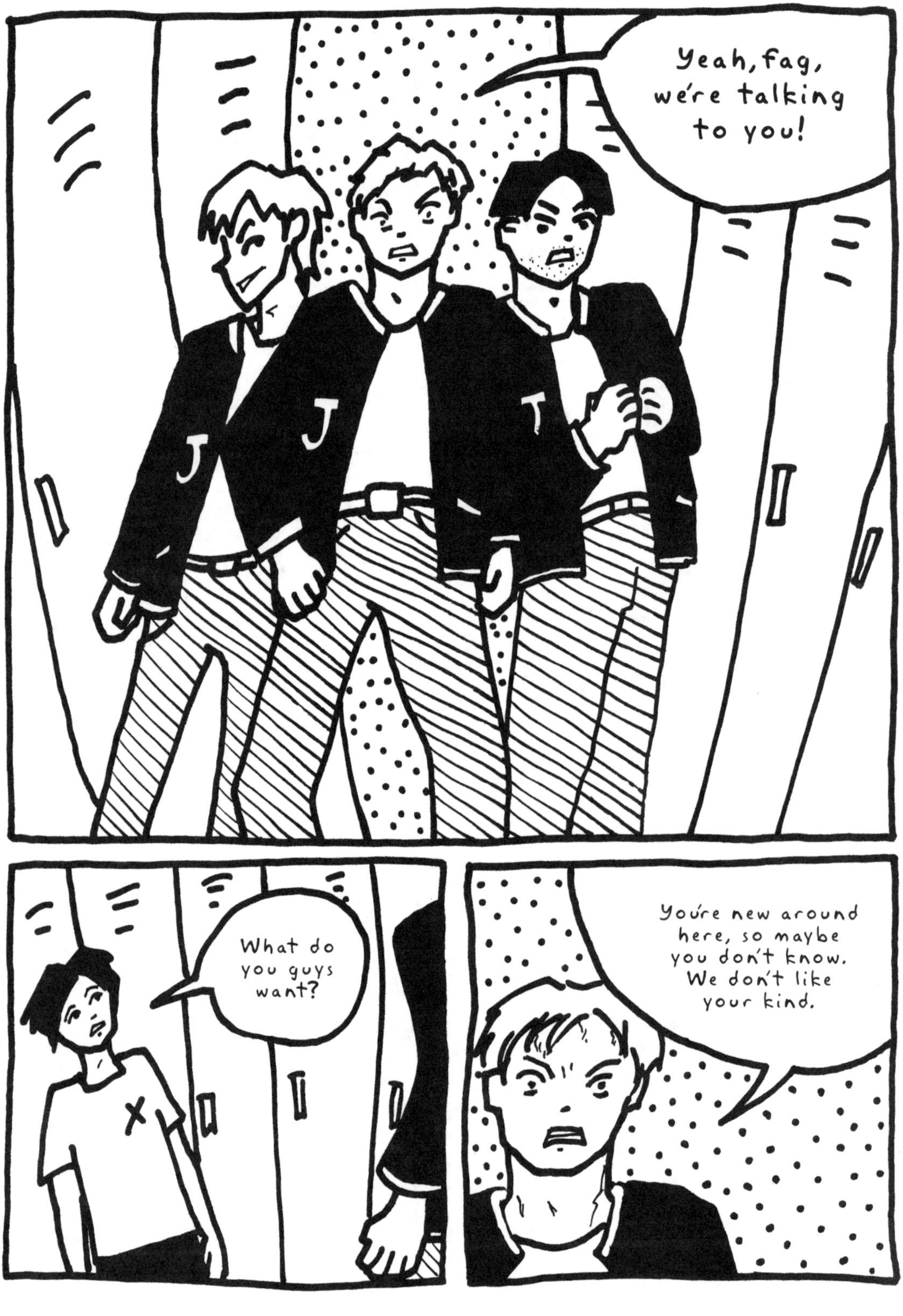
Yeah, fag, we're talking to you!
What do you guys want?
You're new around here, so maybe you don't know. We don't like your kind.

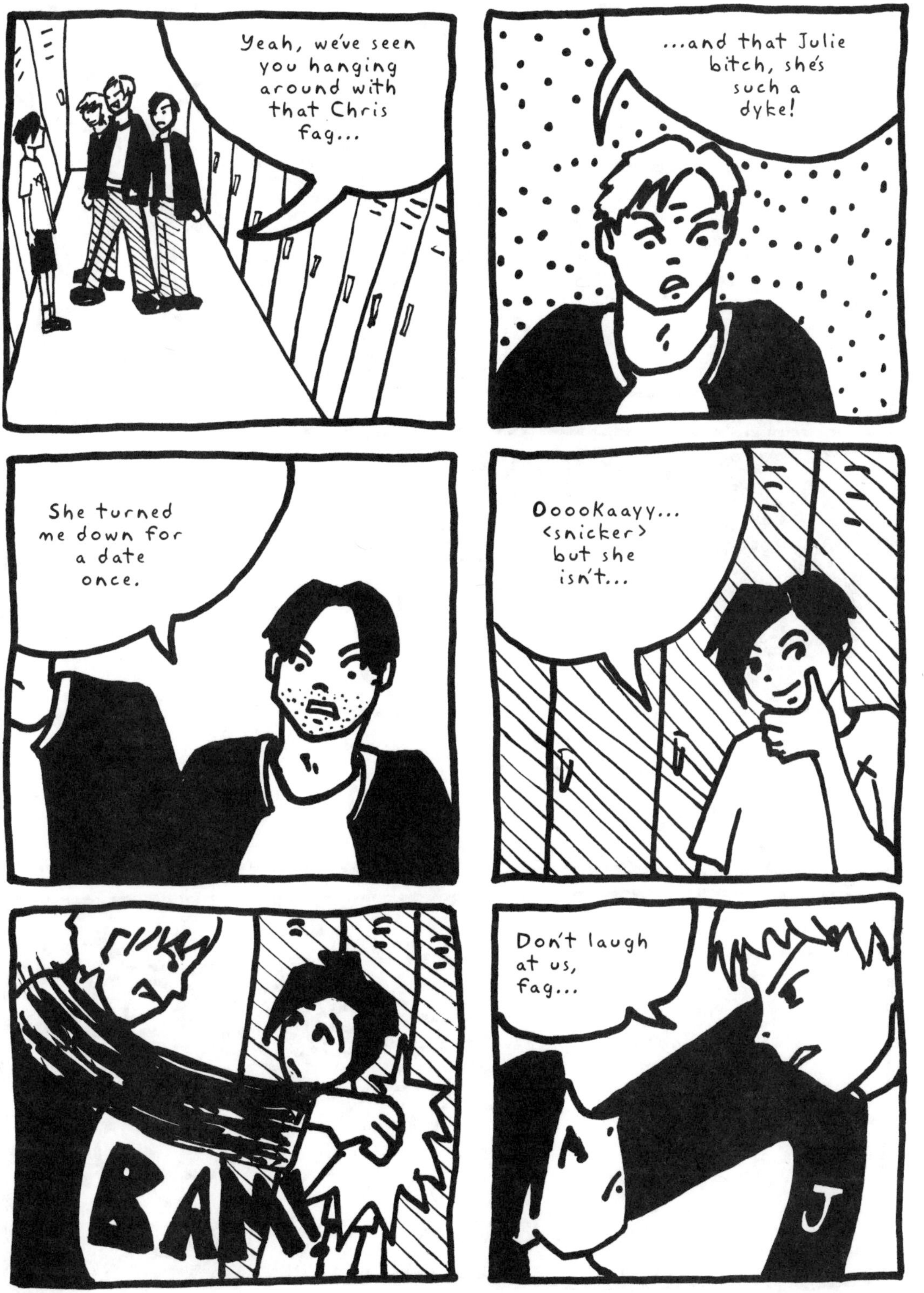
Yeah, we've seen you hanging around with that Chris fag...
...and that Julie bitch, she's such a dyke!
She turned me down for a date once.
OoooKaayy... <snicker> but she isn't...
BAM
Don't laugh at us, fag...
J

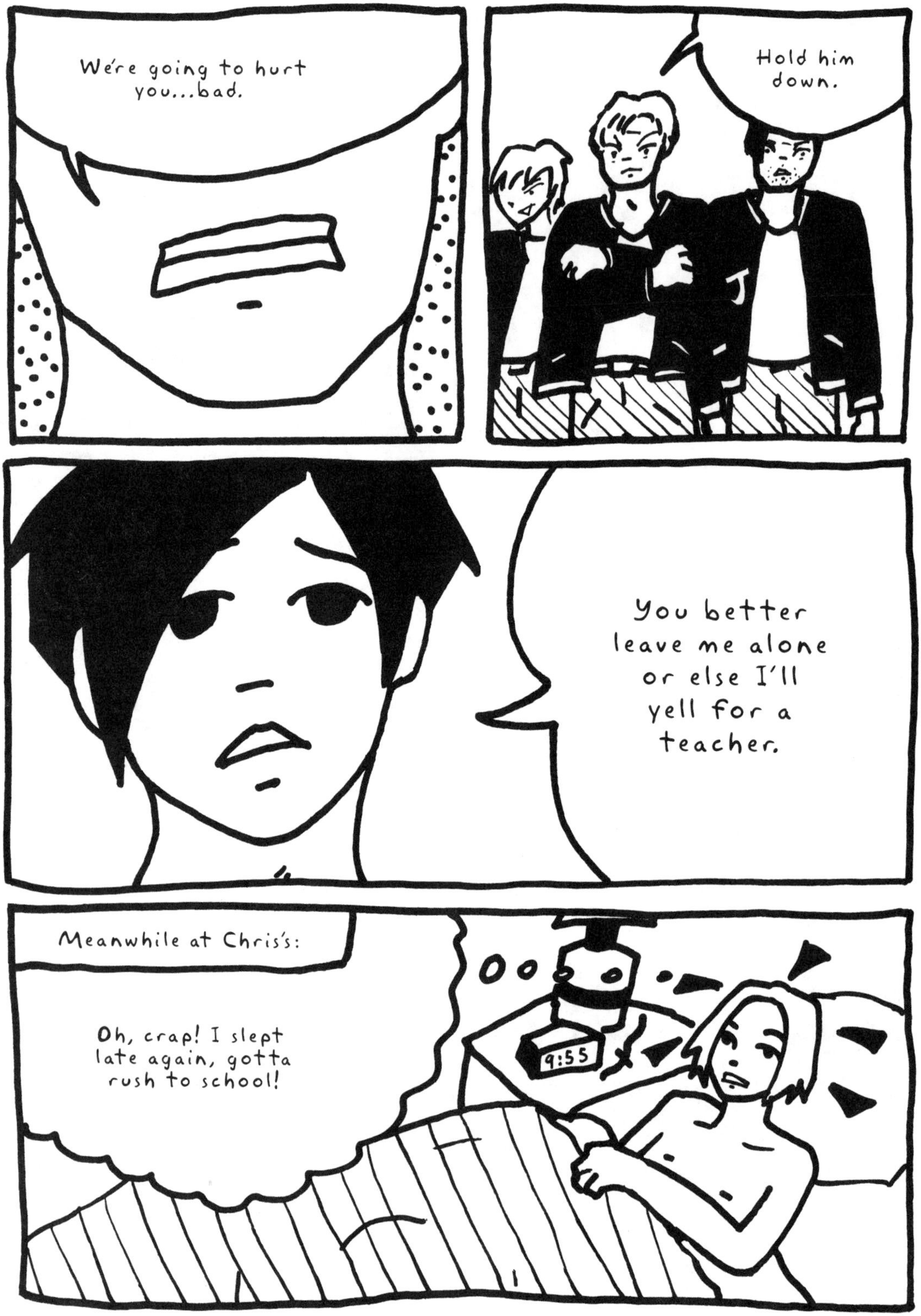
We're going to hurt you...bad.
Hold him down.
You better leave me alone or else I'll yell for a teacher.
Meanwhile at Chris's:
Oh, crap! I slept late again, gotta rush to school!
9:55

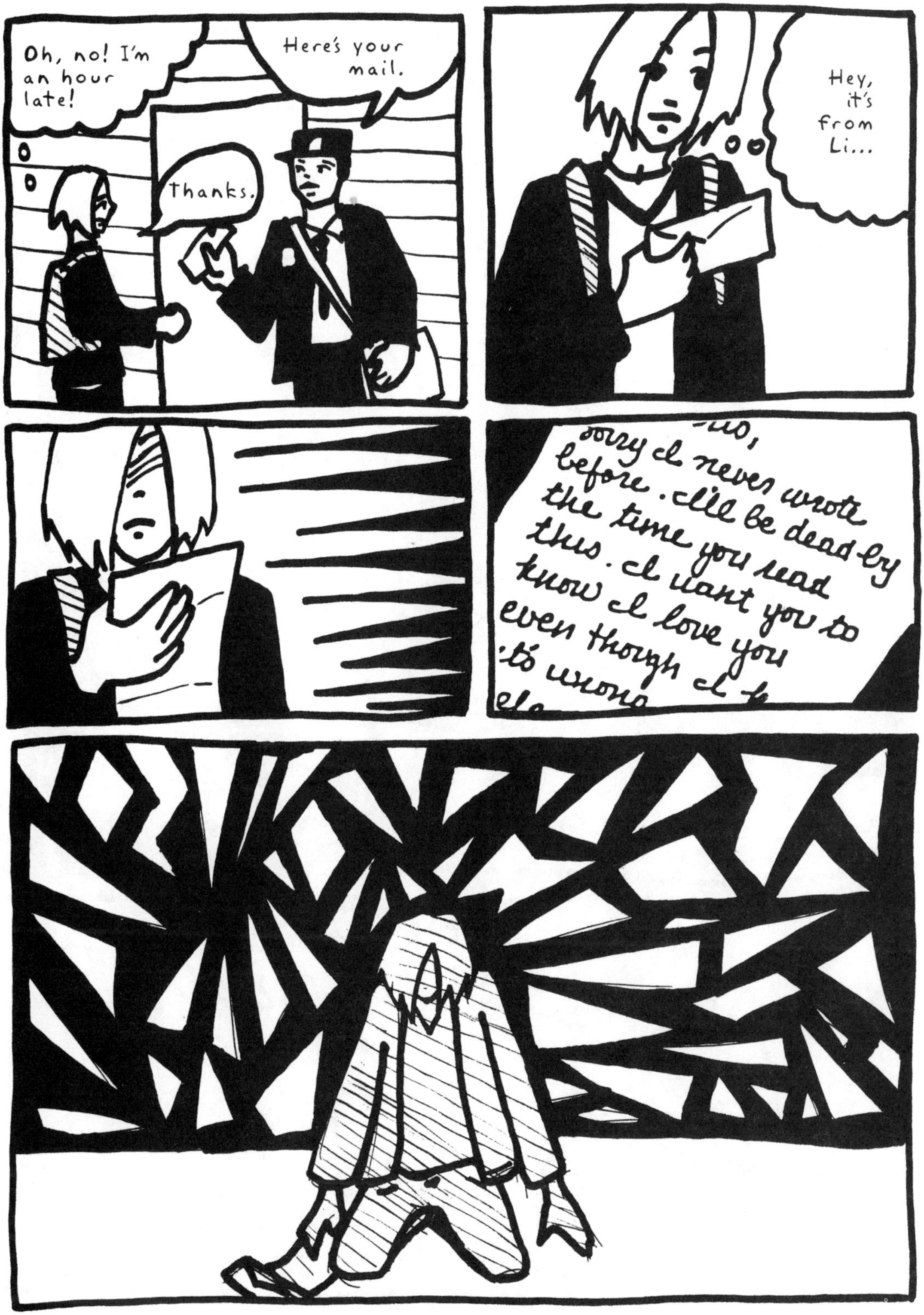
Oh, no! I'm an hour late!
Here's your mail.
Thanks.
Hey, it's from Li...
sorry I never wrote
before. I'll be dead by
the time you read
this. I want you to
know I love you
even though
it's wrong

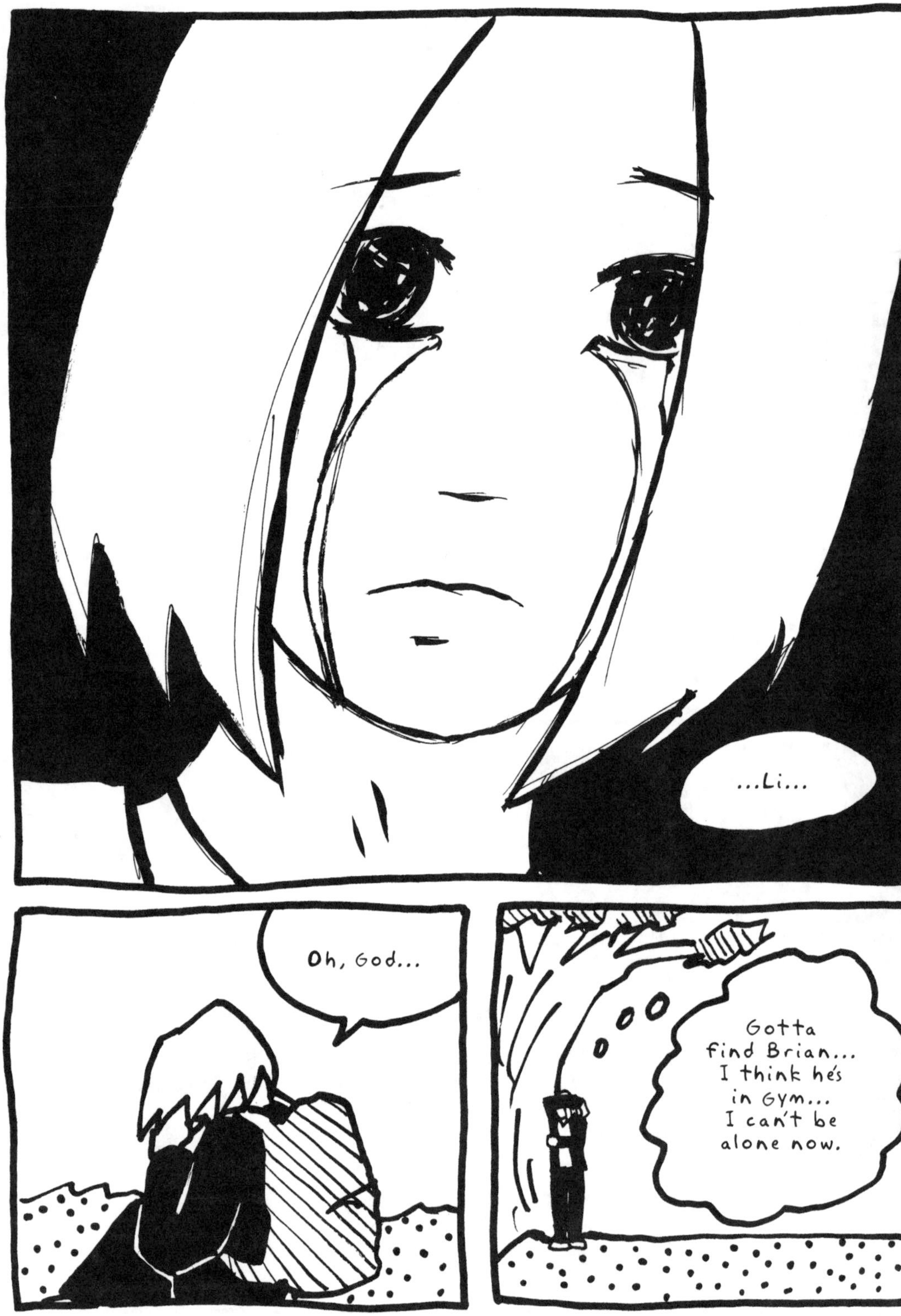
...Li...
Oh, God...
Gotta find Brian... I think he's in Gym... I can't be alone now.

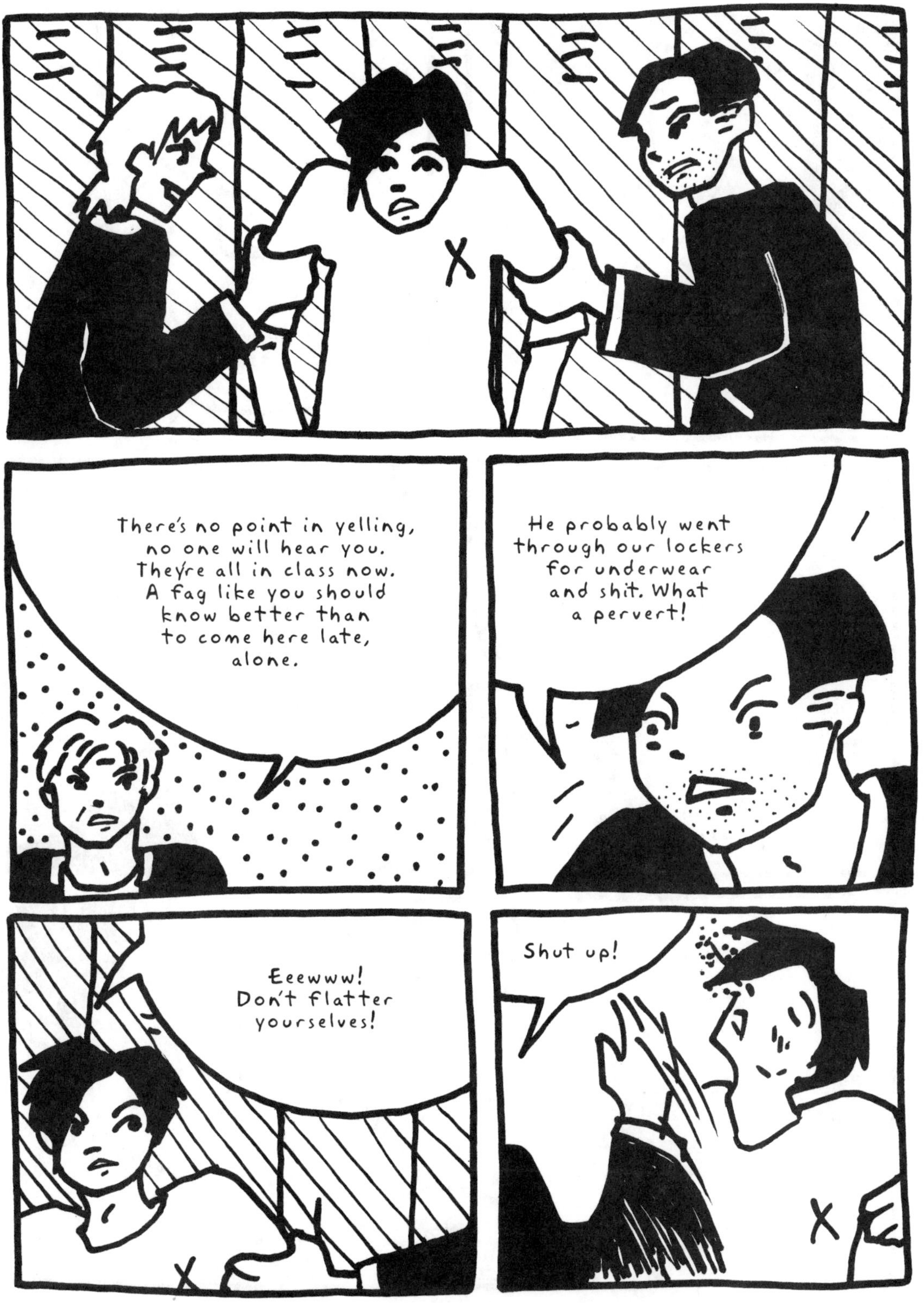
There's no point in yelling, no one will hear you. They're all in class now. A fag like you should know better than to come here late, alone.
He probably went through our lockers for underwear and shit. What a pervert!
Eeewww! Don't flatter yourselves!
Shut up!

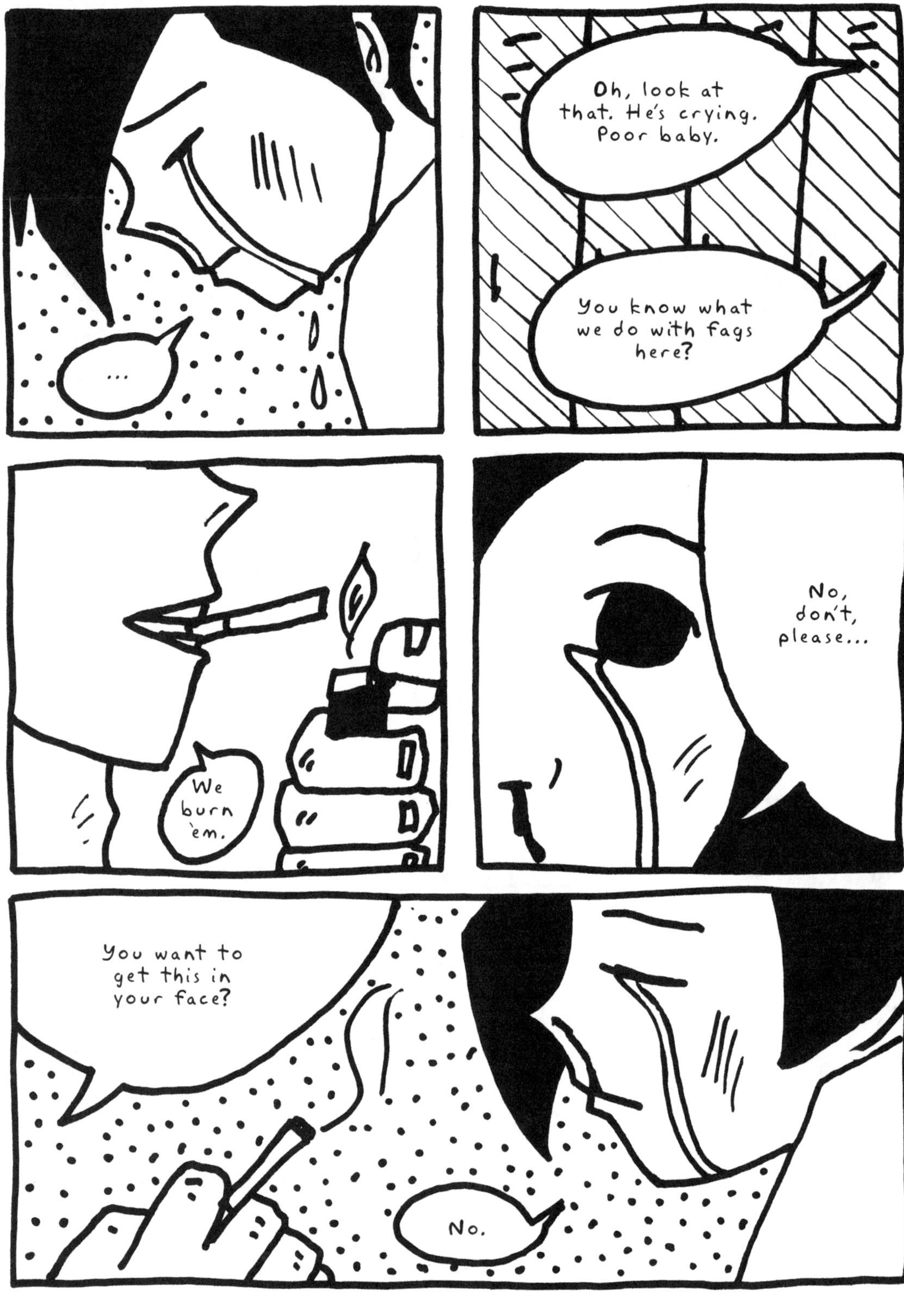
...
Oh, look at that. He's crying. Poor baby.
You know what we do with fags here?
We burn 'em.
No, don't, please...
You want to get this in your face?
No.

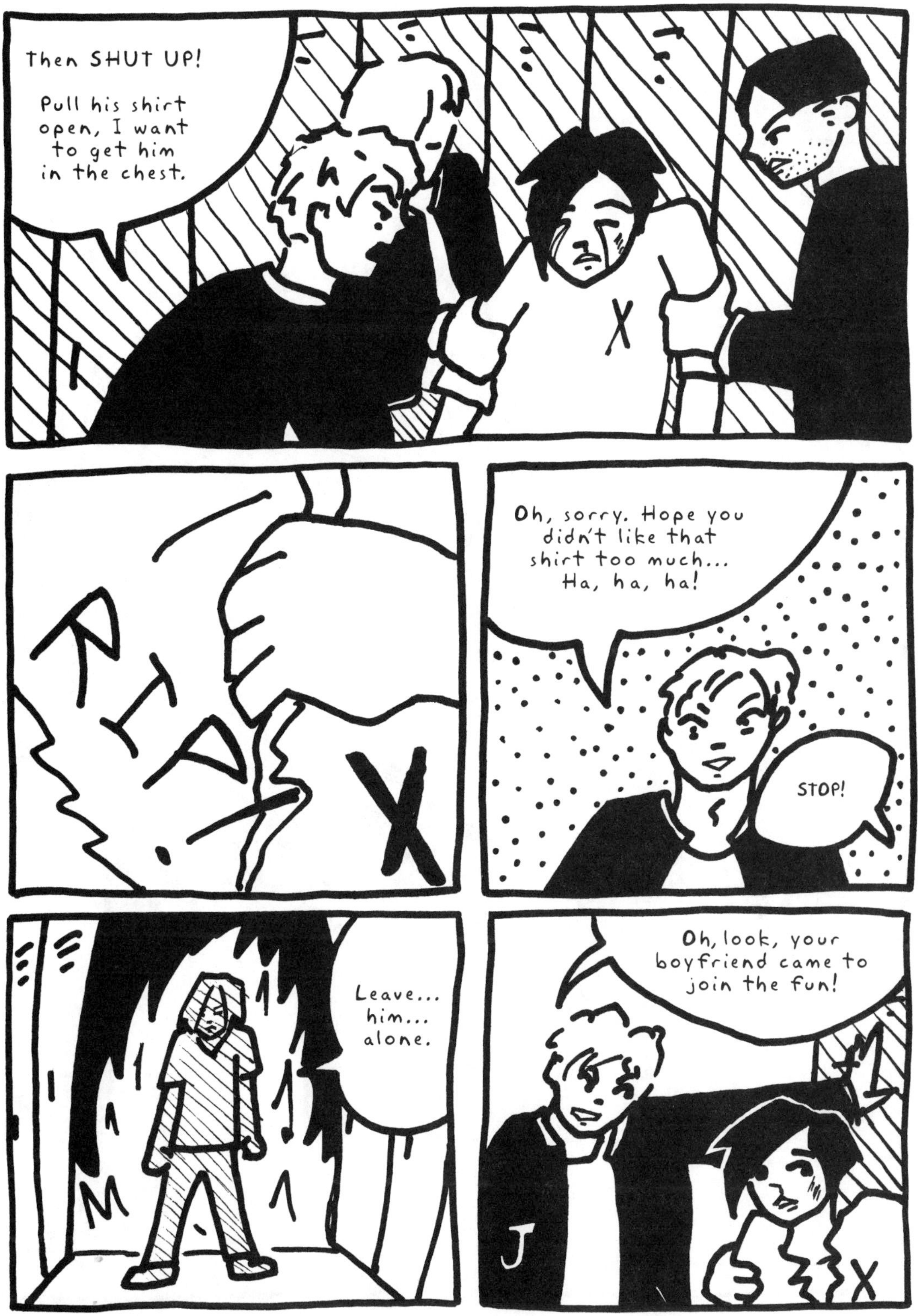
Then SHUT UP!
Pull his shirt open, I want to get him in the chest.
RIP
Oh, sorry. Hope you didn't like that shirt too much... Ha, ha, ha!
STOP!
Leave... him... alone.
Oh, look, your boyfriend came to join the fun!

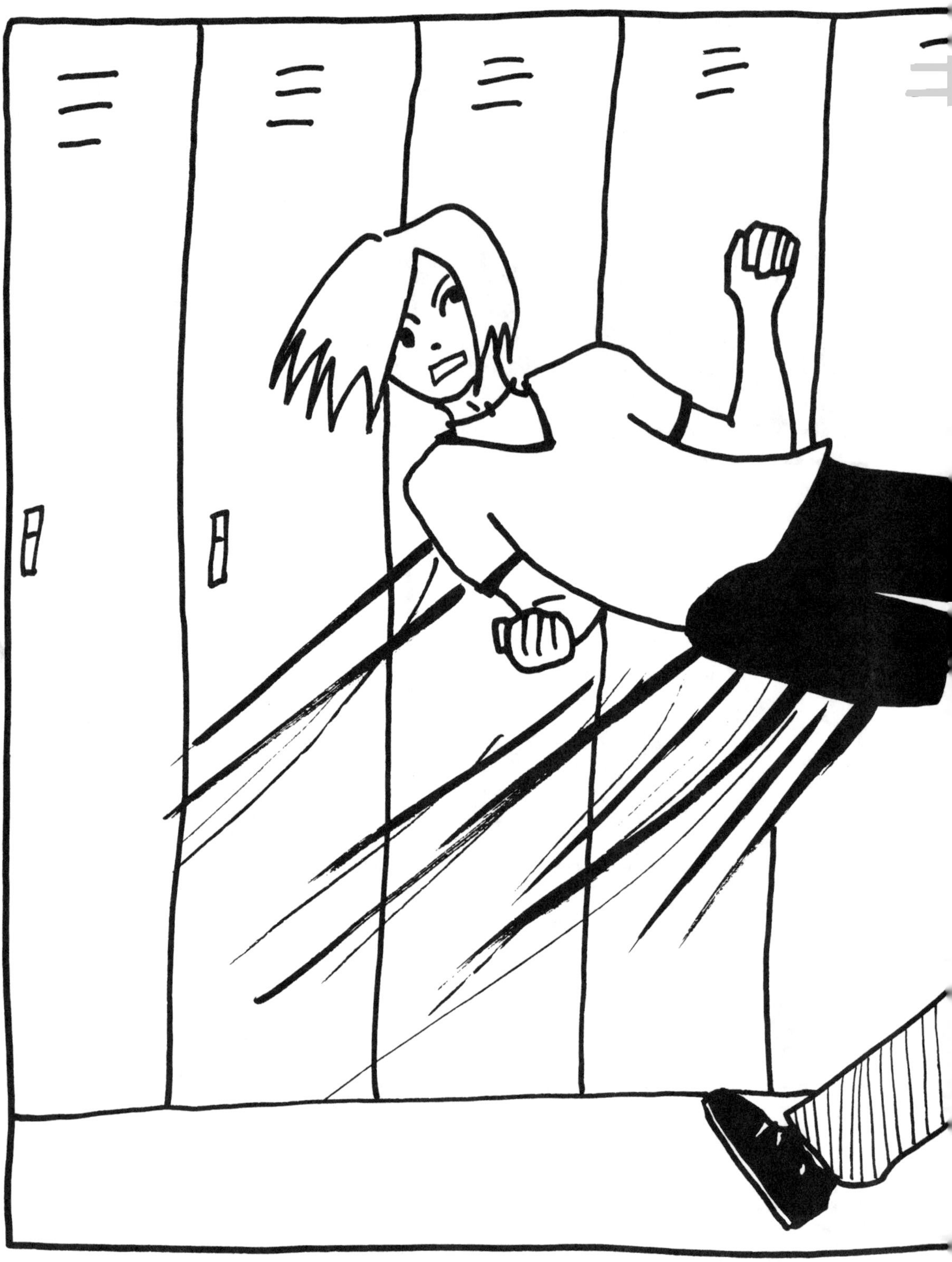

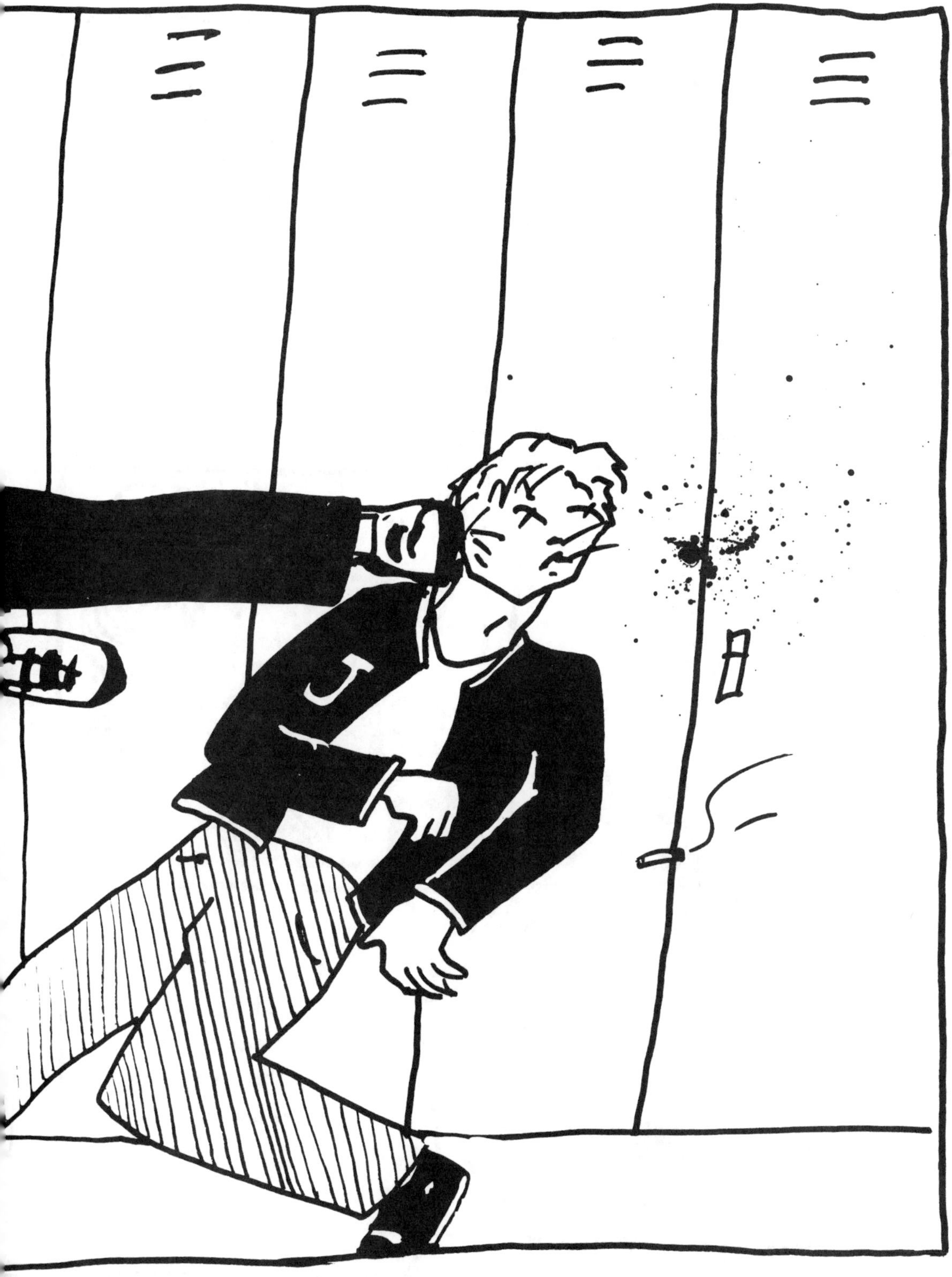

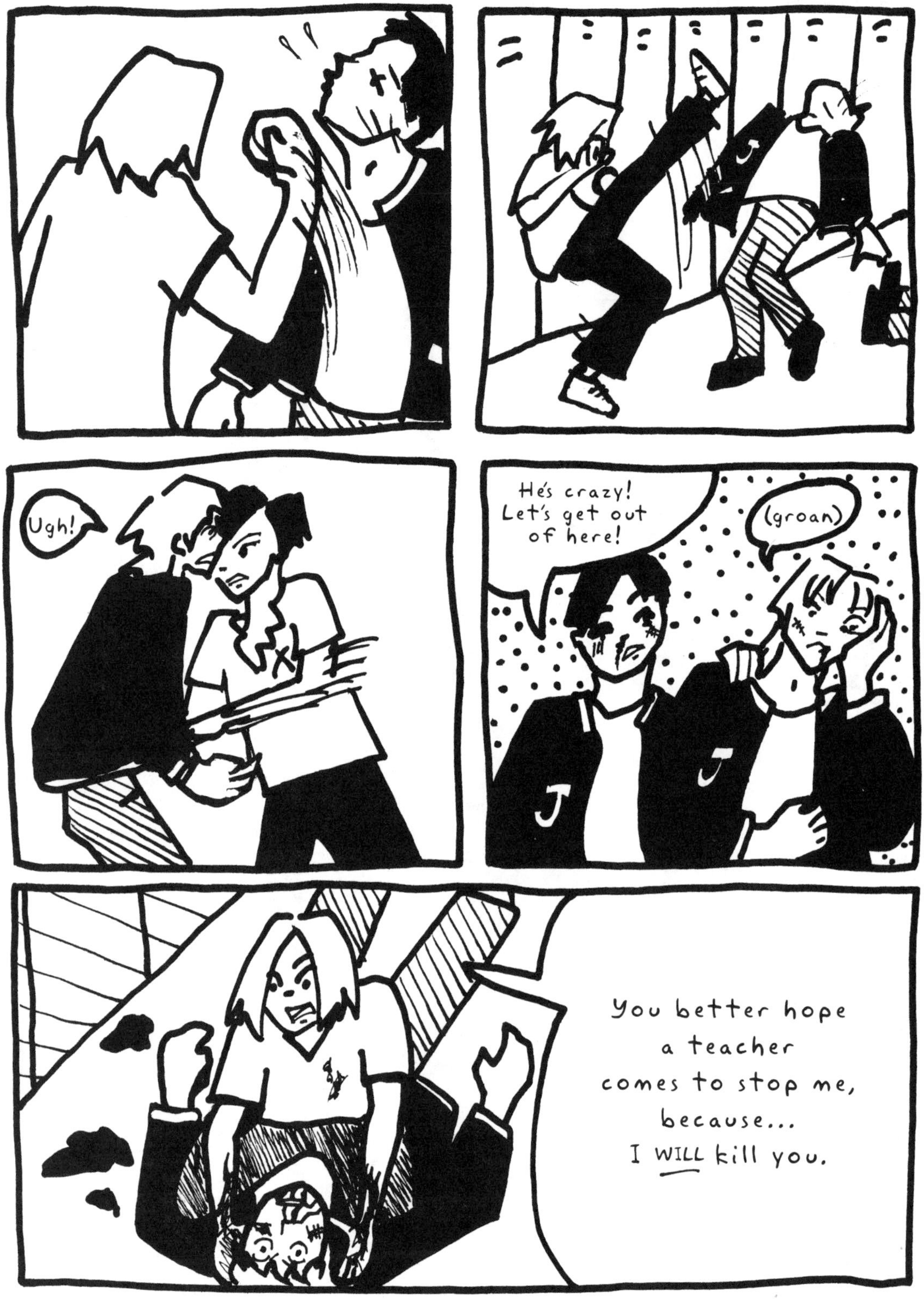
Ugh!
He's crazy! Let's get out of here!
(groan)
You better hope a teacher comes to stop me, because... I WILL kill you.

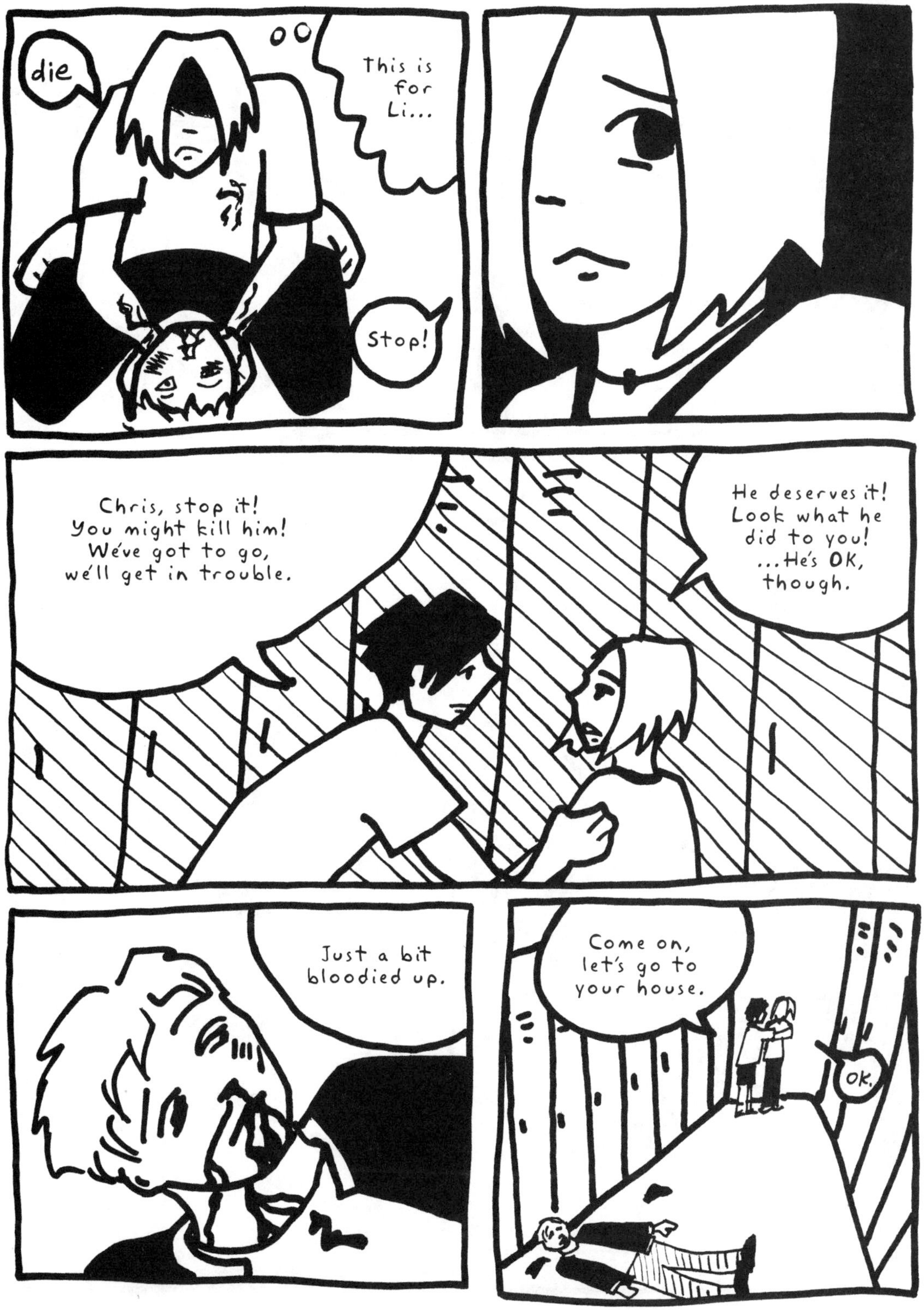

die
This is for Li...
Stop!
Chris, stop it! You might kill him! We've got to go, we'll get in trouble.
He deserves it! Look what he did to you! ...He's OK, though.
Just a bit bloodied up.
Come on, let's go to your house.
OK.

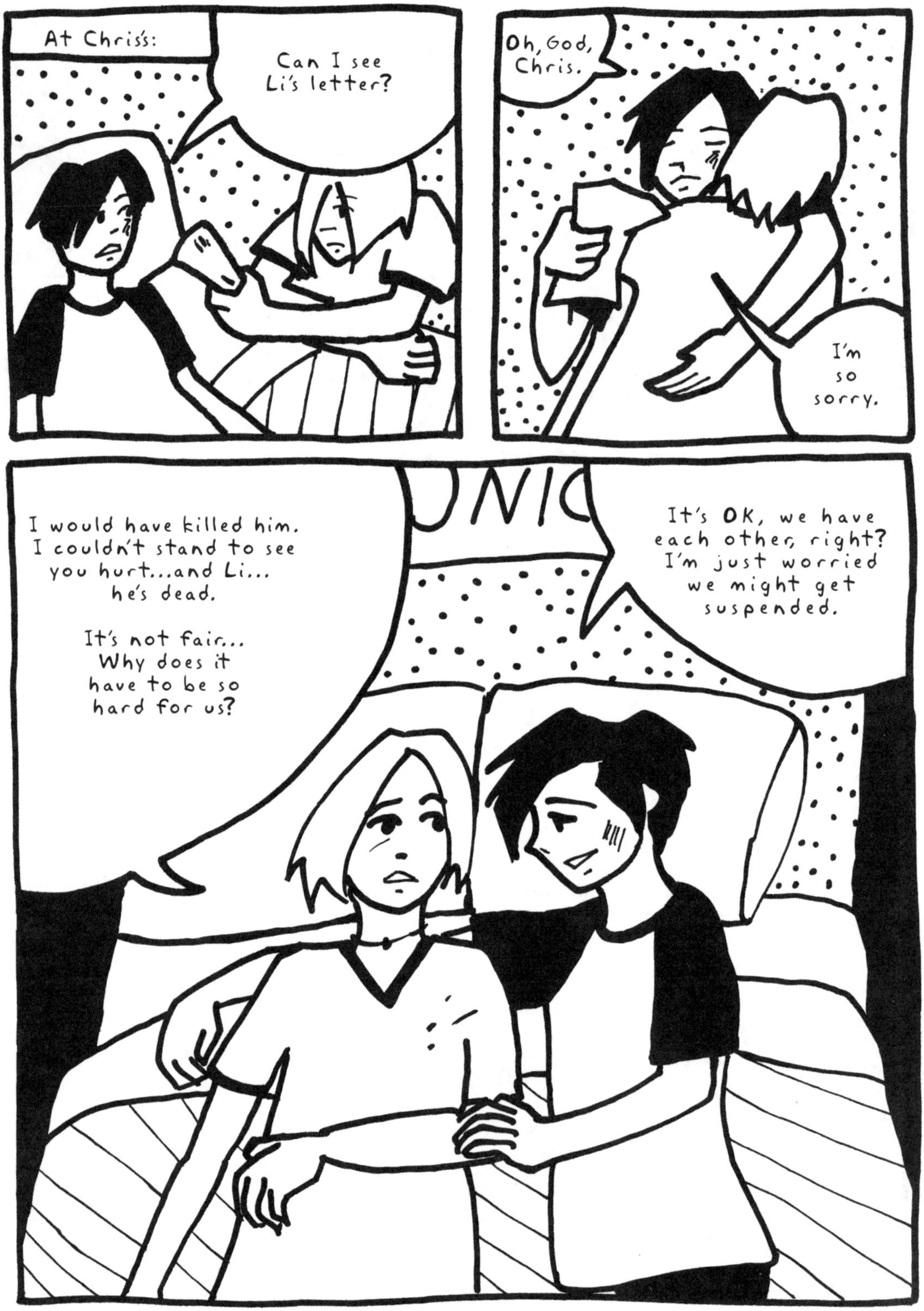
At Chris's:
Can I see Li's letter?
Oh, God, Chris.
I'm so sorry.
ONIC
I would have killed him. I couldn't stand to see you hurt...and Li... he's dead.
It's not fair... Why does it have to be so hard for us?
It's OK, we have each other, right? I'm just worried we might get suspended.

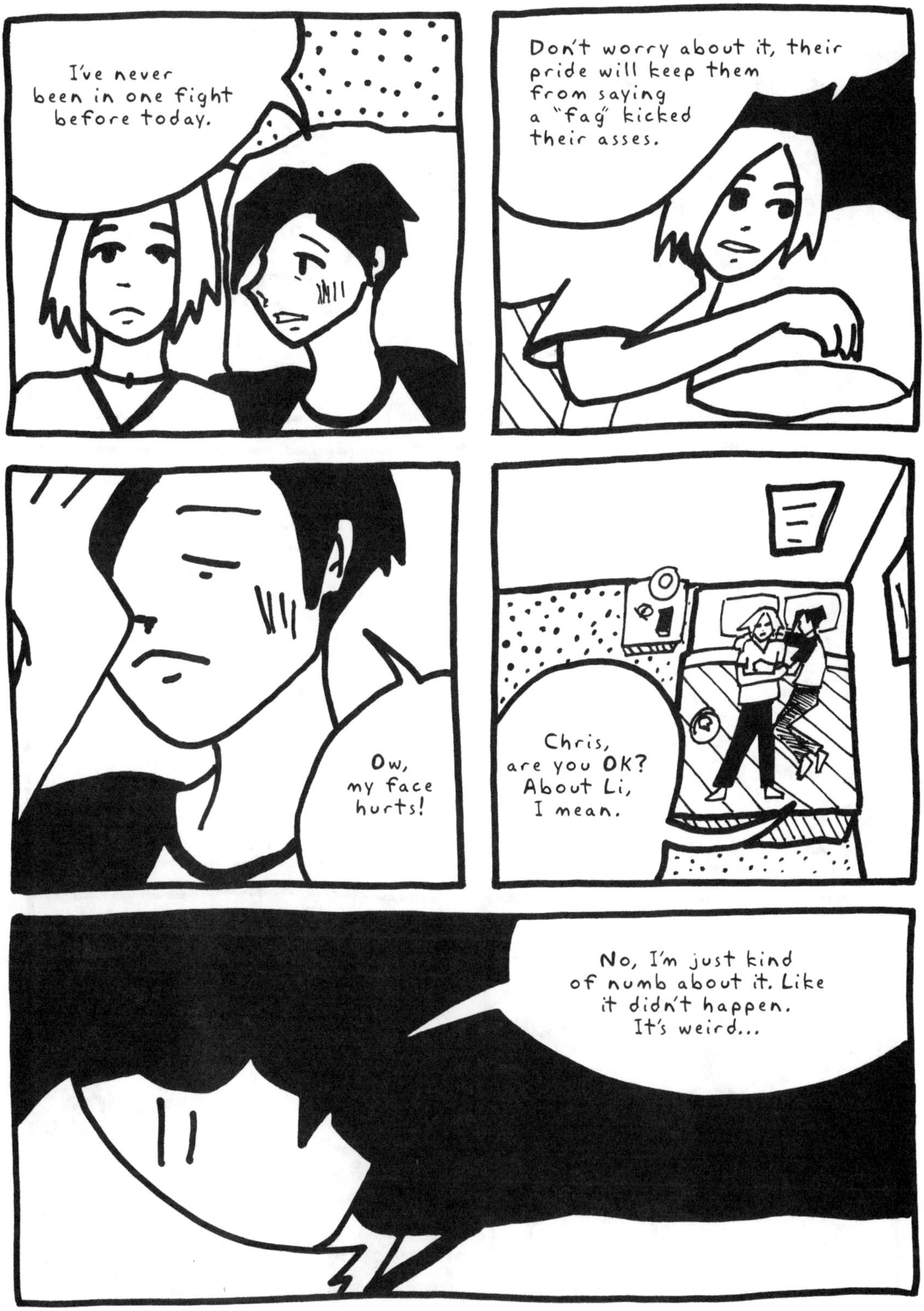
I've never been in one fight before today.
Don't worry about it, their pride will keep them from saying a "fag" kicked their asses.
Ow, my face hurts!
Chris, are you OK? About Li, I mean.
No, I'm just kind of numb about it. Like it didn't happen. It's weird...

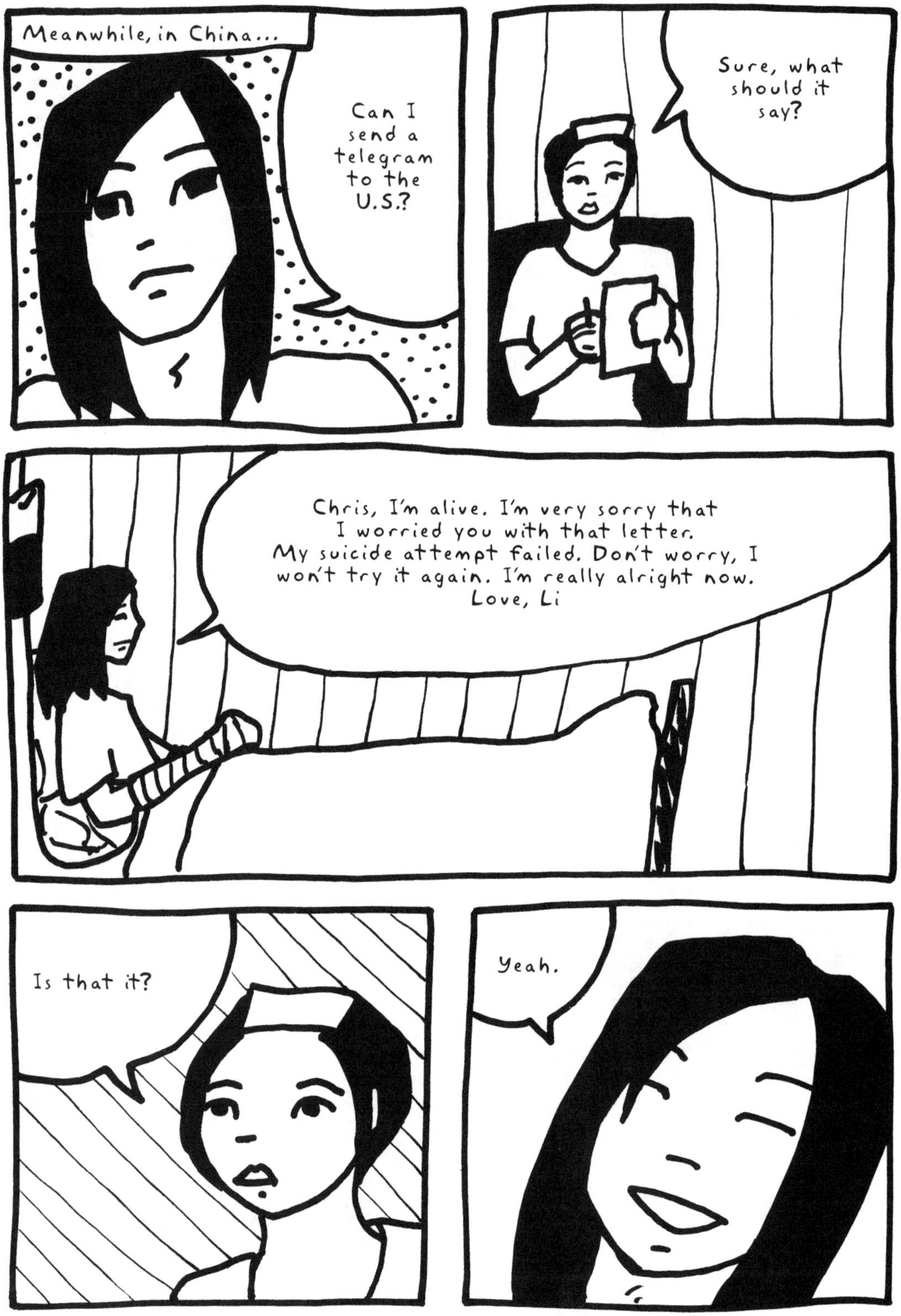
Meanwhile, in China...
Can I send a telegram to the U.S.?
Sure, what should it say?
Chris, I'm alive. I'm very sorry that I worried you with that letter. My suicide attempt failed. Don't worry, I won't try it again. I'm really alright now. Love, Li
Is that it?
Yeah.

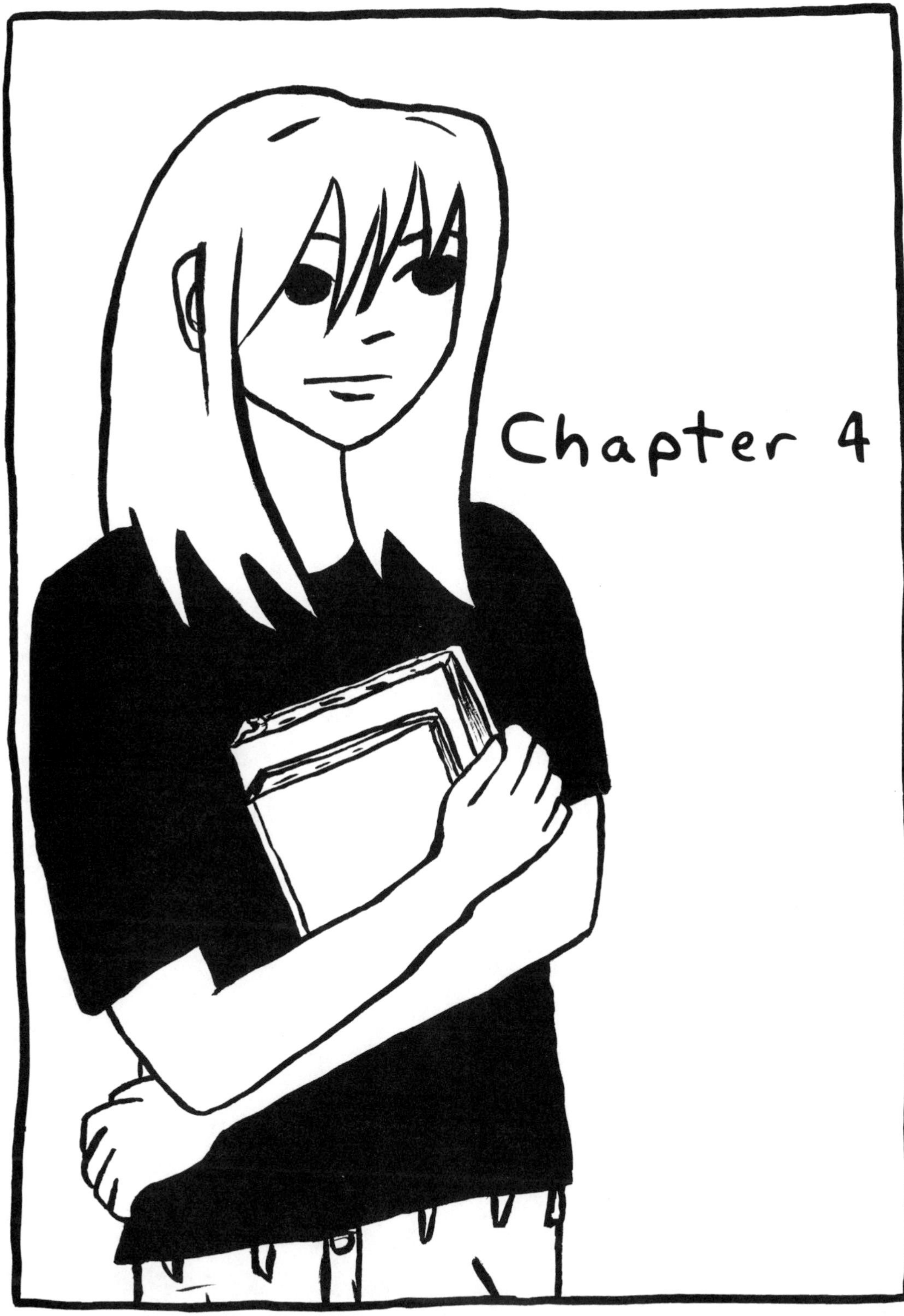
Chapter 4

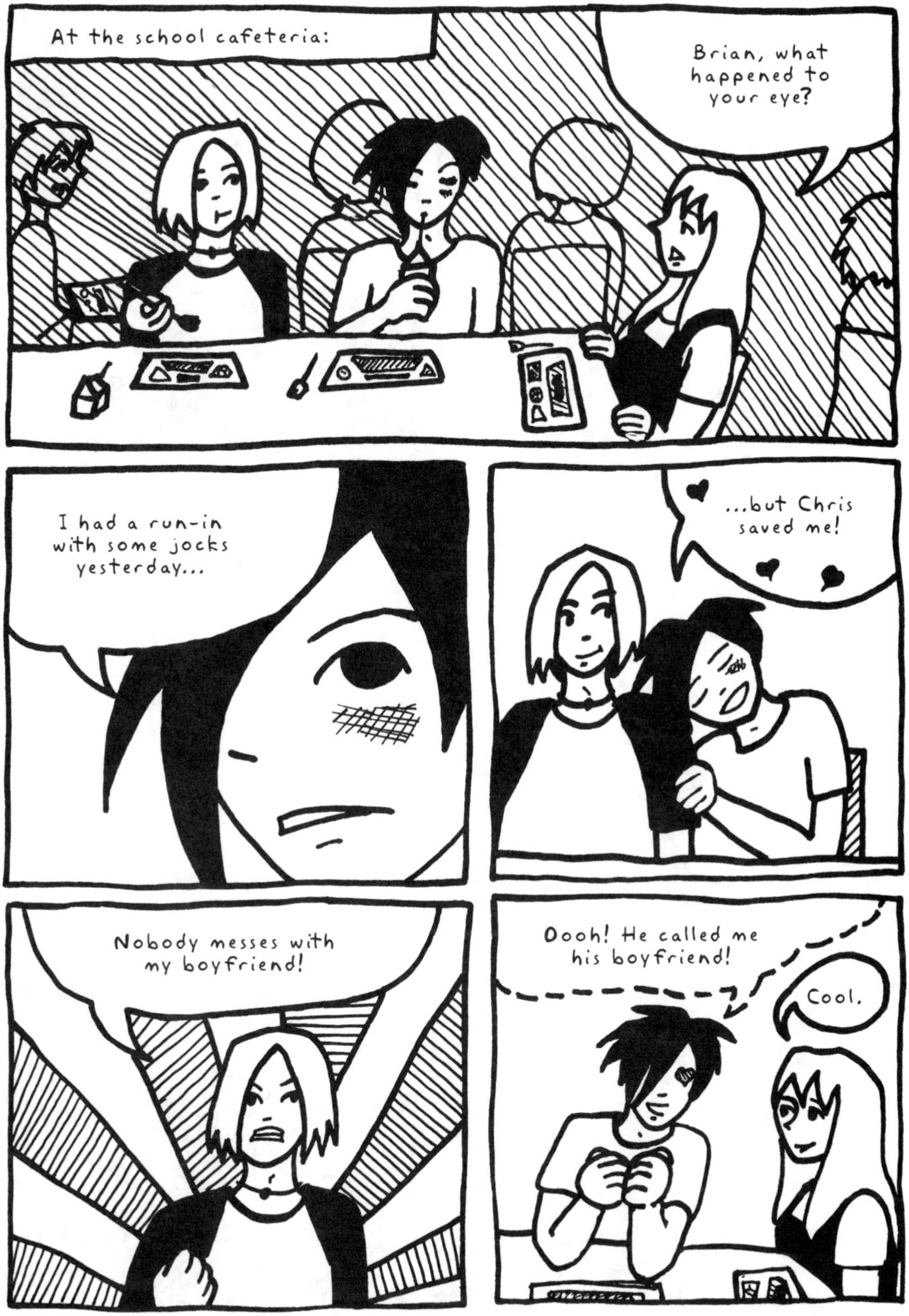
At the school cafeteria:
Brian, what happened to your eye?
I had a run-in with some jocks yesterday...
...but Chris saved me!
Nobody messes with my boyfriend!
Oooh! He called me his boyfriend!
Cool.

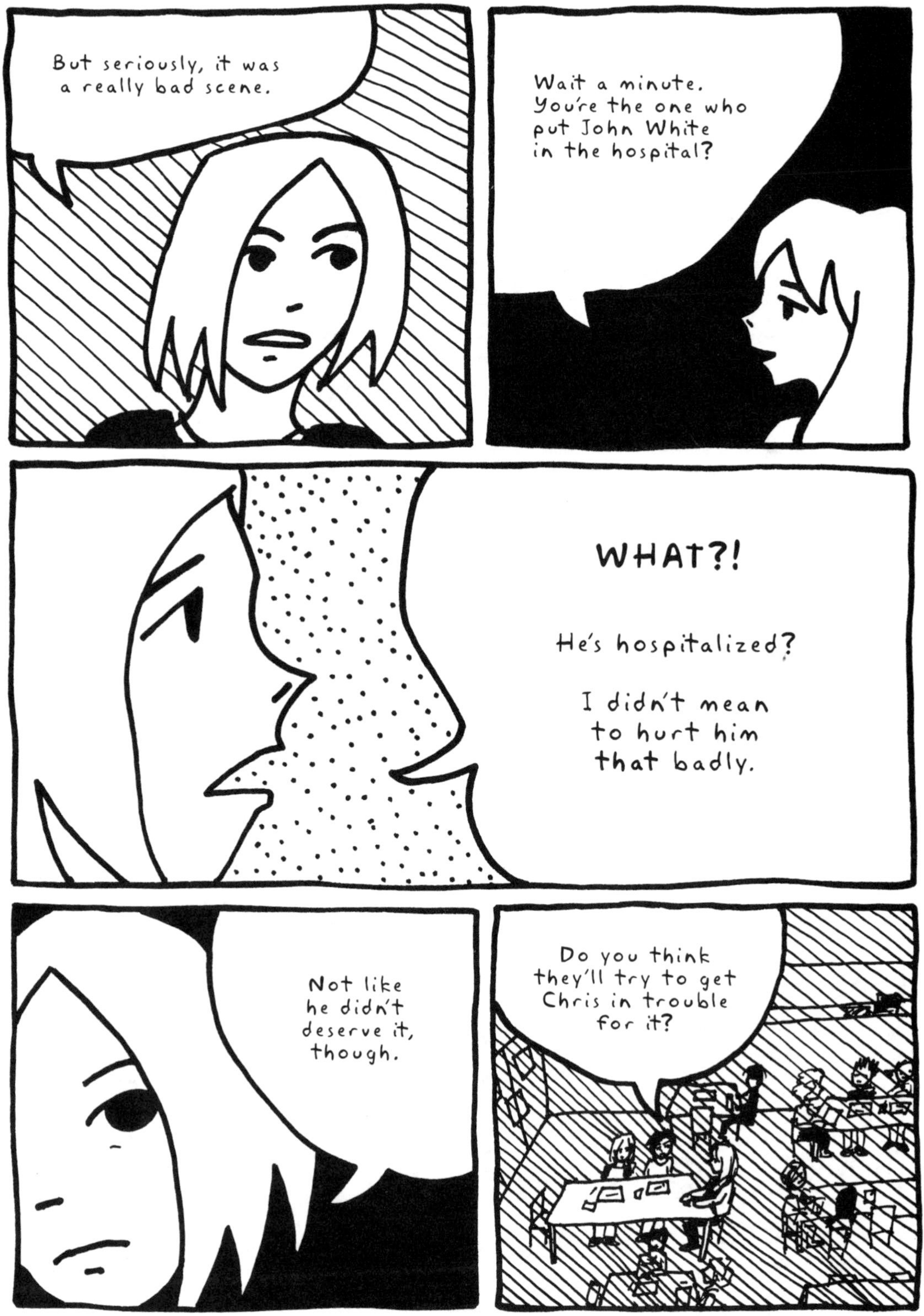
But seriously, it was a really bad scene.
Wait a minute. You're the one who put John White in the hospital?
WHAT?!
He's hospitalized?
I didn't mean to hurt him that badly.
Not like he didn't deserve it, though.
Do you think they'll try to get Chris in trouble for it?

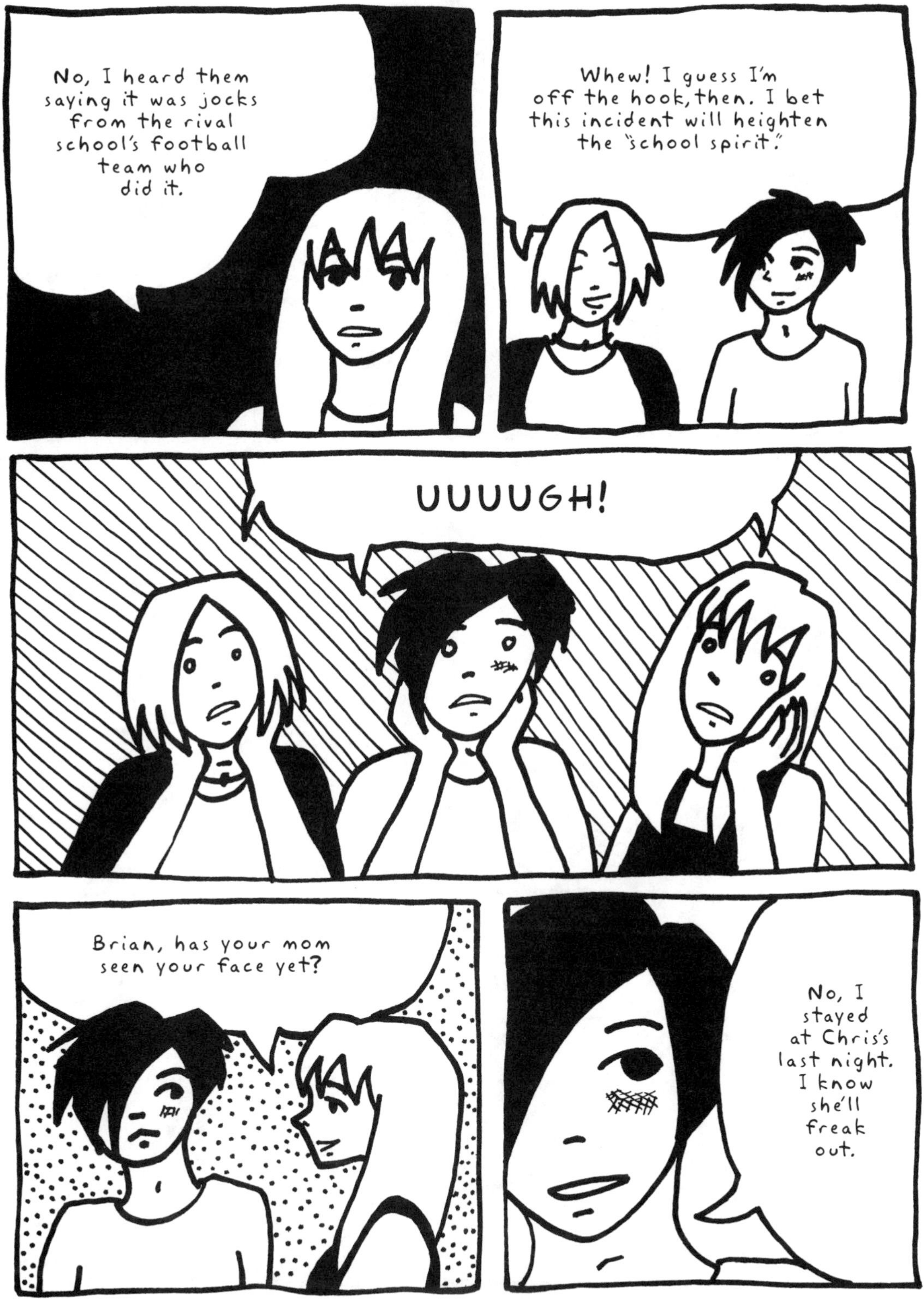
No, I heard them saying it was jocks from the rival school's football team who did it.
Whew! I guess I'm off the hook, then. I bet this incident will heighten the "school spirit."
UUUUGH!
Brian, has your mom seen your face yet?
No, I stayed at Chris's last night. I know she'll freak out.

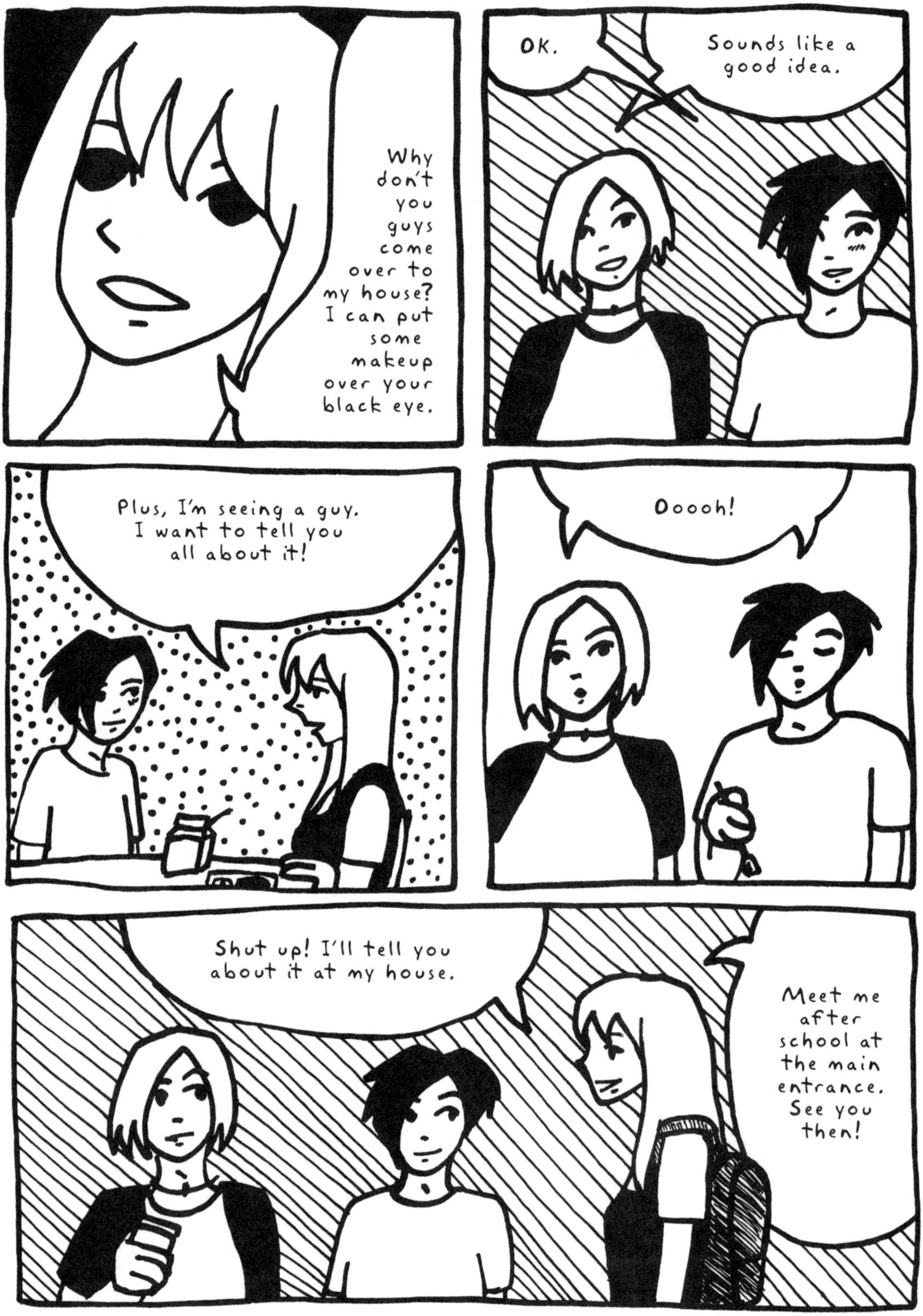
Why don't you guys come over to my house? I can put some makeup over your black eye.
OK.
Sounds like a good idea.
Plus, I'm seeing a guy. I want to tell you all about it!
Ooooh!
Shut up! I'll tell you about it at my house.
Meet me after school at the main entrance. See you then!

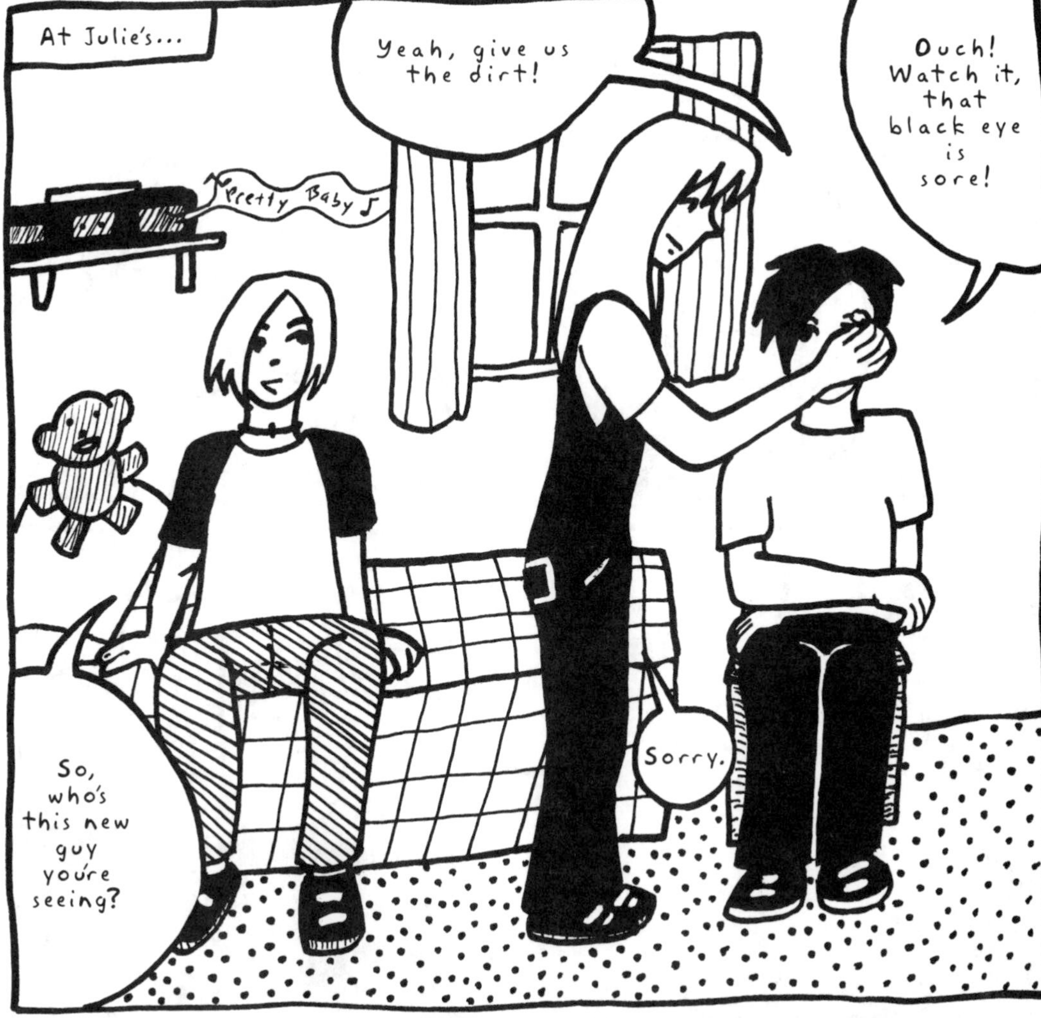
At Julie's...
Yeah, give us the dirt!
Ouch! Watch it, that black eye is sore!
Pretty Baby
Sorry.
So, who's this new guy you're seeing?

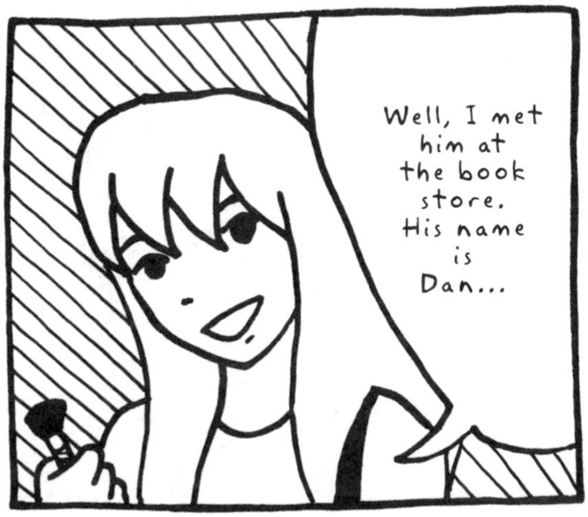
Well, I met him at the book store. His name is Dan...

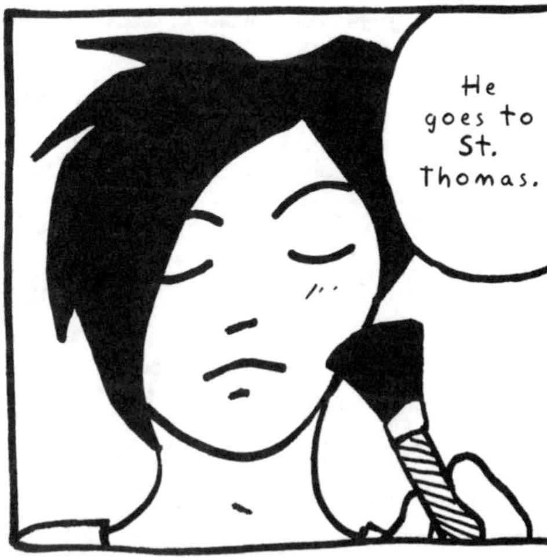
He goes to St. Thomas.

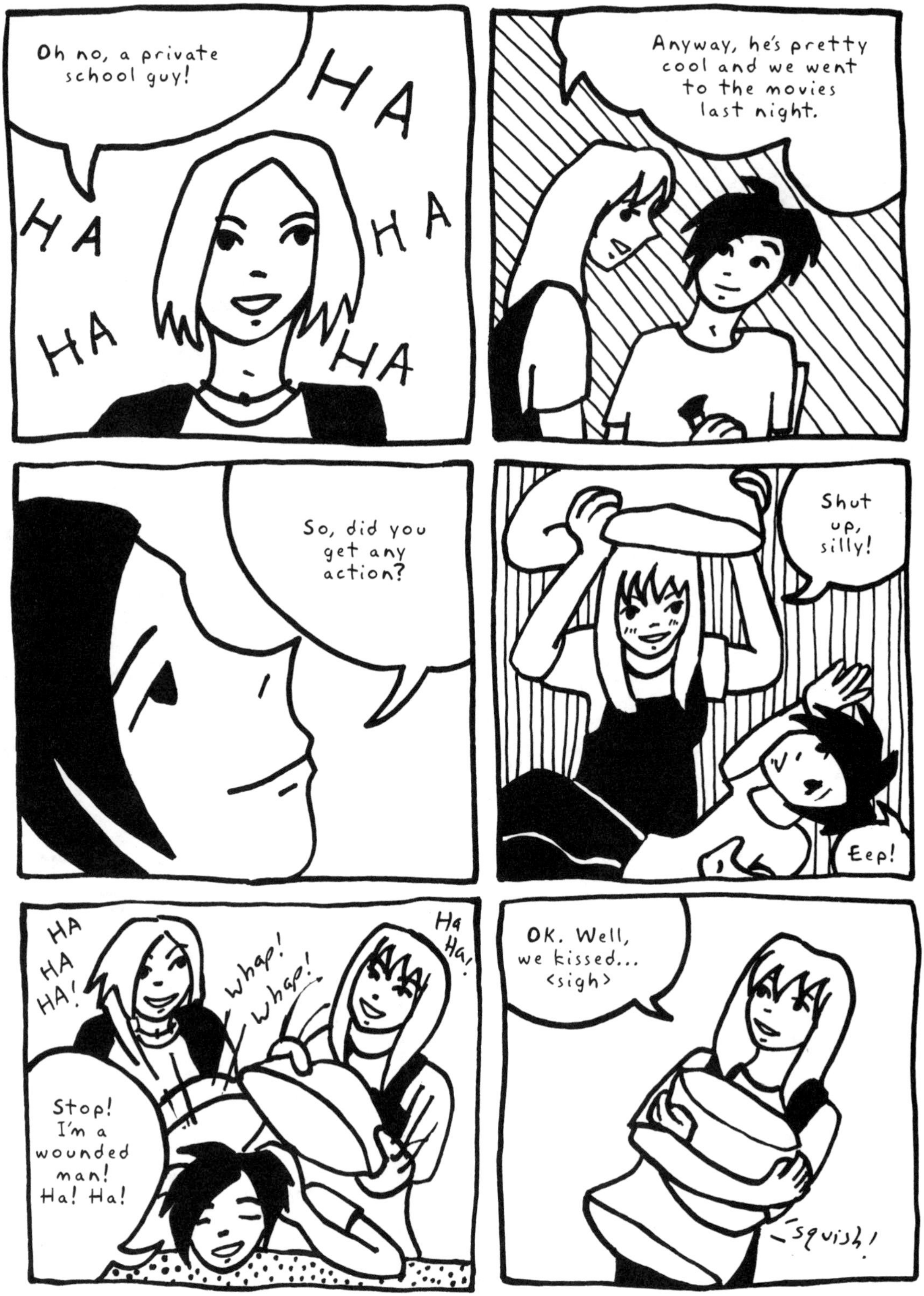
Oh no, a private school guy!
HA HA HA HA HA HA
Anyway, he's pretty cool and we went to the movies last night.
So, did you get any action?
Shut up, silly!
Eep!
HA HA HA!
Whap! Whap!
Ha Ha!
Stop! I'm a wounded man! Ha! Ha!
OK. Well, we kissed... <sigh>
Squish!

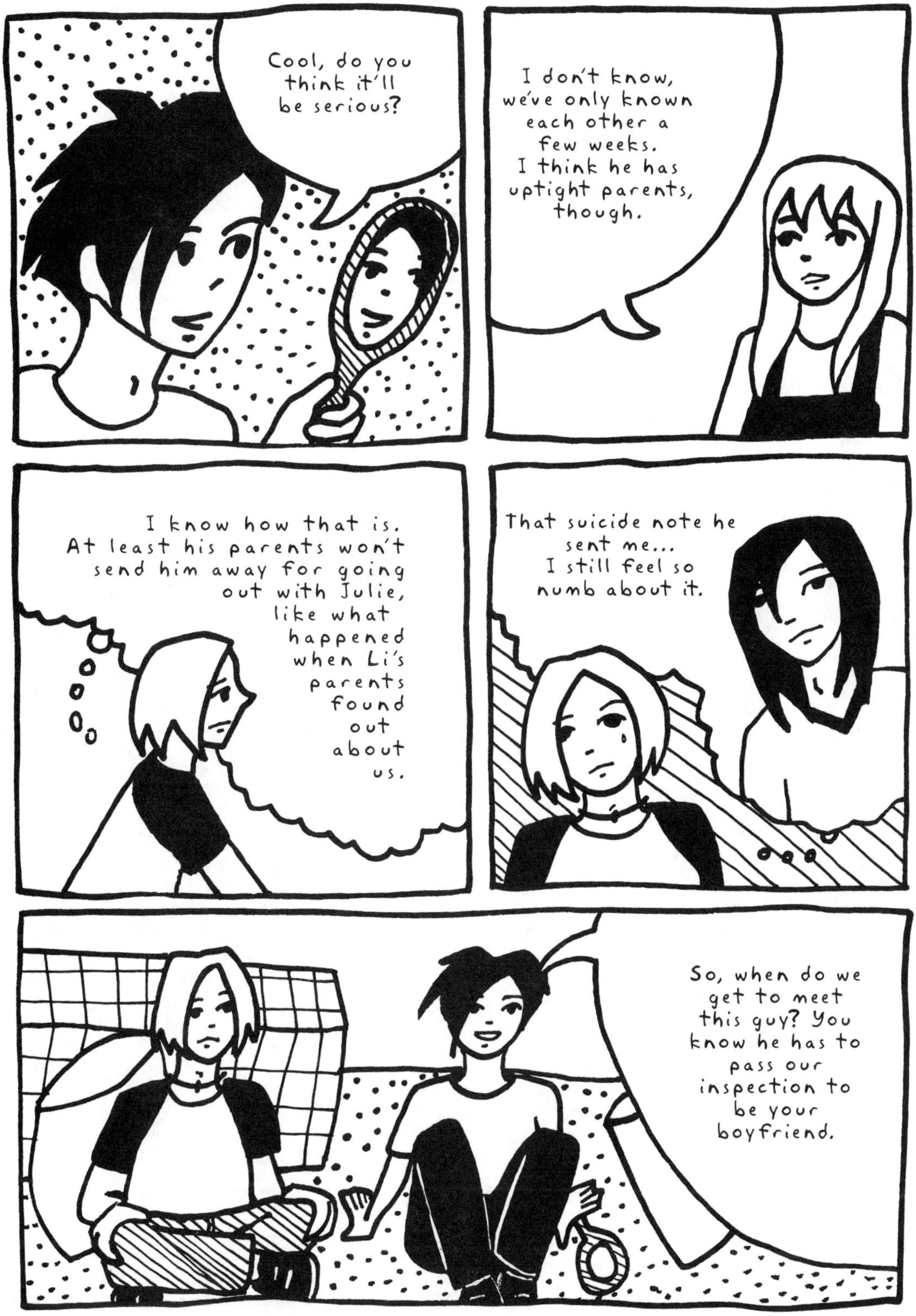
Cool, do you think it'll be serious?
I don't know, we've only known each other a few weeks. I think he has uptight parents, though.
I know how that is. At least his parents won't send him away for going out with Julie, like what happened when Li's parents found out about us.
That suicide note he sent me... I still feel so numb about it.
So, when do we get to meet this guy? You know he has to pass our inspection to be your boyfriend.

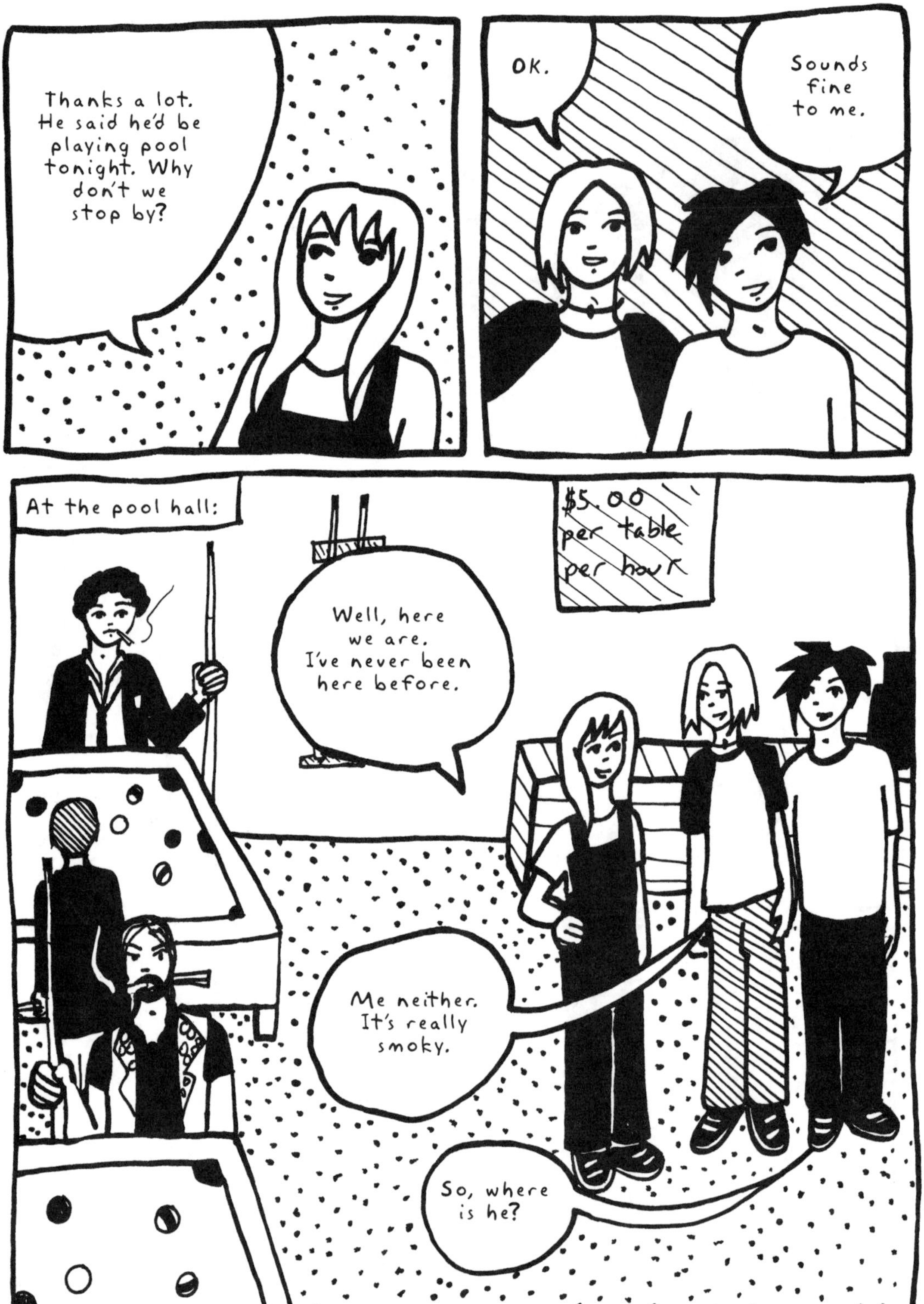
Thanks a lot. He said he'd be playing pool tonight. Why don't we stop by?
OK.
Sounds fine to me.
At the pool hall:
$5.00 per table per hour
Well, here we are. I've never been here before.
Me neither. It's really smoky.
So, where is he?

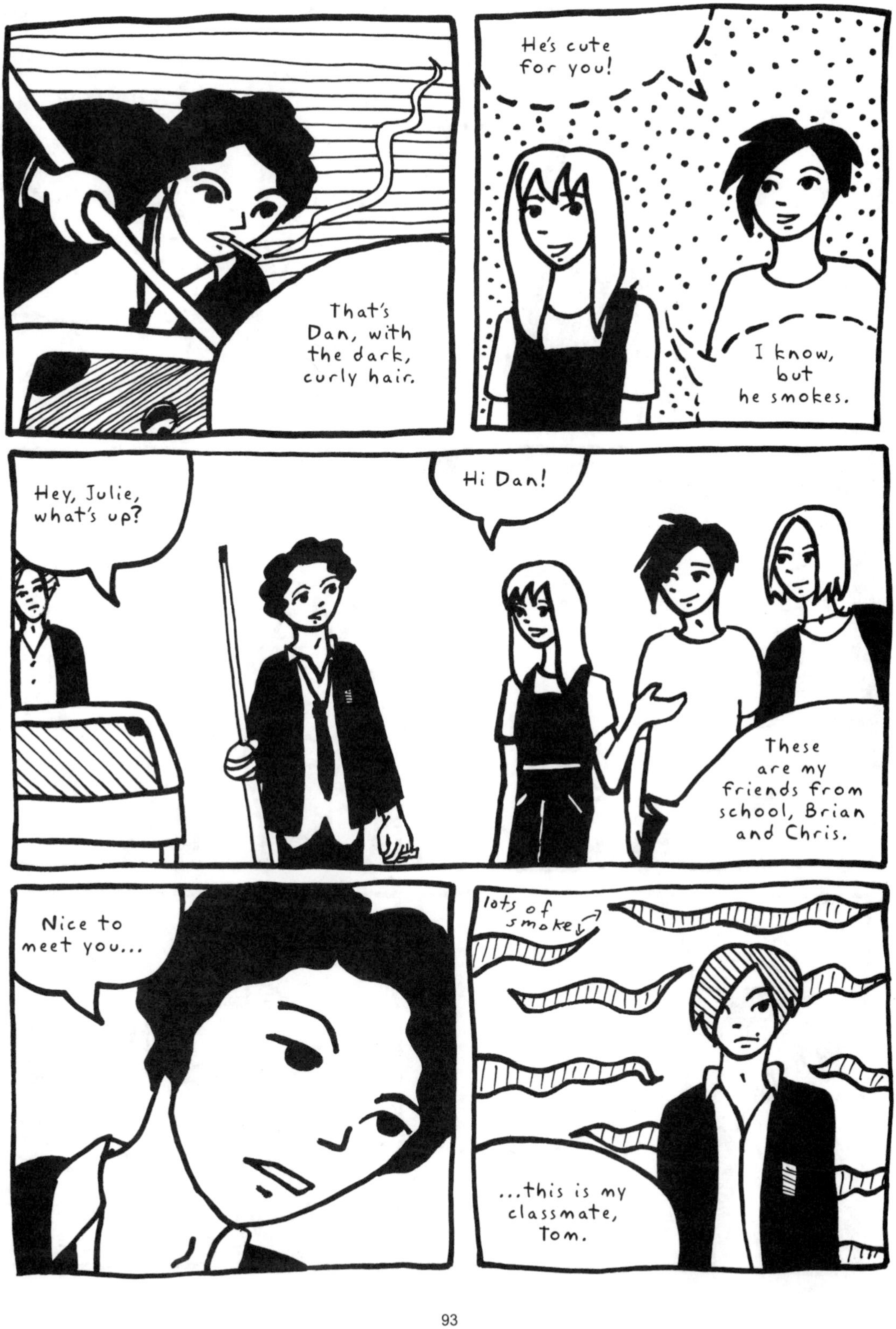
That's Dan, with the dark, curly hair.
He's cute for you!
I know, but he smokes.
Hey, Julie, what's up?
Hi Dan!
These are my friends from school, Brian and Chris.
Nice to meet you...
lots of smoke
...this is my classmate, Tom.

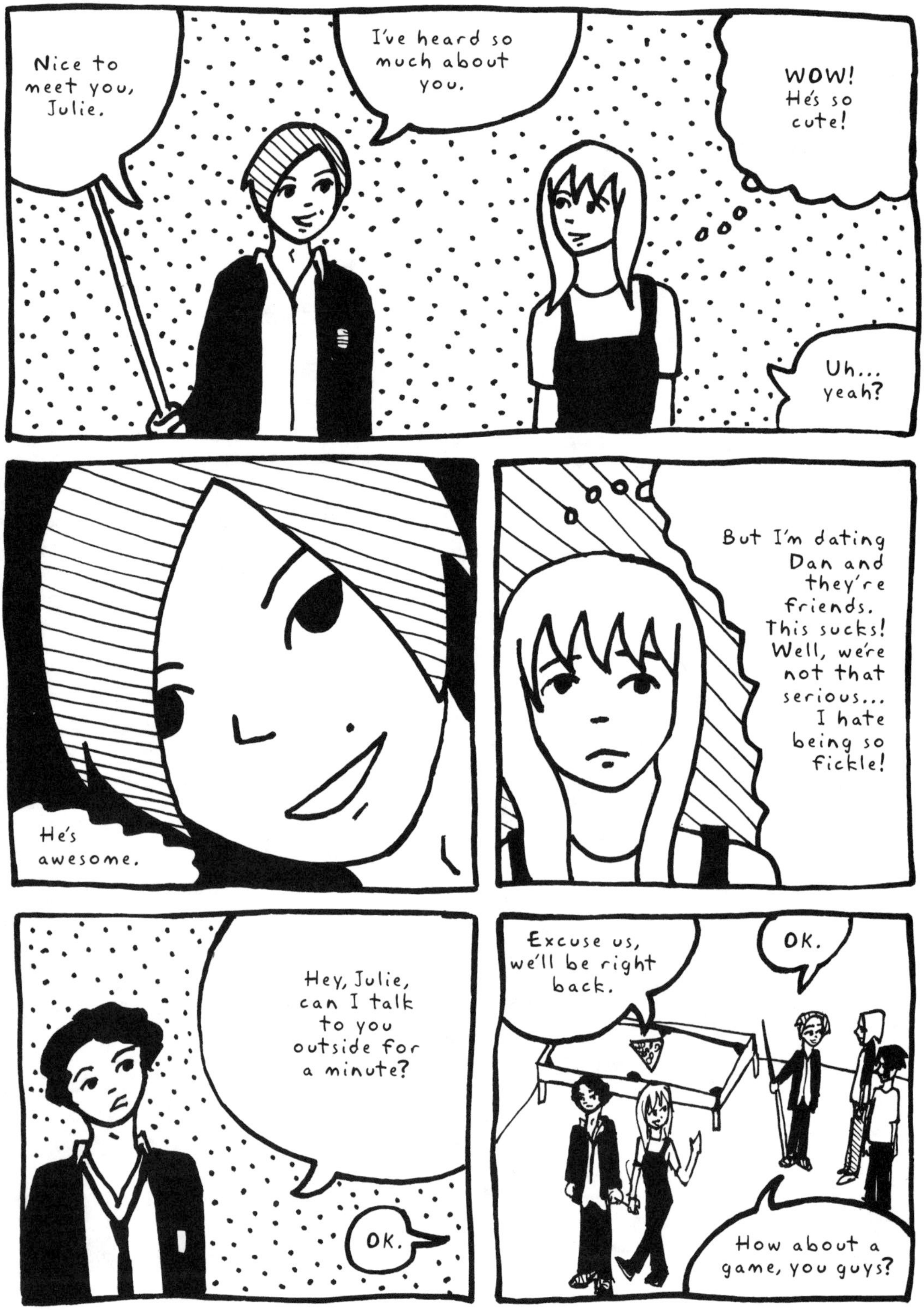
Nice to meet you, Julie.
I've heard so much about you.
WOW! He's so cute!
Uh... yeah?
He's awesome.
But I'm dating Dan and they're friends. This sucks! Well, we're not that serious... I hate being so fickle!
Hey, Julie, can I talk to you outside for a minute?
OK.
Excuse us, we'll be right back.
OK.
How about a game, you guys?

POOL HALL
Julie, what's up with those guys you brought? I don't like you hanging out with other guys!
You're MY girlfriend!
First of all, I didn't know we're "boyfriend/girlfriend", we never discussed it! Second of all, they're my friends, and believe me, you have nothing to worry about!
What? Are they fags or something?
What do I say?

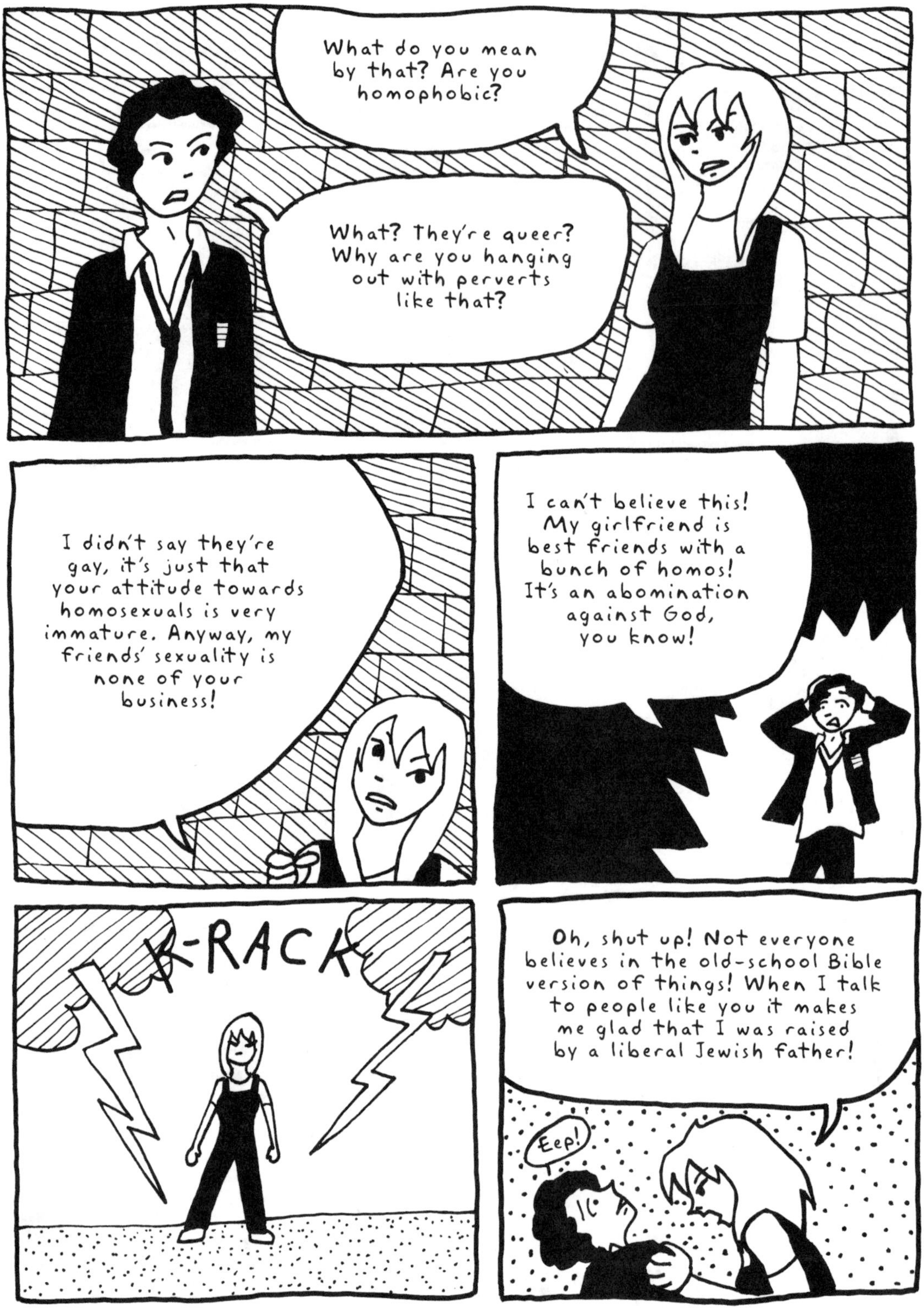
What do you mean by that? Are you homophobic?
What? They're queer? Why are you hanging out with perverts like that?
I didn't say they're gay, it's just that your attitude towards homosexuals is very immature. Anyway, my friends' sexuality is none of your business!
I can't believe this! My girlfriend is best friends with a bunch of homos! It's an abomination against God, you know!
K-RACK
Oh, shut up! Not everyone believes in the old-school Bible version of things! When I talk to people like you it makes me glad that I was raised by a liberal Jewish father!
Eep!

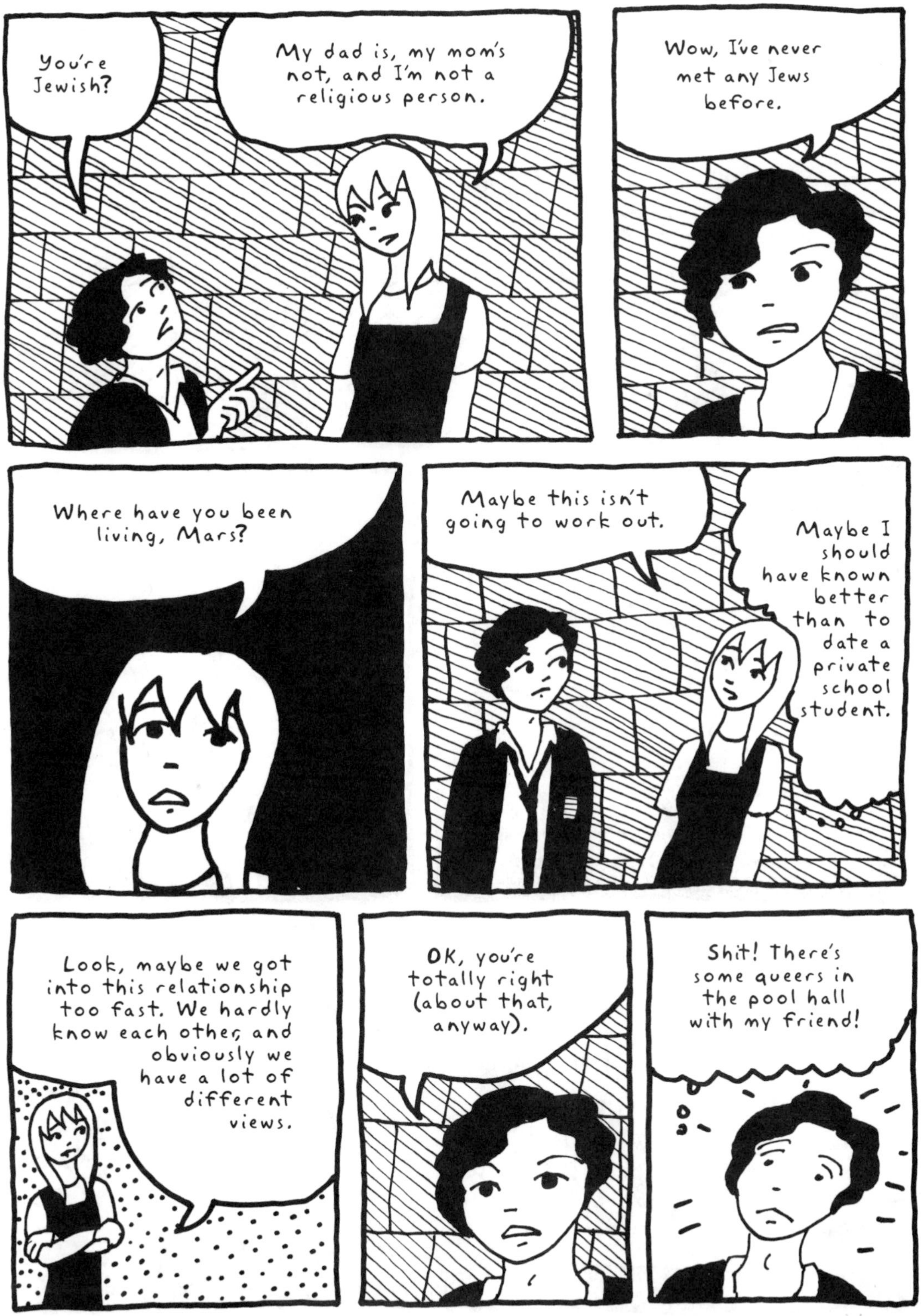
You're Jewish?
My dad is, my mom's not, and I'm not a religious person.
Wow, I've never met any Jews before.
Where have you been living, Mars?
Maybe this isn't going to work out.
Maybe I should have known better than to date a private school student.
Look, maybe we got into this relationship too fast. We hardly know each other, and obviously we have a lot of different views.
OK, you're totally right (about that, anyway).
Shit! There's some queers in the pool hall with my friend!

Queer Love

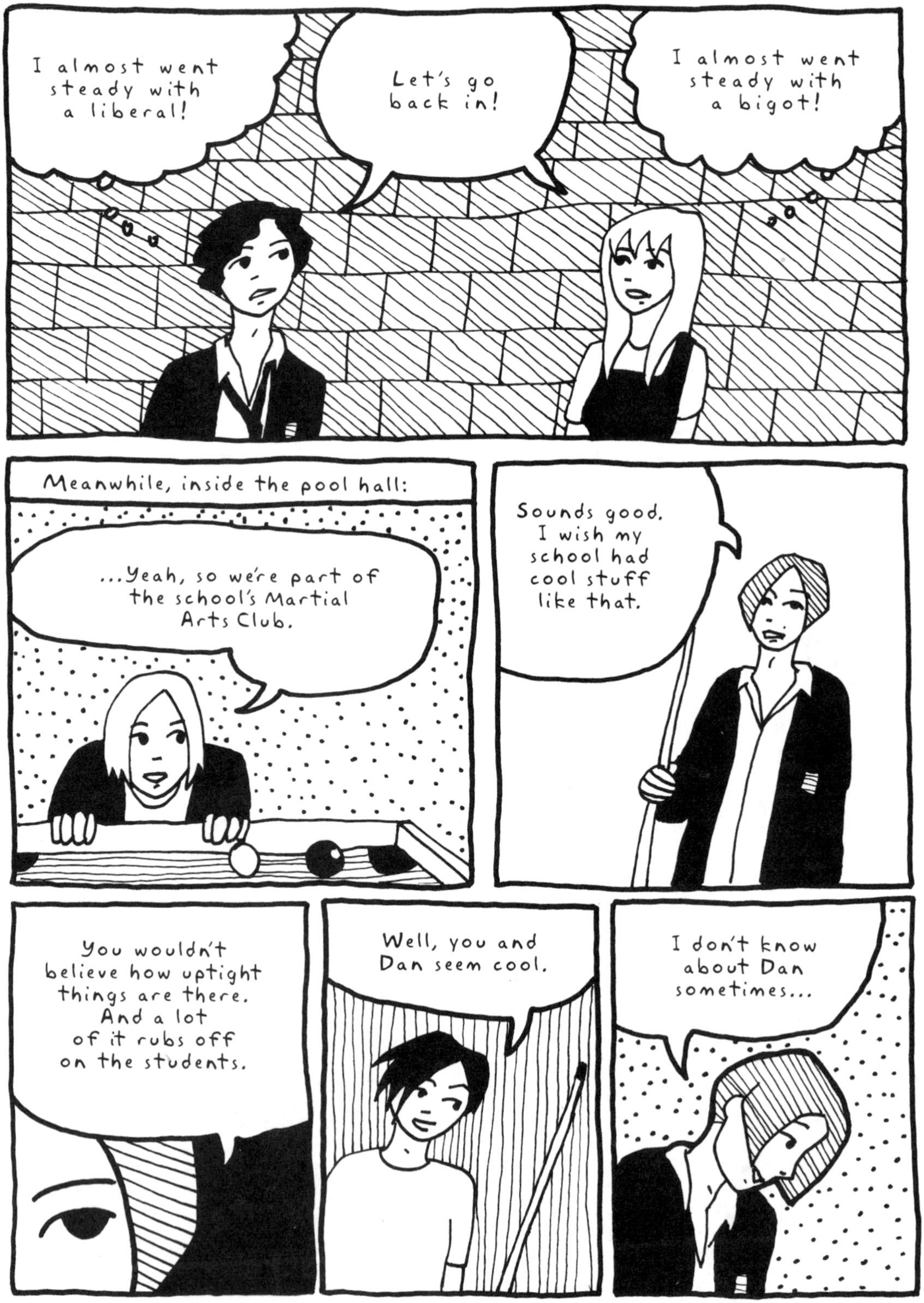
I almost went steady with a liberal!
Let's go back in!
I almost went steady with a bigot!
Meanwhile, inside the pool hall:
...Yeah, so we're part of the school's Martial Arts Club.
Sounds good. I wish my school had cool stuff like that.
You wouldn't believe how uptight things are there. And a lot of it rubs off on the students.
Well, you and Dan seem cool.
I don't know about Dan sometimes...

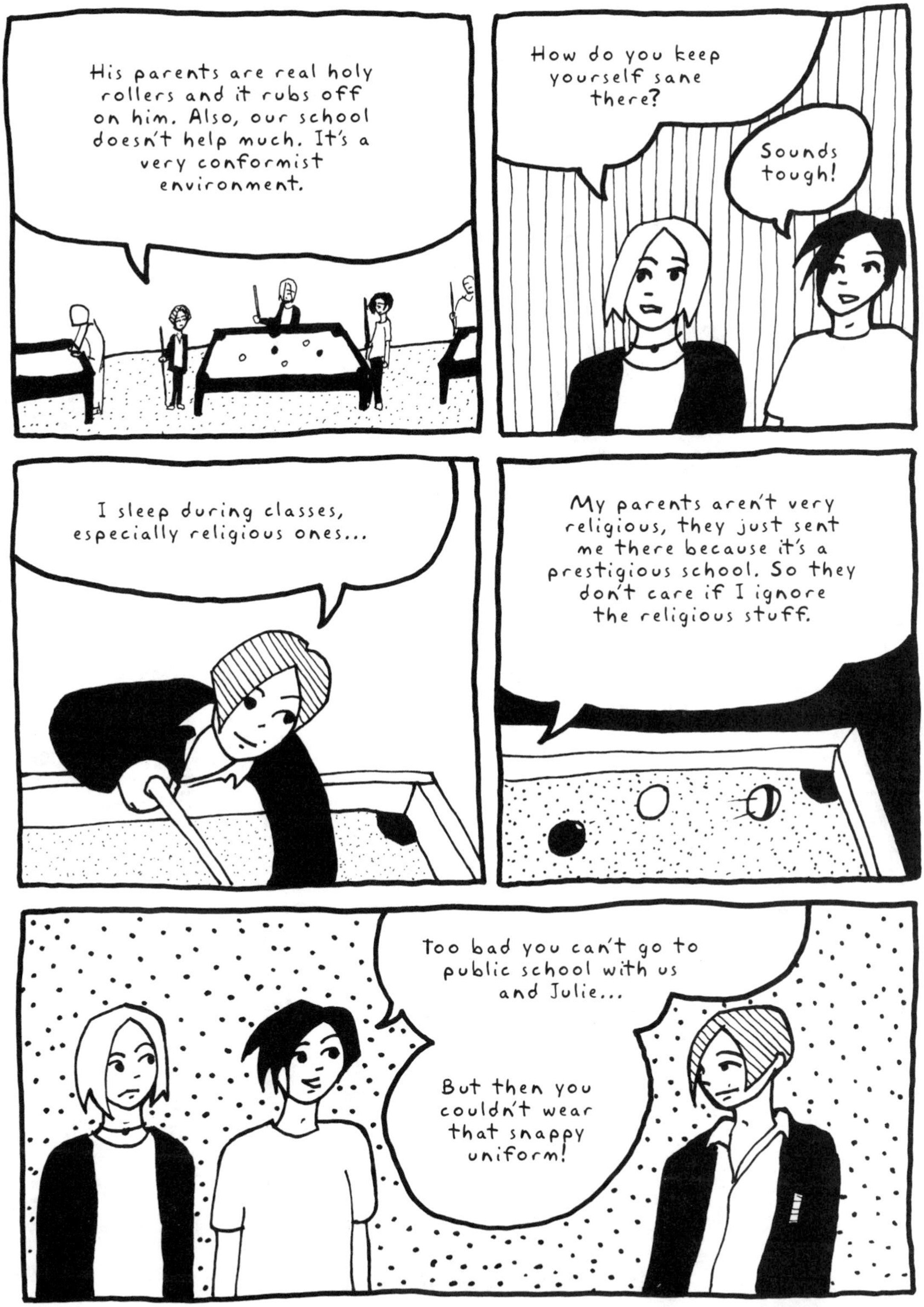
His parents are real holy rollers and it rubs off on him. Also, our school doesn't help much. It's a very conformist environment.
How do you keep yourself sane there?
Sounds tough!
I sleep during classes, especially religious ones...
My parents aren't very religious, they just sent me there because it's a prestigious school. So they don't care if I ignore the religious stuff.
Too bad you can't go to public school with us and Julie...
But then you couldn't wear that snappy uniform!

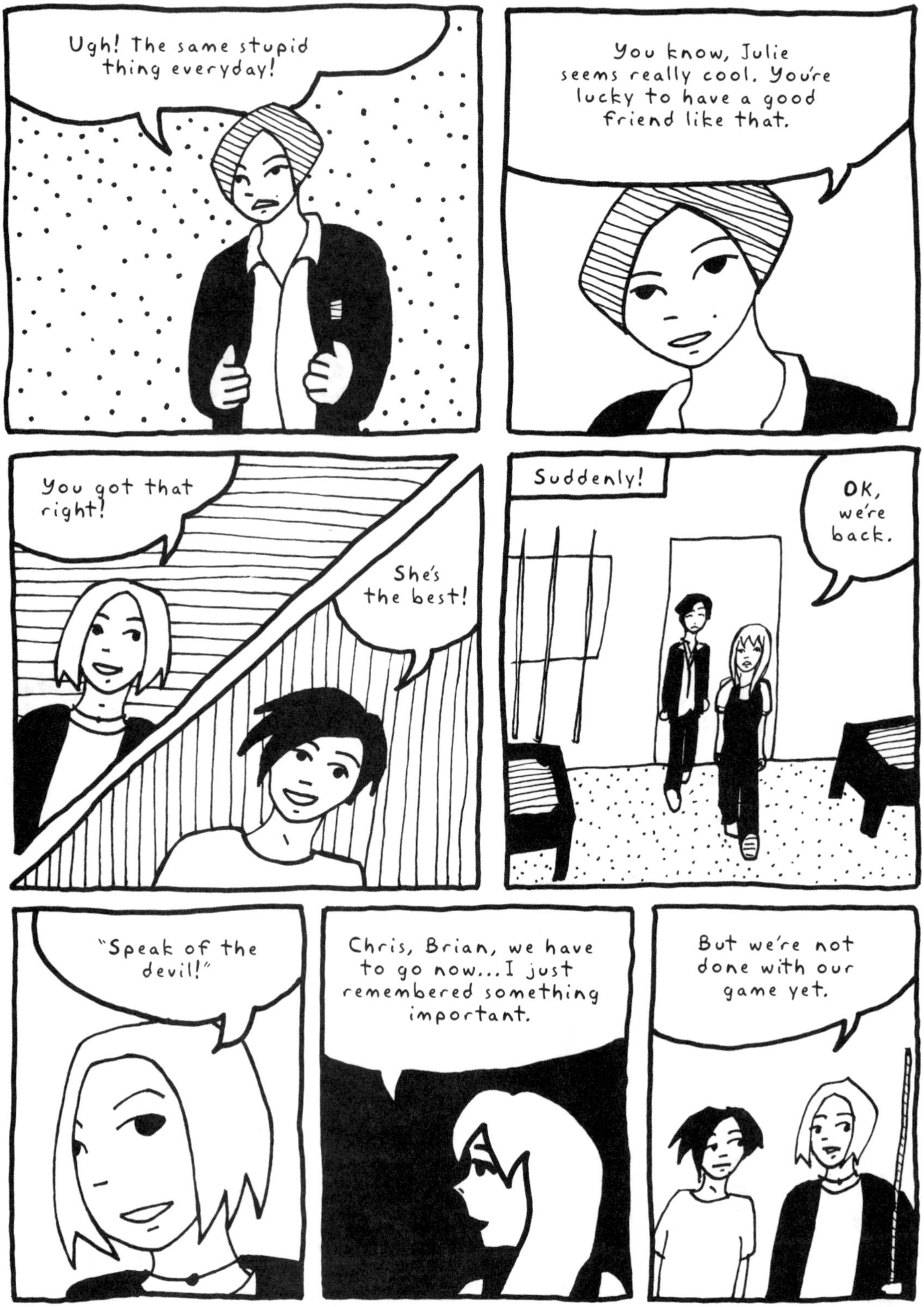

Ugh! The same stupid thing everyday!
You know, Julie seems really cool. You're lucky to have a good friend like that.
You got that right!
She's the best!
Suddenly!
OK, we're back.
"Speak of the devil!"
Chris, Brian, we have to go now...I just remembered something important.
But we're not done with our game yet.

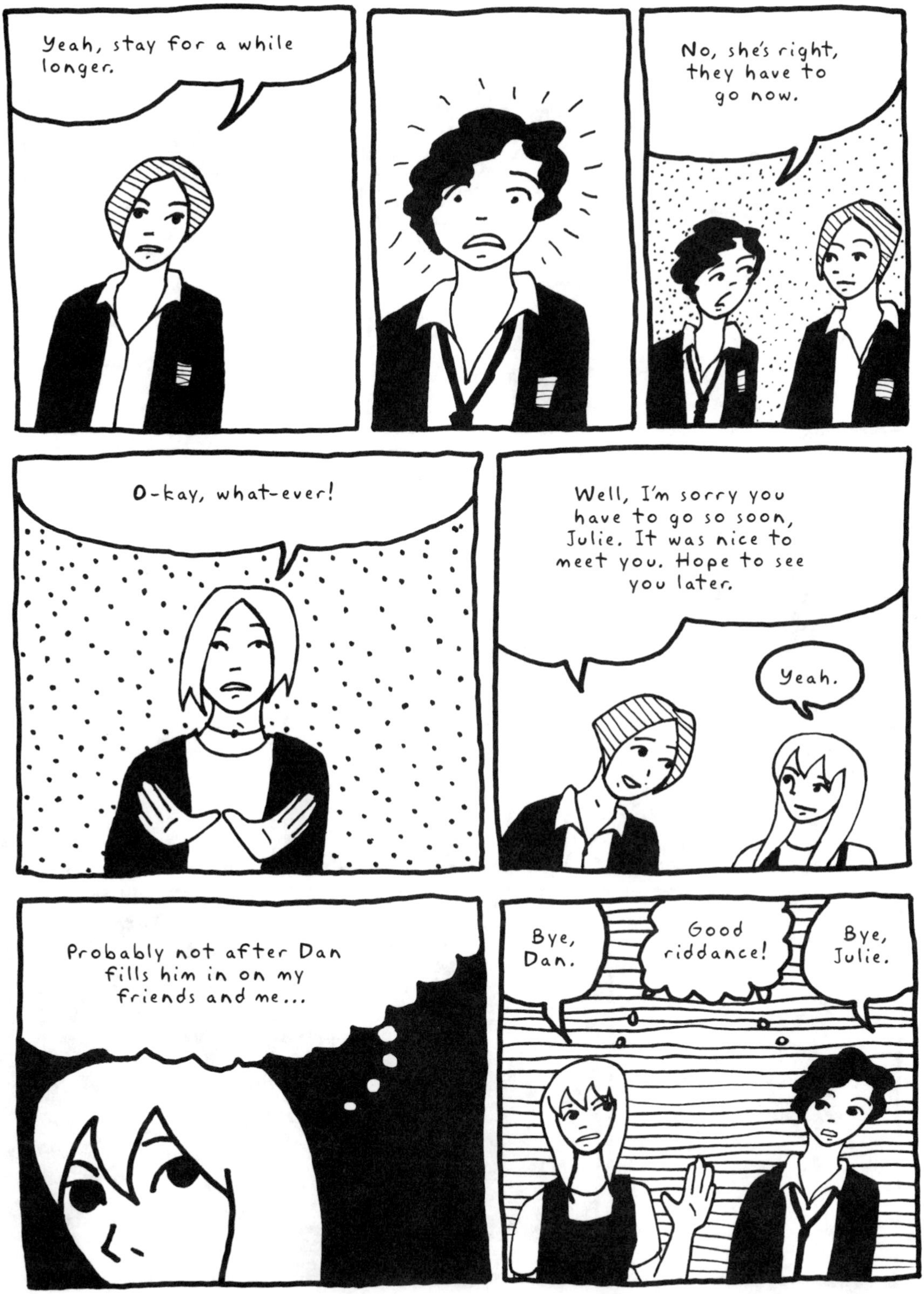
Yeah, stay for a while longer.
No, she's right, they have to go now.
O-kay, what-ever!
Well, I'm sorry you have to go so soon, Julie. It was nice to meet you. Hope to see you later.
Yeah.
Probably not after Dan fills him in on my friends and me...
Bye, Dan.
Good riddance!
Bye, Julie.

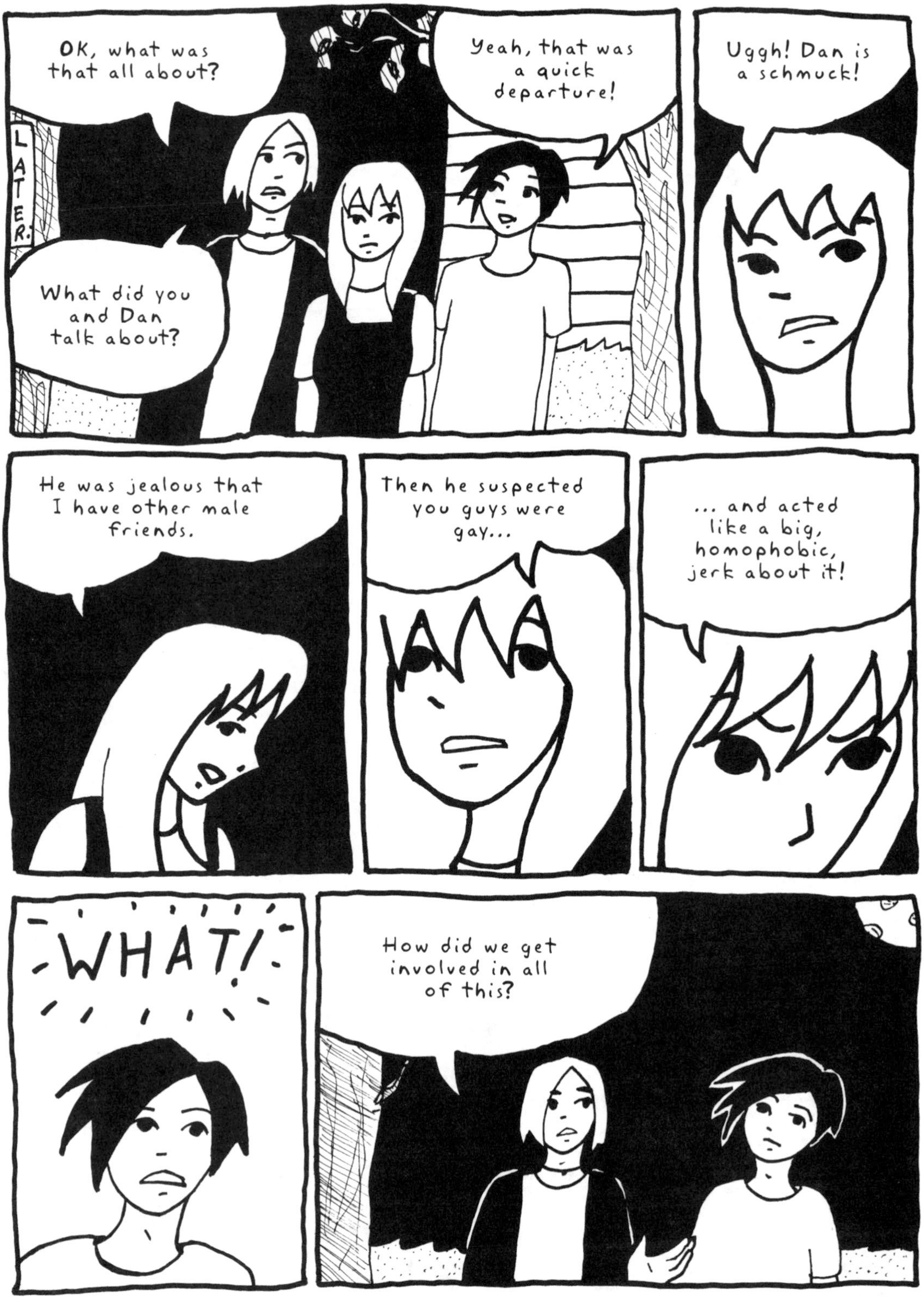
OK, what was that all about?
LATER.
What did you and Dan talk about?
Yeah, that was a quick departure!
Uggh! Dan is a schmuck!
He was jealous that I have other male friends.
Then he suspected you guys were gay...
... and acted like a big, homophobic, jerk about it!
WHAT!
How did we get involved in all of this?

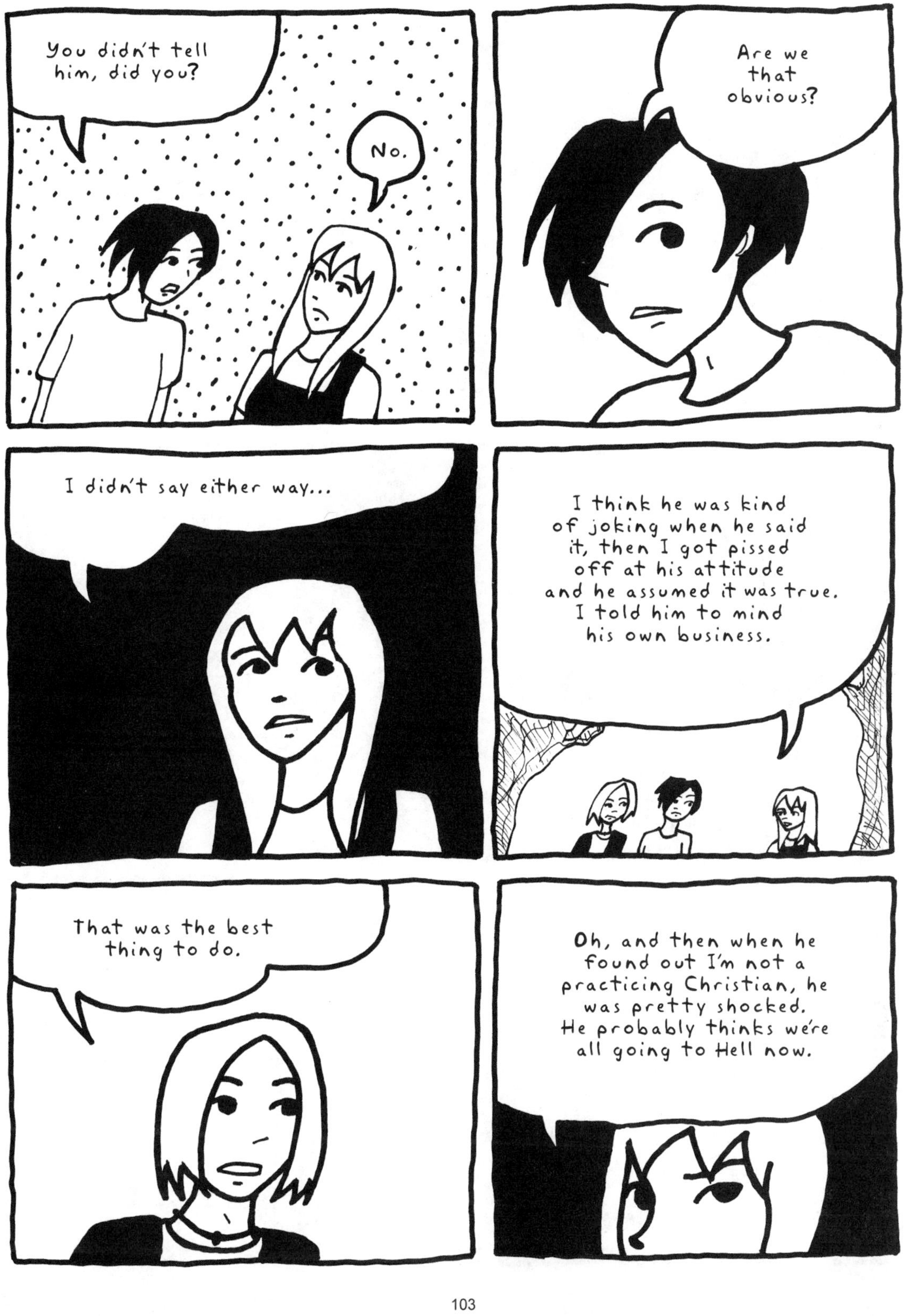
You didn't tell him, did you?
No.
Are we that obvious?
I didn't say either way...
I think he was kind of joking when he said it, then I got pissed off at his attitude and he assumed it was true. I told him to mind his own business.
That was the best thing to do.
Oh, and then when he found out I'm not a practicing Christian, he was pretty shocked. He probably thinks we're all going to Hell now.

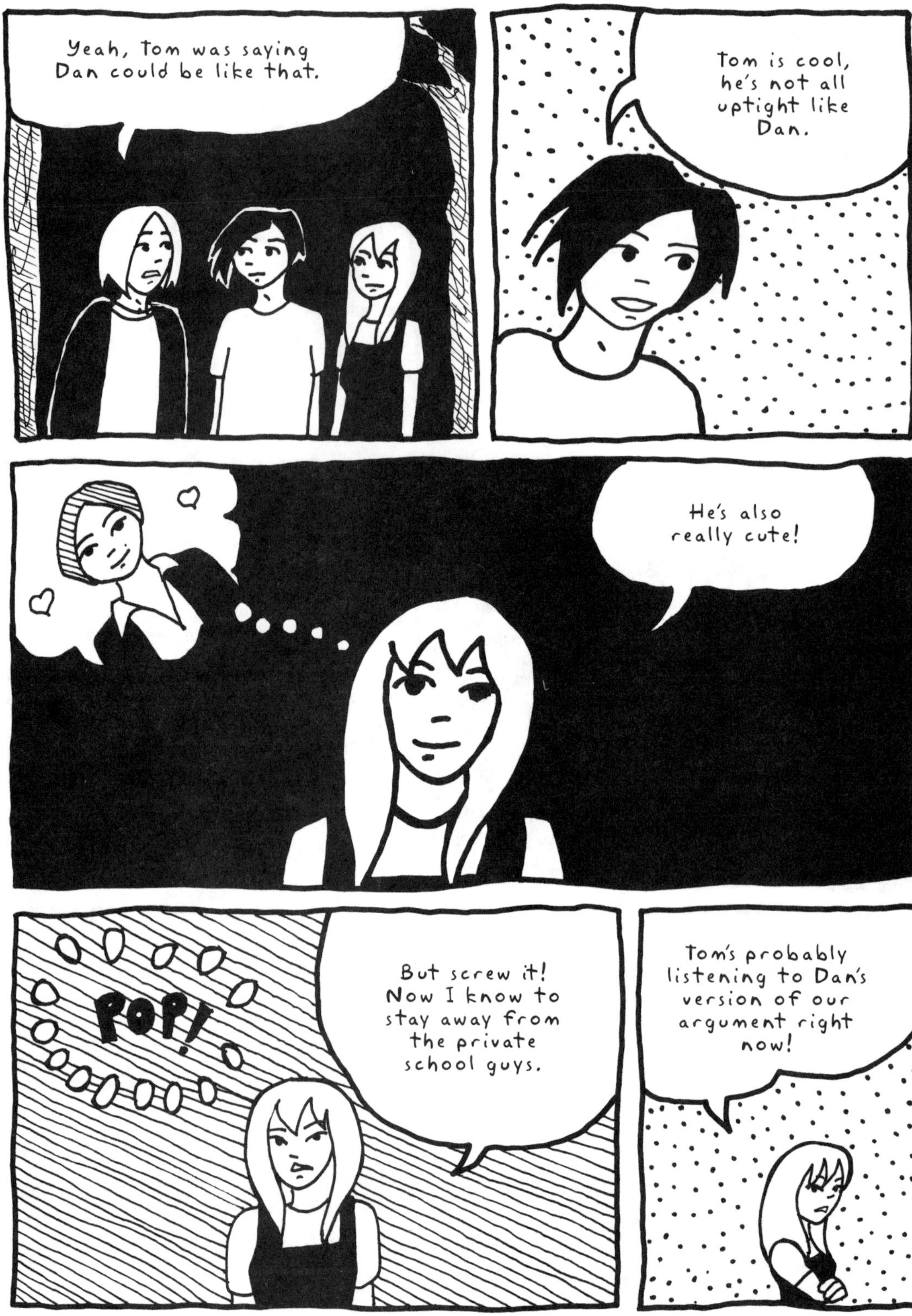
Yeah, Tom was saying Dan could be like that.
Tom is cool, he's not all uptight like Dan.
He's also really cute!
POP!
But screw it! Now I know to stay away from the private school guys.
Tom's probably listening to Dan's version of our argument right now!

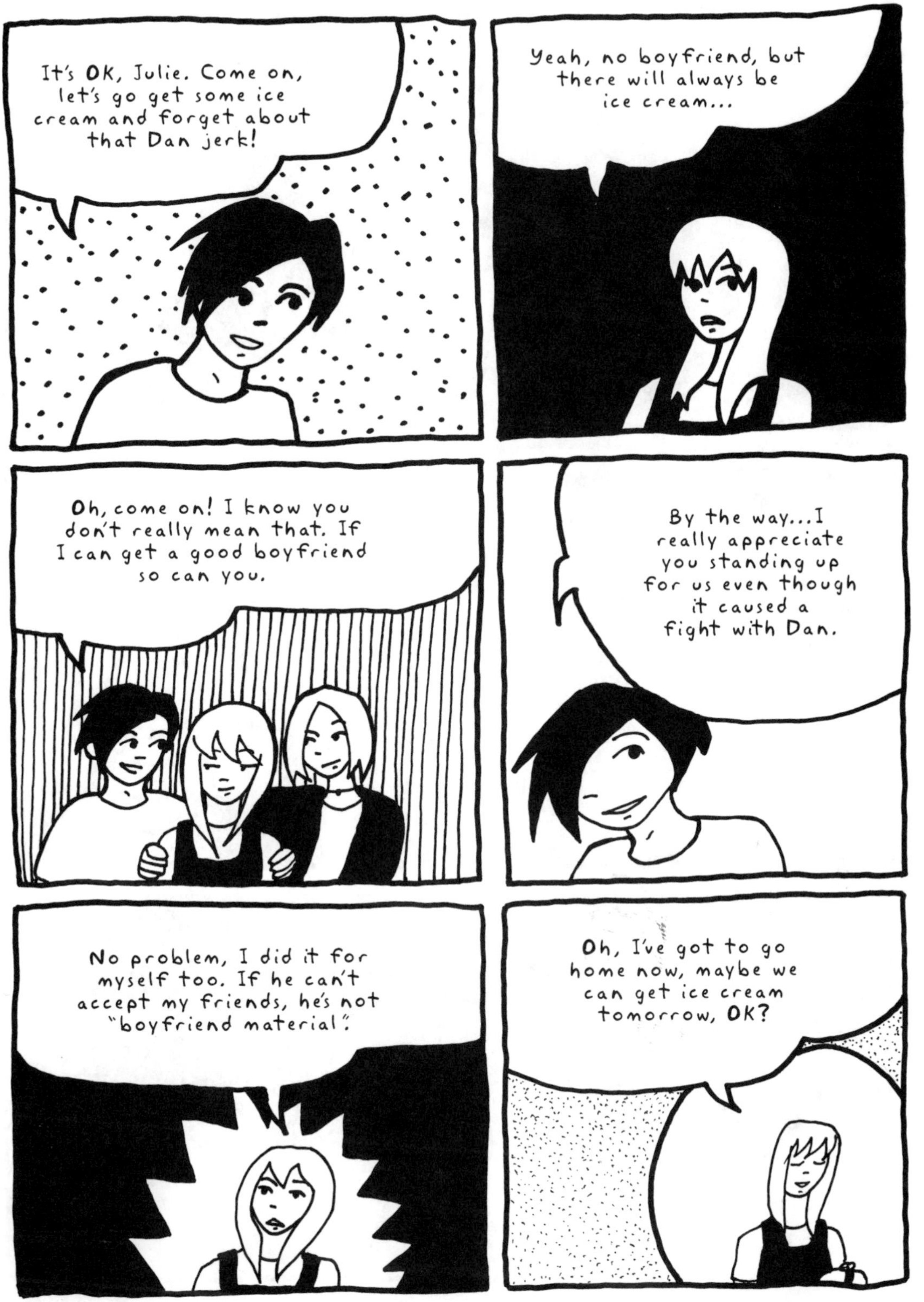
It's OK, Julie. Come on, let's go get some ice cream and forget about that Dan jerk!
Yeah, no boyfriend, but there will always be ice cream...
Oh, come on! I know you don't really mean that. If I can get a good boyfriend so can you.
By the way...I really appreciate you standing up for us even though it caused a fight with Dan.
No problem, I did it for myself too. If he can't accept my friends, he's not "boyfriend material".
Oh, I've got to go home now, maybe we can get ice cream tomorrow, OK?

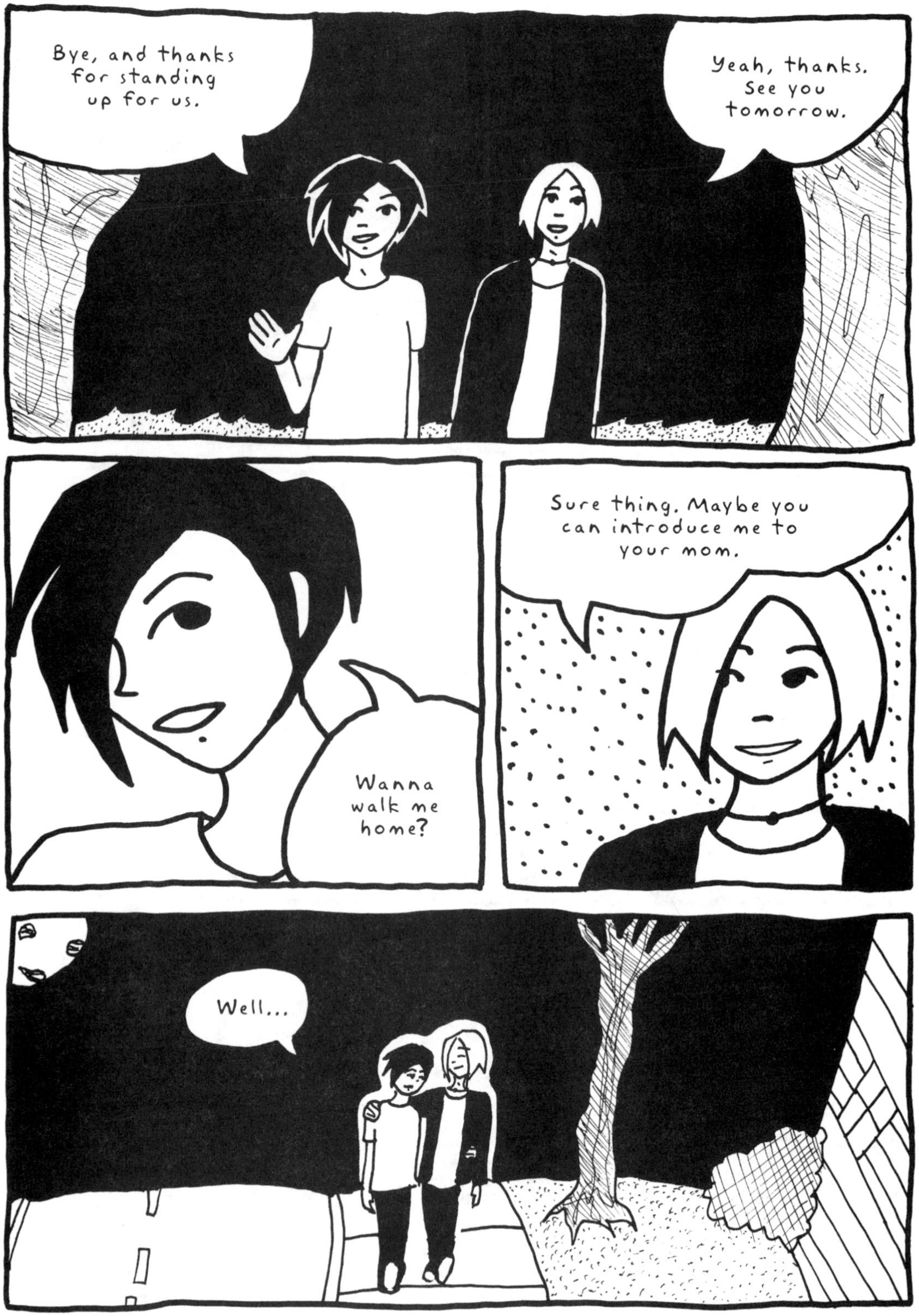
Bye, and thanks for standing up for us.
Yeah, thanks. See you tomorrow.
Wanna walk me home?
Sure thing. Maybe you can introduce me to your mom.
Well...

Chapter 5

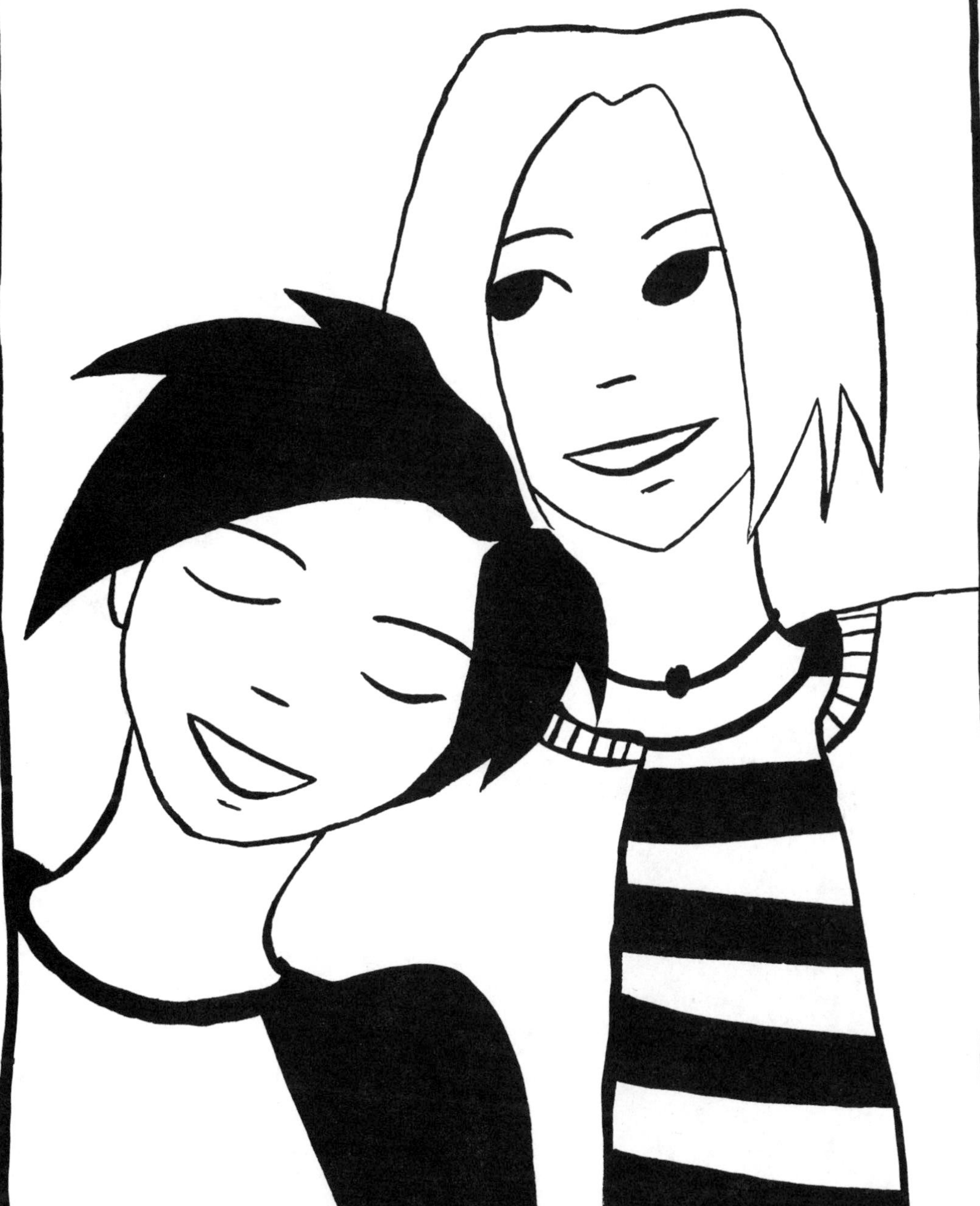

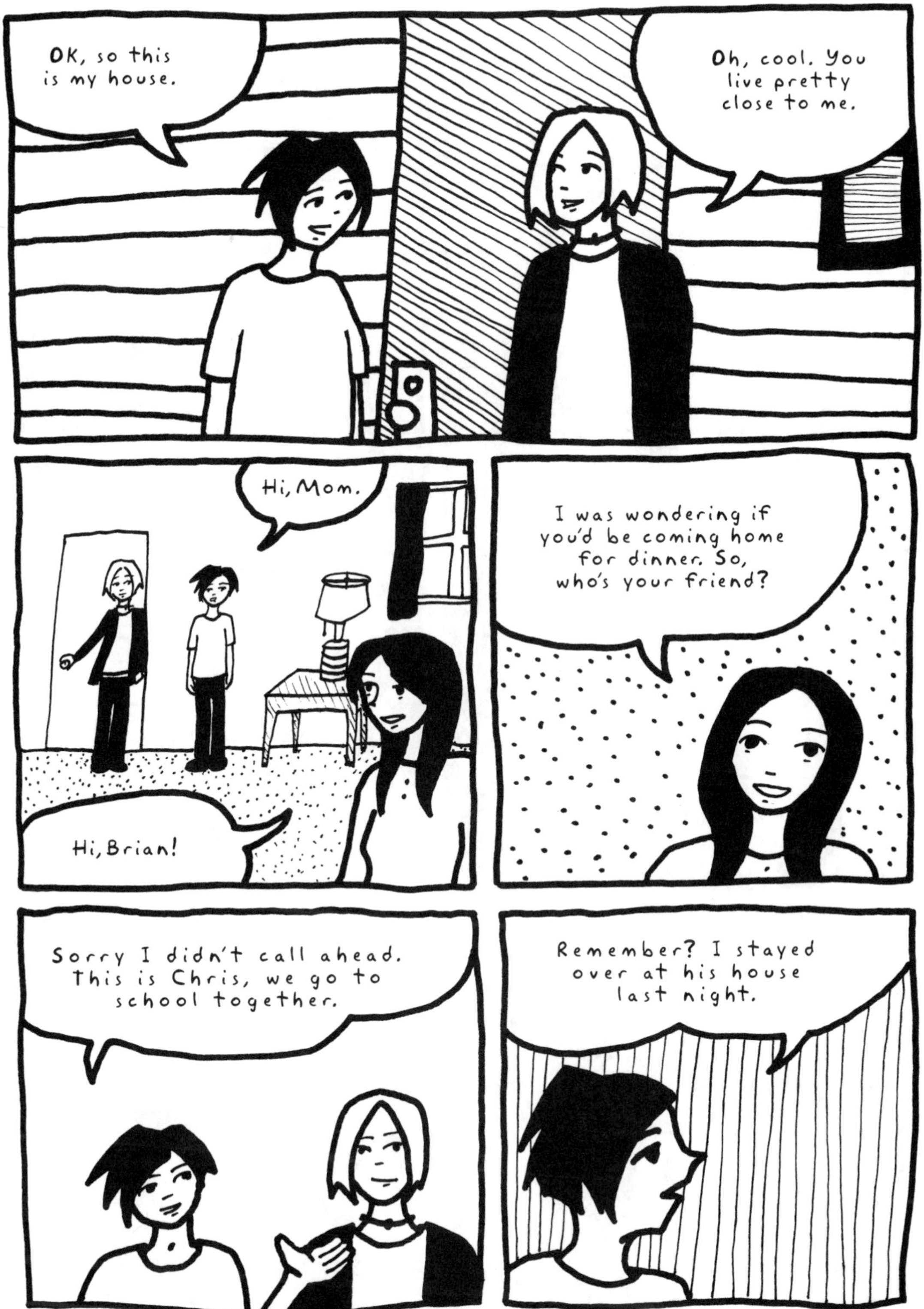
OK, so this is my house.
Oh, cool. You live pretty close to me.
Hi, Mom.
Hi, Brian!
I was wondering if you'd be coming home for dinner. So, who's your friend?
Sorry I didn't call ahead. This is Chris, we go to school together.
Remember? I stayed over at his house last night.

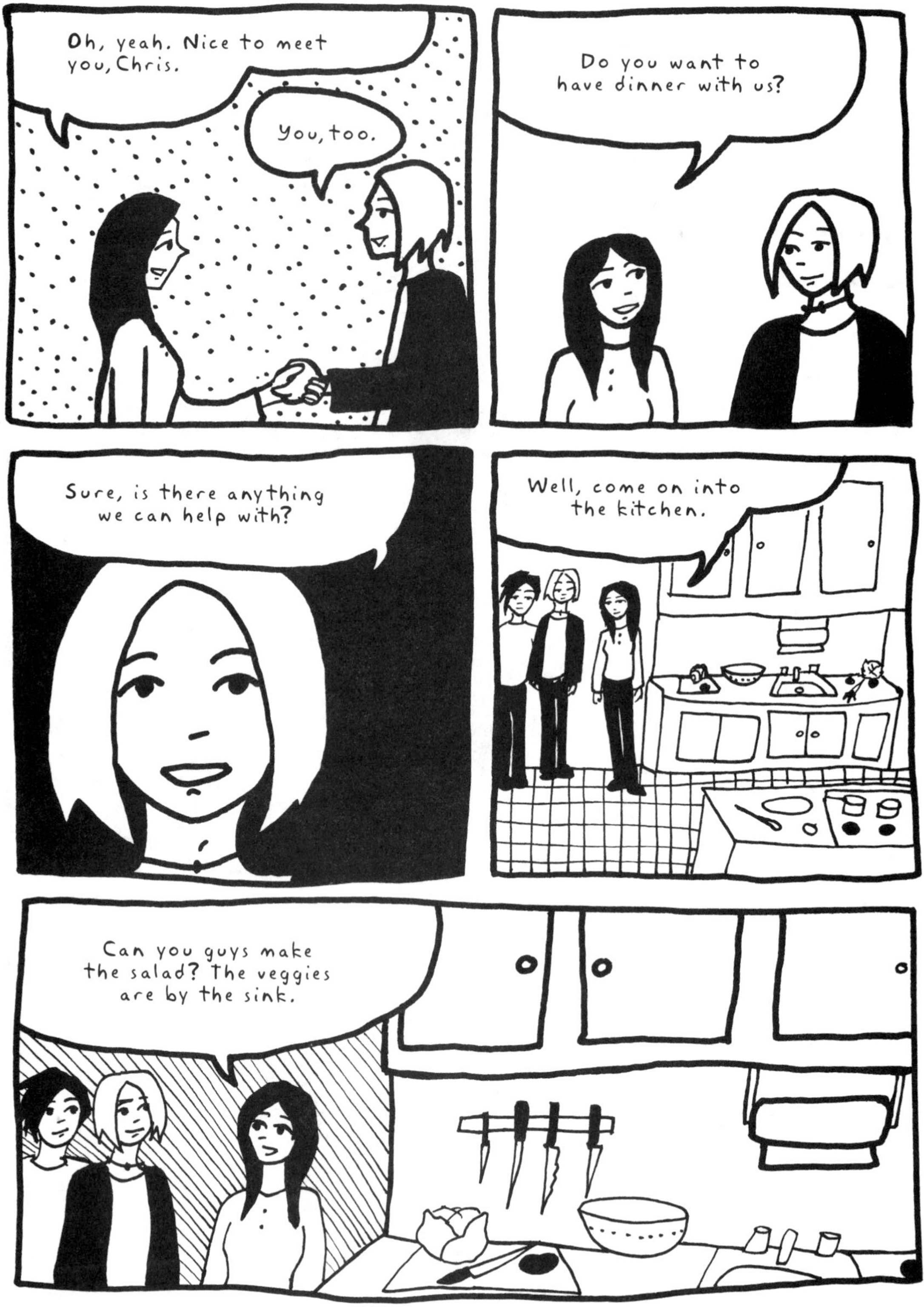

Oh, yeah. Nice to meet you, Chris.
You, too.
Do you want to have dinner with us?
Sure, is there anything we can help with?
Well, come on into the kitchen.
Can you guys make the salad? The veggies are by the sink.

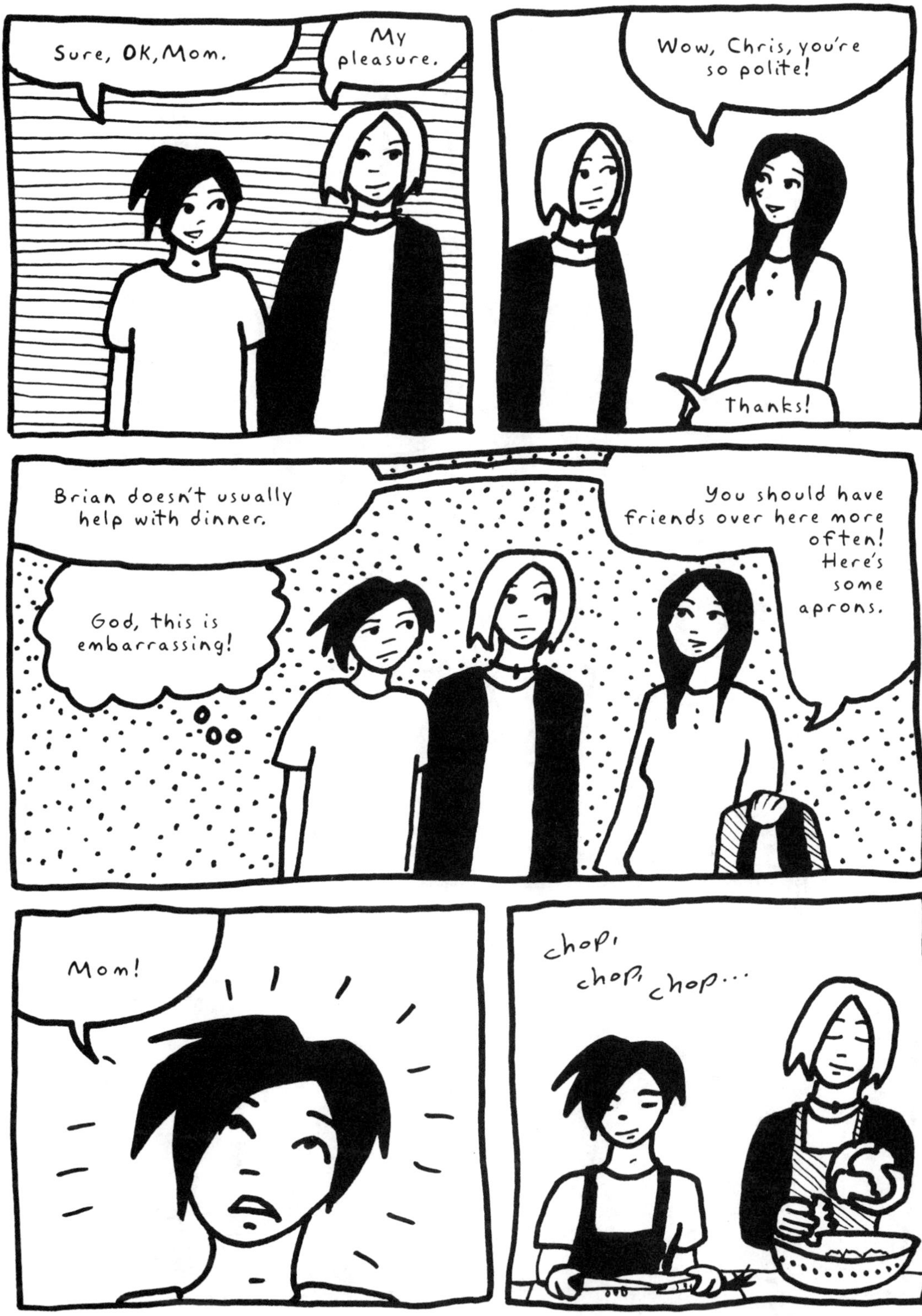
Sure, OK, Mom.
My pleasure.
Wow, Chris, you're so polite!
Thanks!
Brian doesn't usually help with dinner.
You should have friends over here more often! Here's some aprons.
God, this is embarrassing!
Mom!
chop, chop, chop...

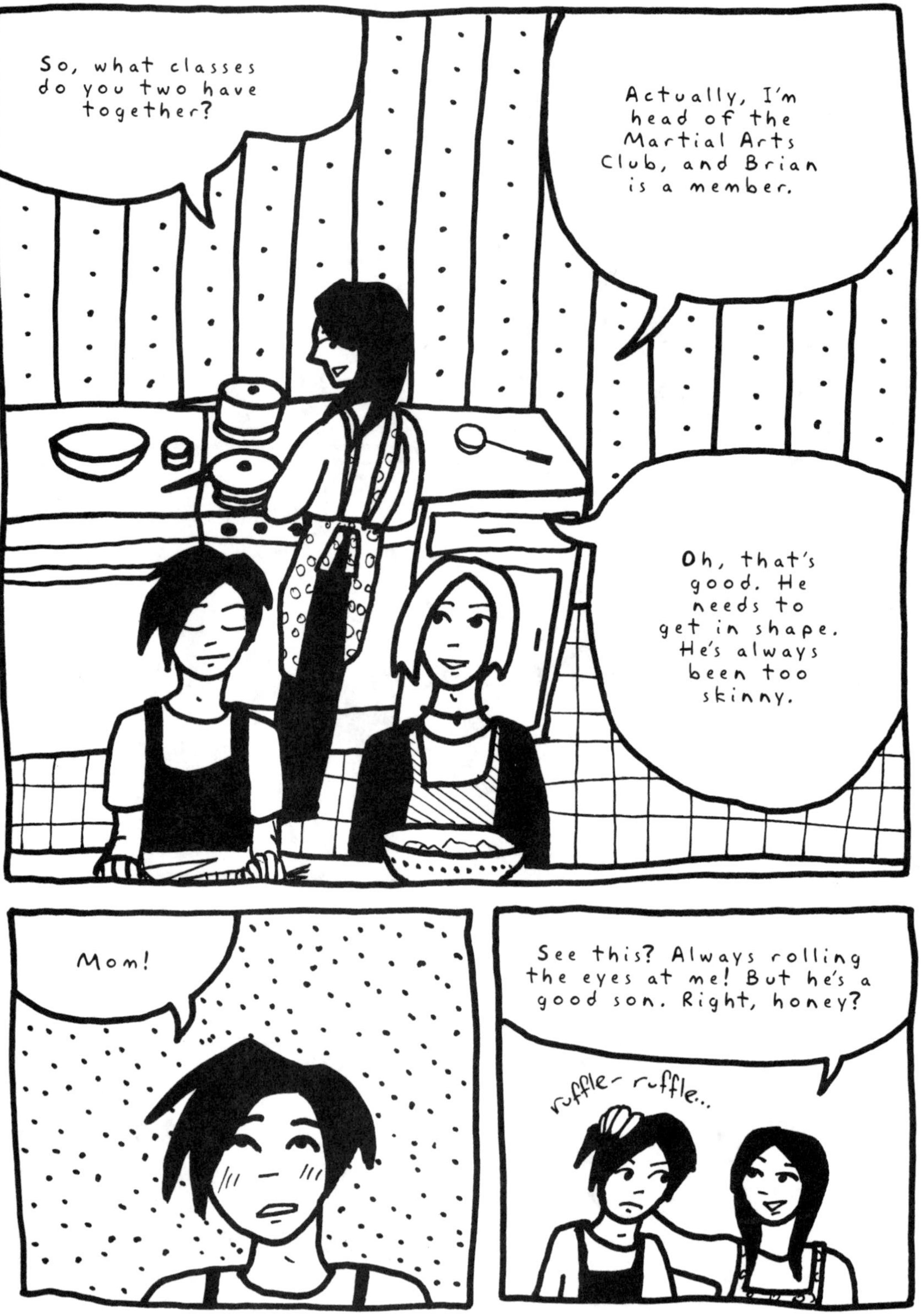
So, what classes do you two have together?
Actually, I'm head of the Martial Arts Club, and Brian is a member.
Oh, that's good. He needs to get in shape. He's always been too skinny.
Mom!
See this? Always rolling the eyes at me! But he's a good son. Right, honey?
ruffle- ruffle...

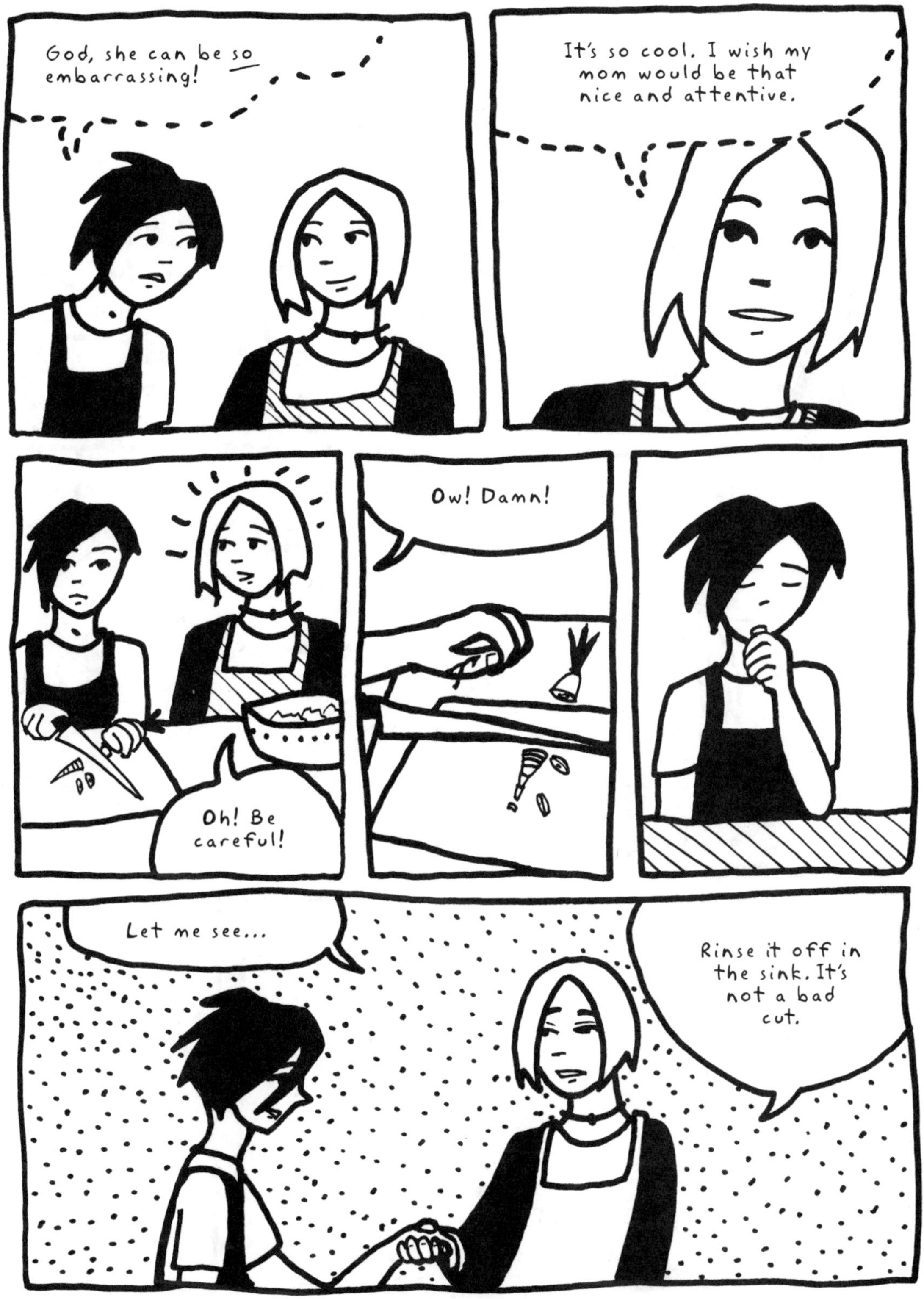
God, she can be so embarrassing!
It's so cool. I wish my mom would be that nice and attentive.
Oh! Be careful!
Ow! Damn!
Let me see...
Rinse it off in the sink. It's not a bad cut.

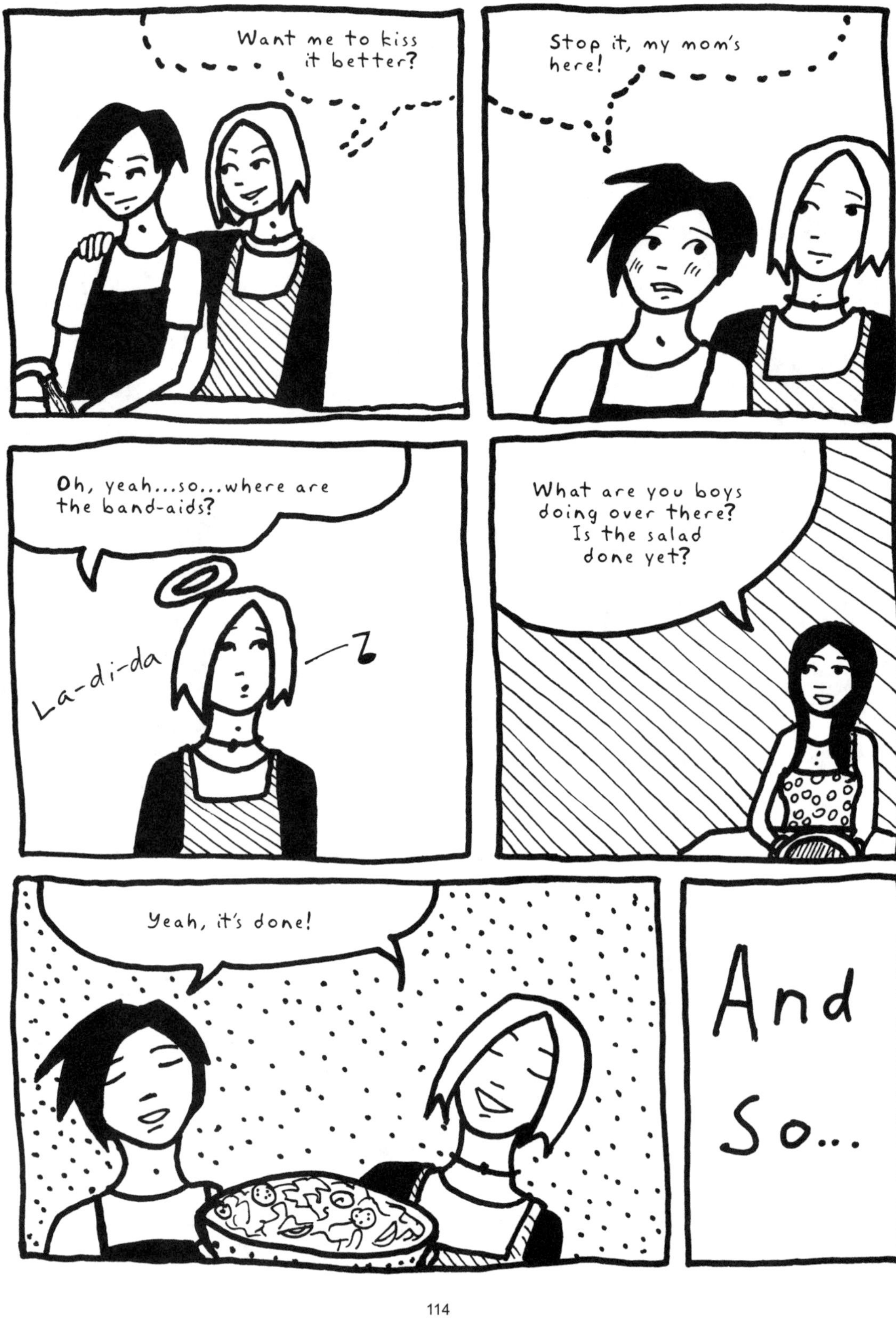

Want me to kiss it better?
Stop it, my mom's here!
Oh, yeah...so...where are the band-aids?
La-di-da
What are you boys doing over there? Is the salad done yet?
Yeah, it's done!
And So...

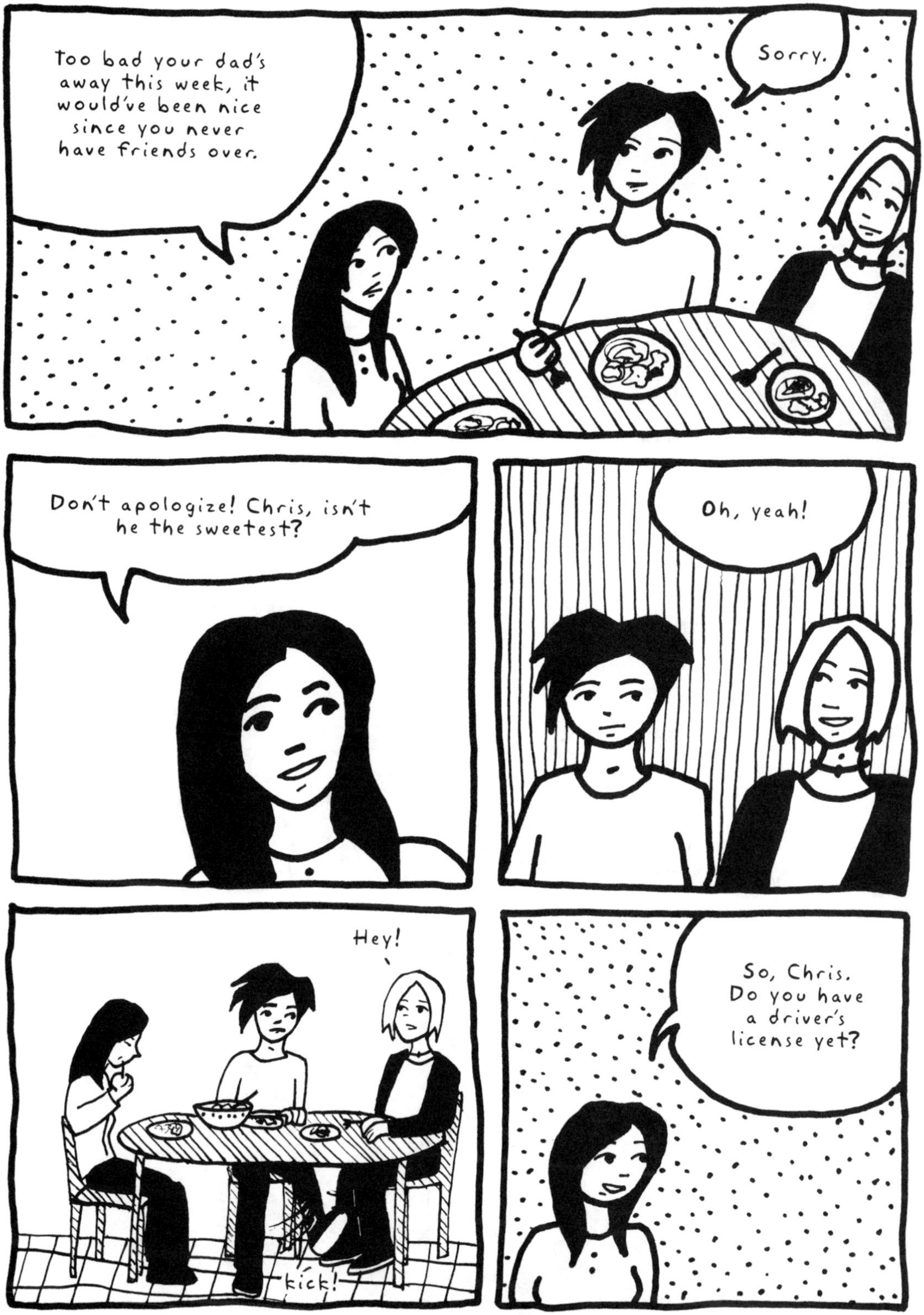
Too bad your dad's away this week, it would've been nice since you never have friends over.
Sorry.
Don't apologize! Chris, isn't he the sweetest?
Oh, yeah!
Hey!
kick!
So, Chris. Do you have a driver's license yet?

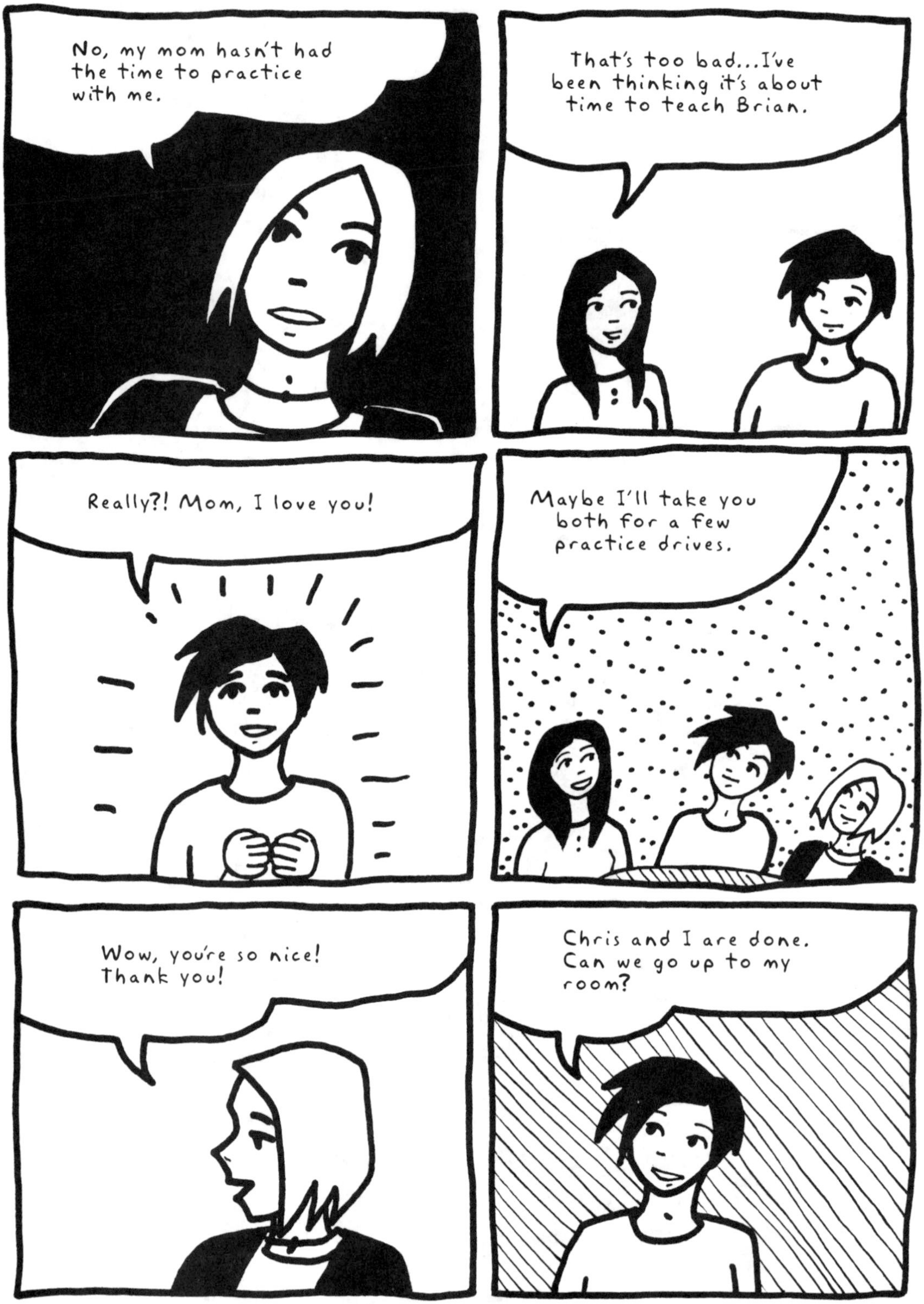

No, my mom hasn't had the time to practice with me.
That's too bad...I've been thinking it's about time to teach Brian.
Really?! Mom, I love you!
Maybe I'll take you both for a few practice drives.
Wow, you're so nice! Thank you!
Chris and I are done. Can we go up to my room?

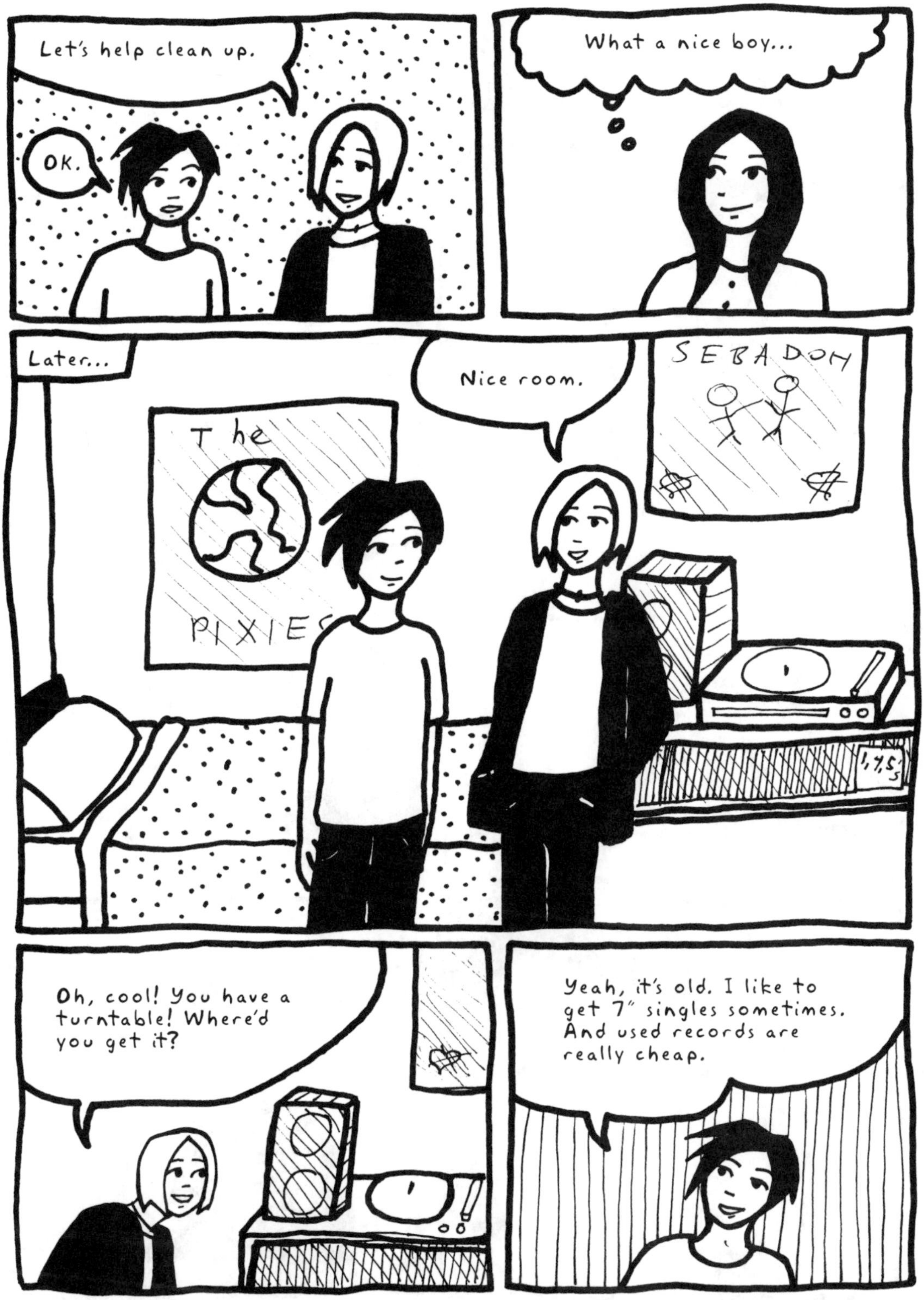
Let's help clean up.
OK.
What a nice boy...
Later...
Nice room.
The
PIXIES
SEBADOH
Oh, cool! You have a turntable! Where'd you get it?
Yeah, it's old. I like to get 7" singles sometimes. And used records are really cheap.

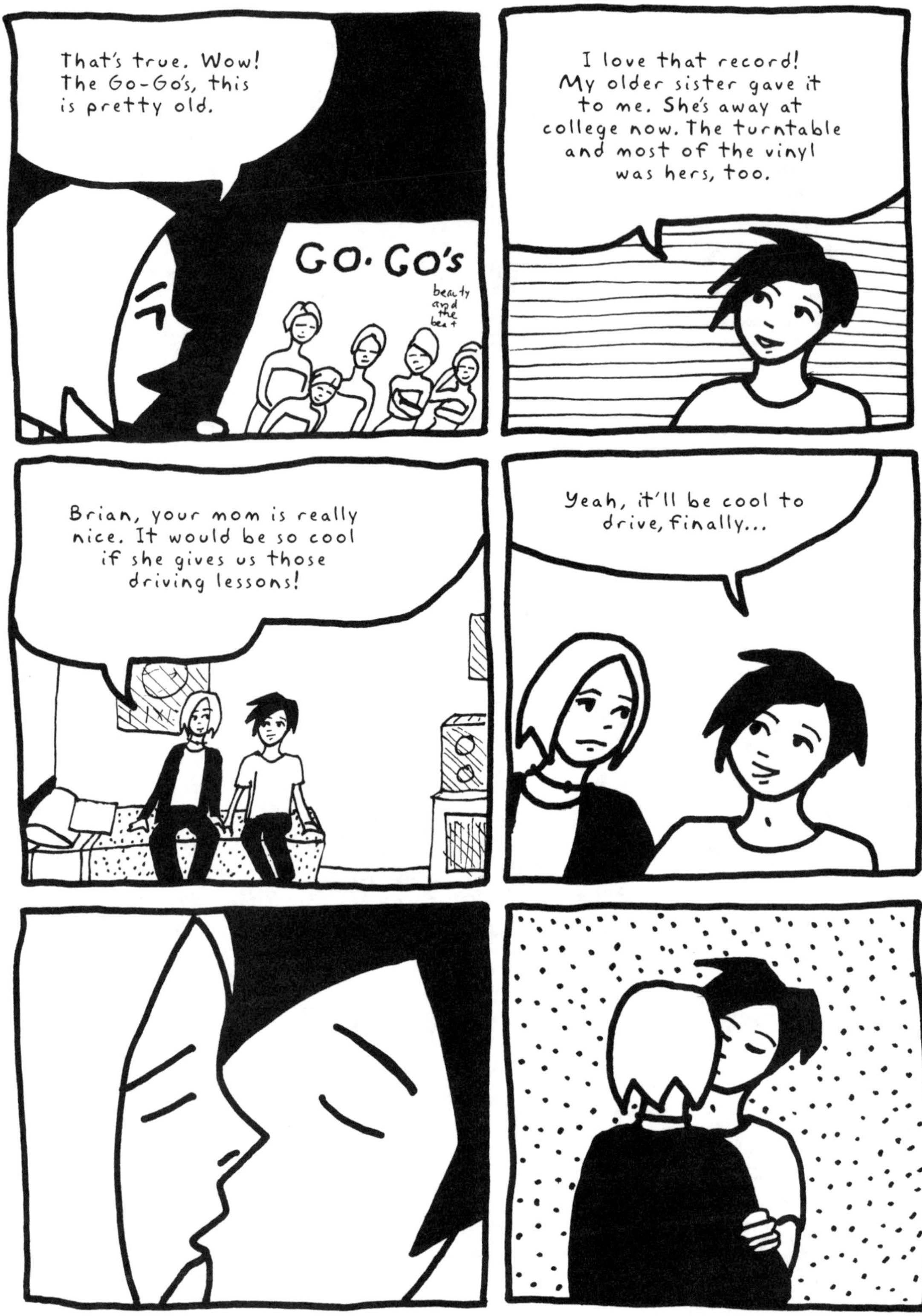
That's true. Wow! The Go-Go's, this is pretty old.
GO·GO's
beauty and the beat
I love that record! My older sister gave it to me. She's away at college now. The turntable and most of the vinyl was hers, too.
Brian, your mom is really nice. It would be so cool if she gives us those driving lessons!
Yeah, it'll be cool to drive, finally...

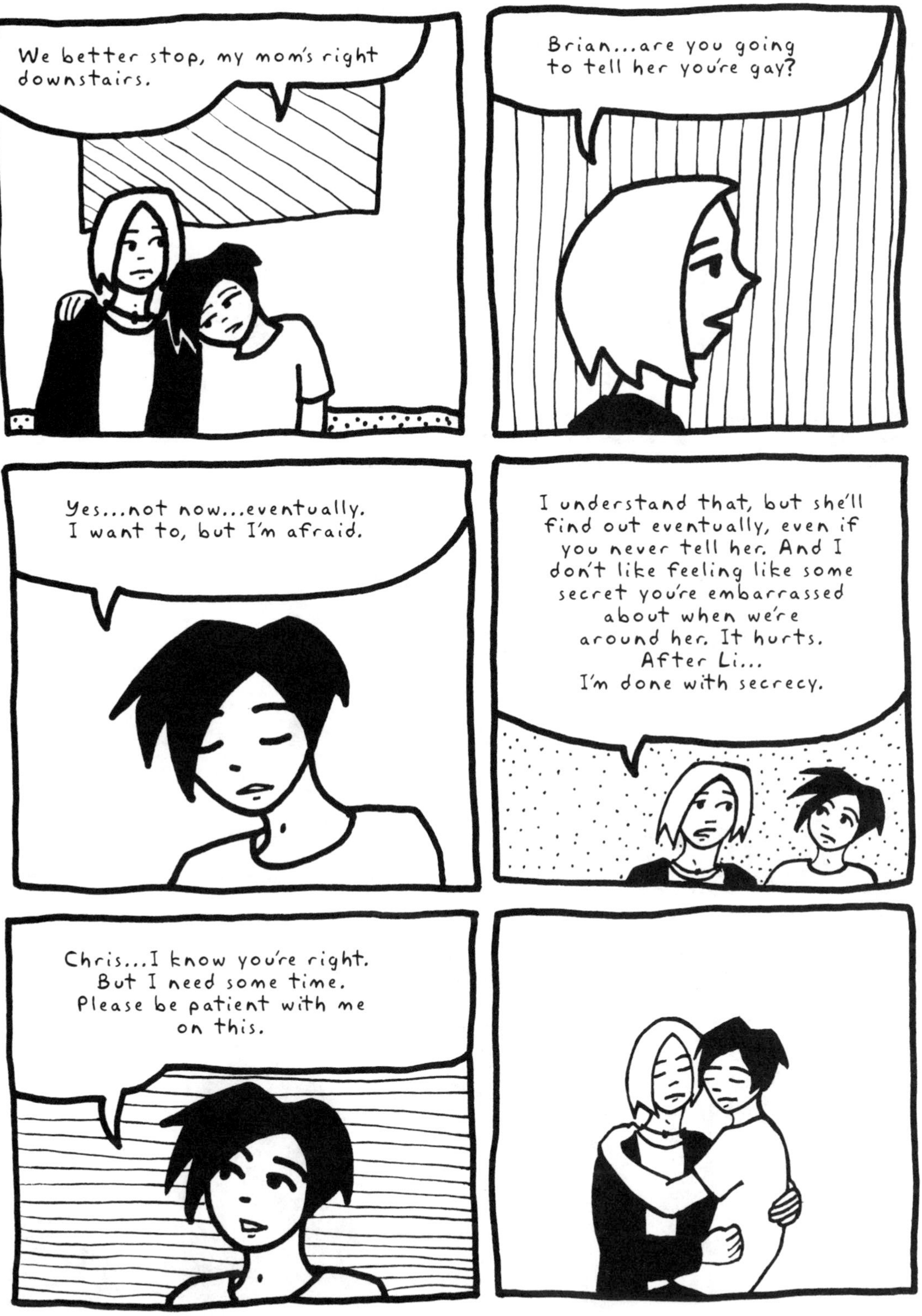
We better stop, my mom's right downstairs.
Brian...are you going to tell her you're gay?
Yes...not now...eventually. I want to, but I'm afraid.
I understand that, but she'll find out eventually, even if you never tell her. And I don't like feeling like some secret you're embarrassed about when we're around her. It hurts. After Li... I'm done with secrecy.
Chris...I know you're right. But I need some time. Please be patient with me on this.

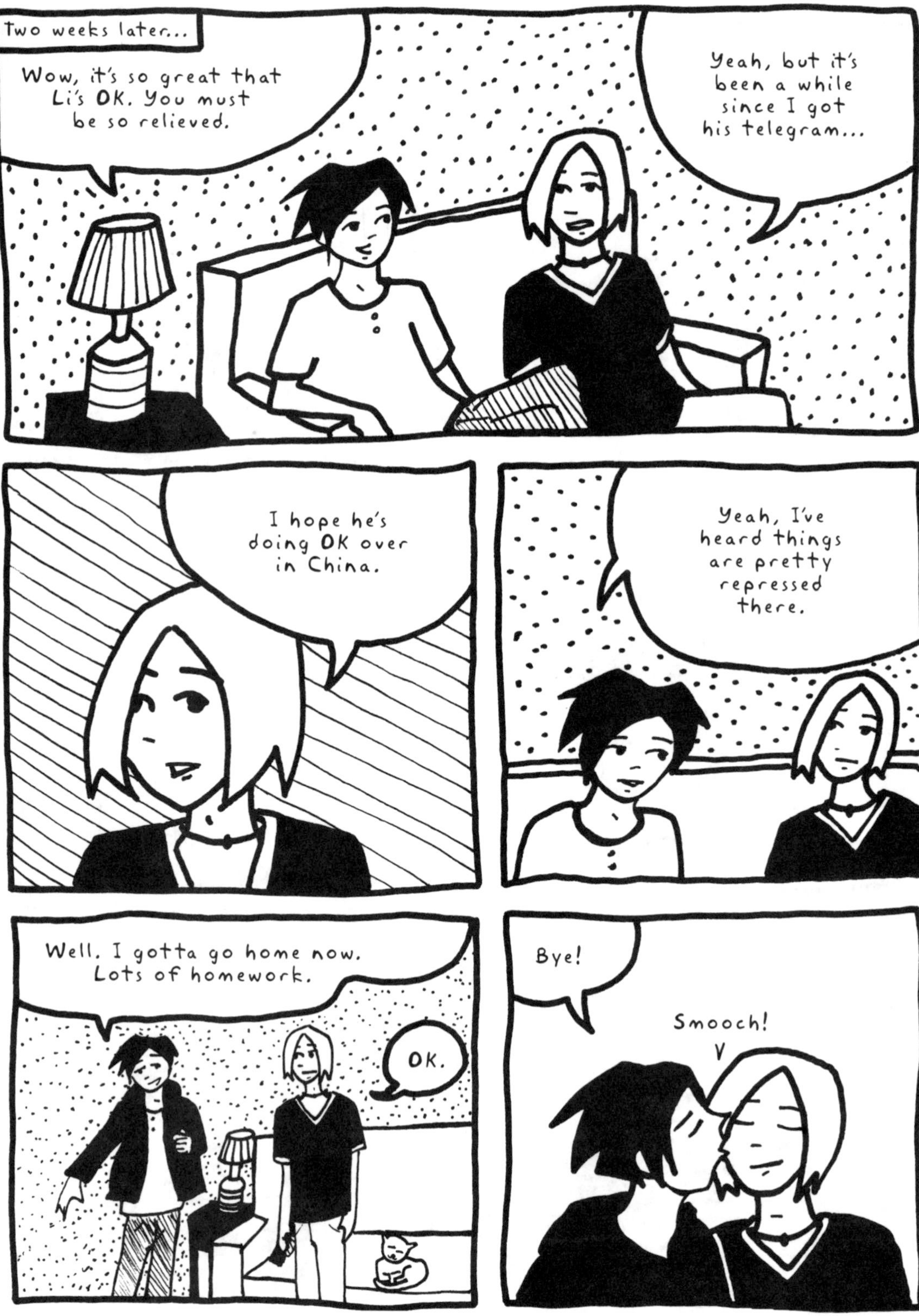
Two weeks later...
Wow, it's so great that Li's OK. You must be so relieved.
Yeah, but it's been a while since I got his telegram...
I hope he's doing OK over in China.
Yeah, I've heard things are pretty repressed there.
Well. I gotta go home now. Lots of homework.
OK.
Bye!
Smooch!

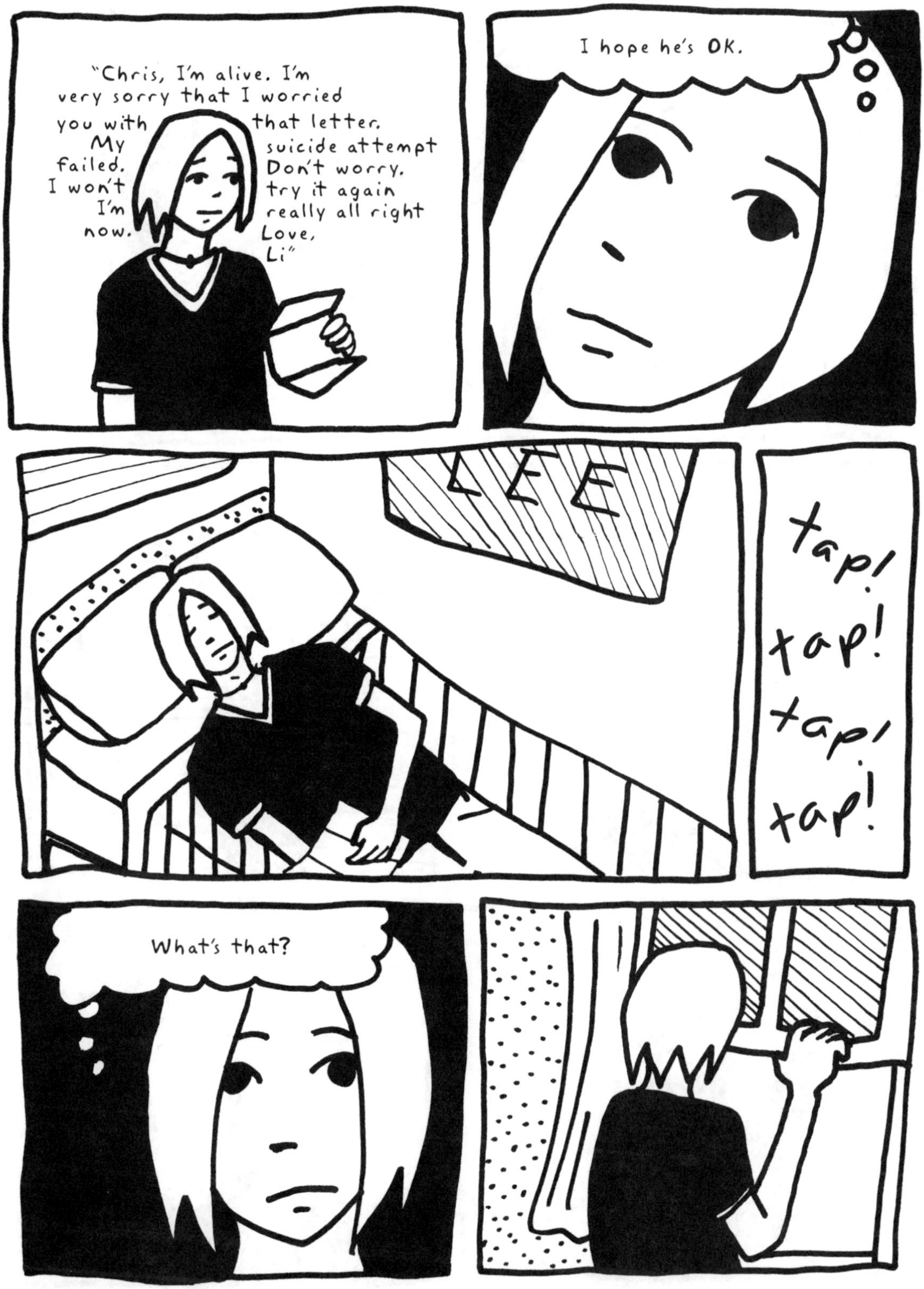
"Chris, I'm alive. I'm very sorry that I worried you with that letter. My suicide attempt failed. Don't worry. I won't try it again I'm really all right now. Love, Li"
I hope he's OK.
LEE
tap! tap! tap! tap!
What's that?

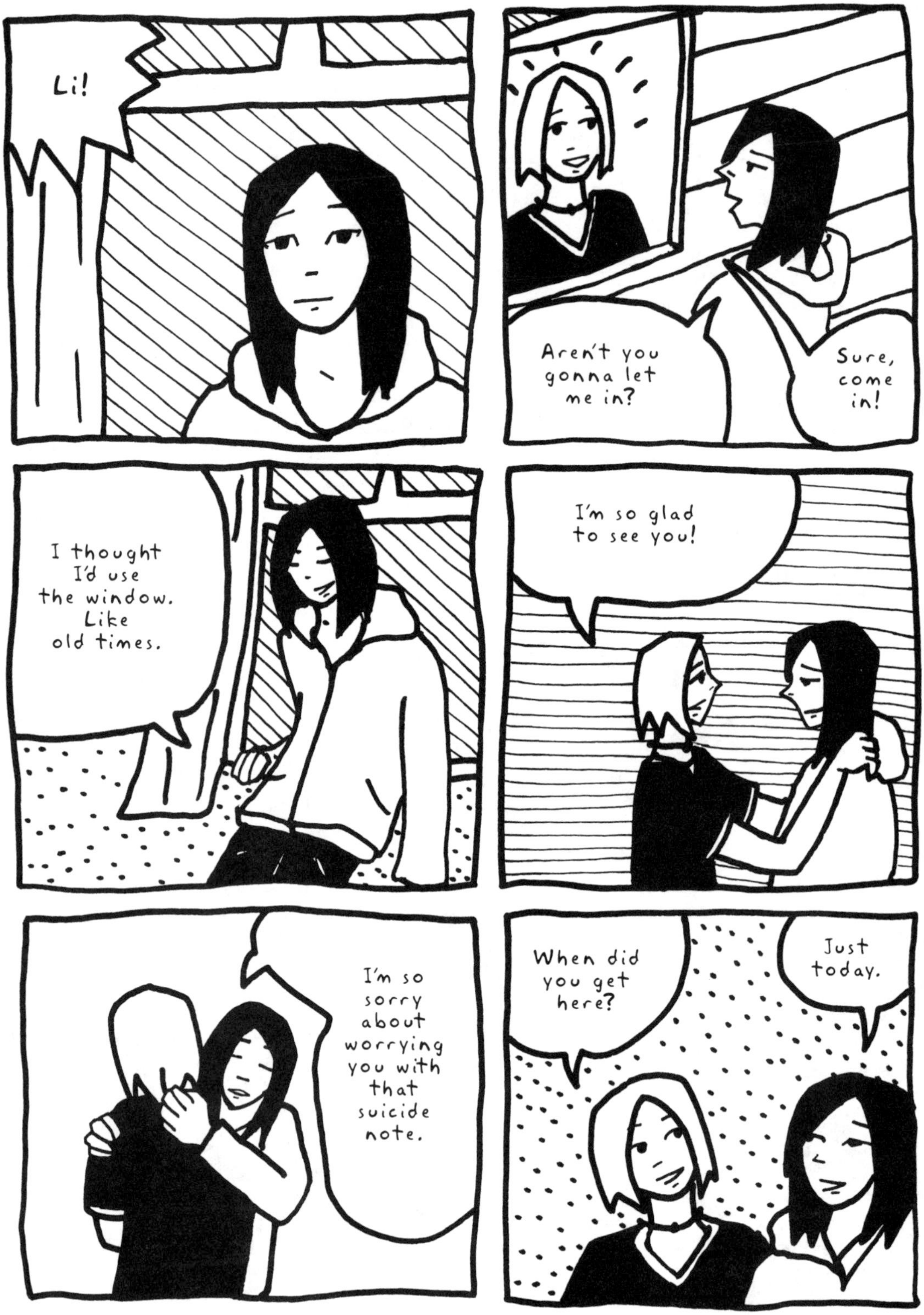
Li!
Aren't you gonna let me in?
Sure, come in!
I thought I'd use the window. Like old times.
I'm so glad to see you!
I'm so sorry about worrying you with that suicide note.
When did you get here?
Just today.

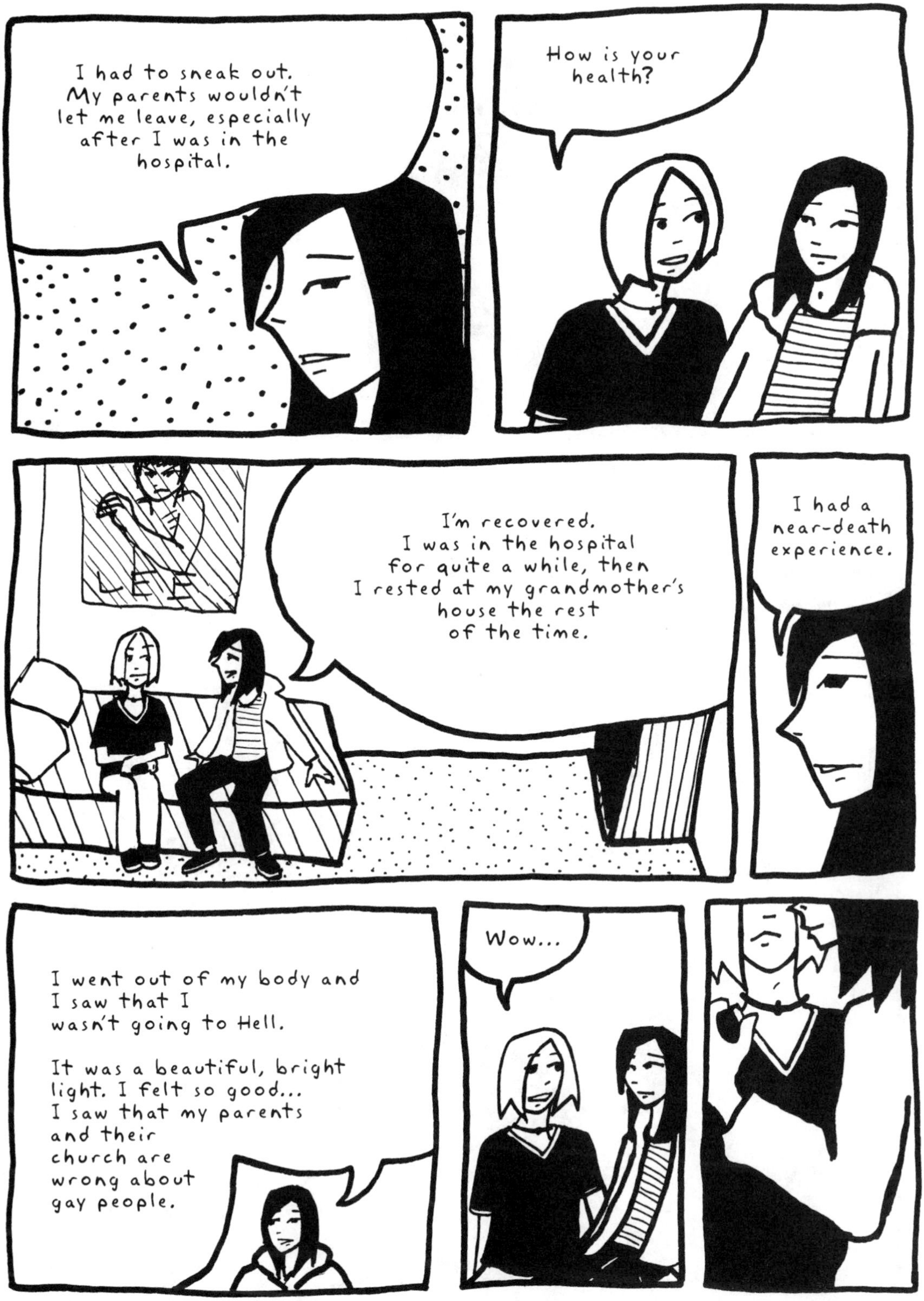

I had to sneak out. My parents wouldn't let me leave, especially after I was in the hospital.
How is your health?
LEE
I'm recovered. I was in the hospital for quite a while, then I rested at my grandmother's house the rest of the time.
I had a near-death experience.
I went out of my body and I saw that I wasn't going to Hell.
It was a beautiful, bright light. I felt so good... I saw that my parents and their church are wrong about gay people.
Wow...

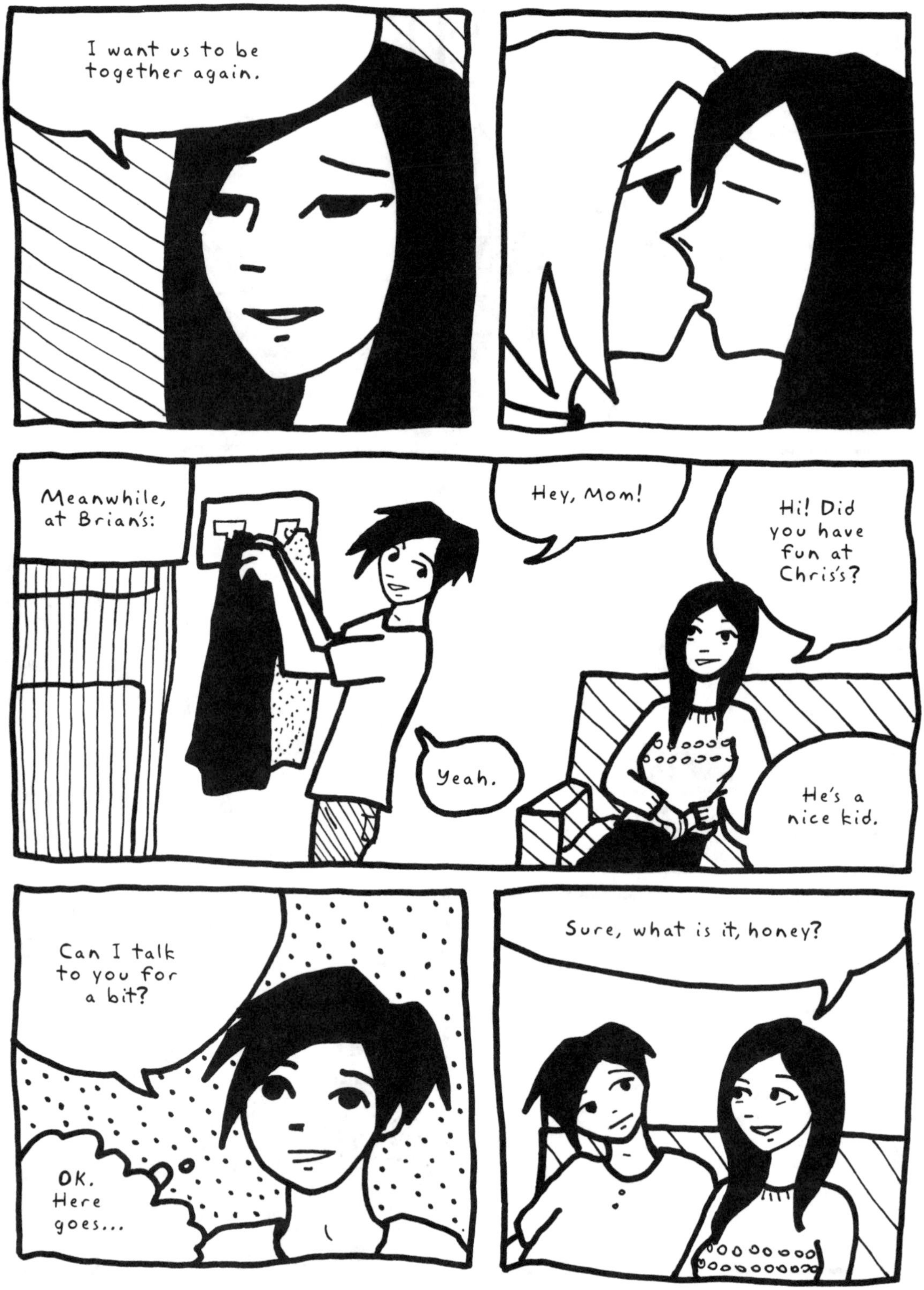
I want us to be together again.
Meanwhile, at Brian's:
Hey, Mom!
Hi! Did you have fun at Chris's?
Yeah.
He's a nice kid.
Can I talk to you for a bit?
OK. Here goes...
Sure, what is it, honey?

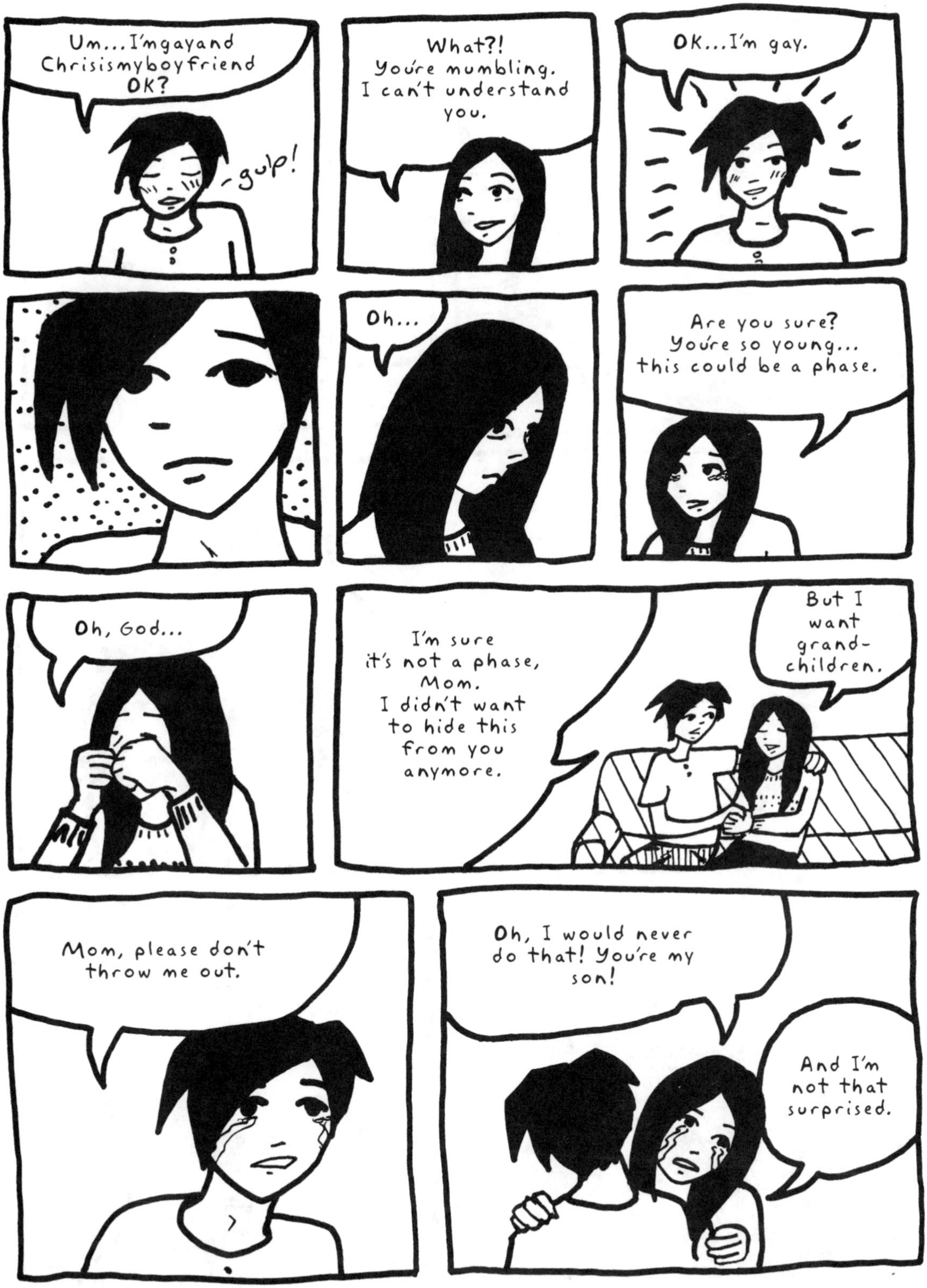

Um...I'mgayand Chrisismyboyfriend OK?
-gulp!
What?! You're mumbling. I can't understand you.
OK...I'm gay.
Oh...
Are you sure? You're so young... this could be a phase.
Oh, God...
I'm sure it's not a phase, Mom. I didn't want to hide this from you anymore.
But I want grand-children.
Mom, please don't throw me out.
Oh, I would never do that! You're my son!
And I'm not that surprised.

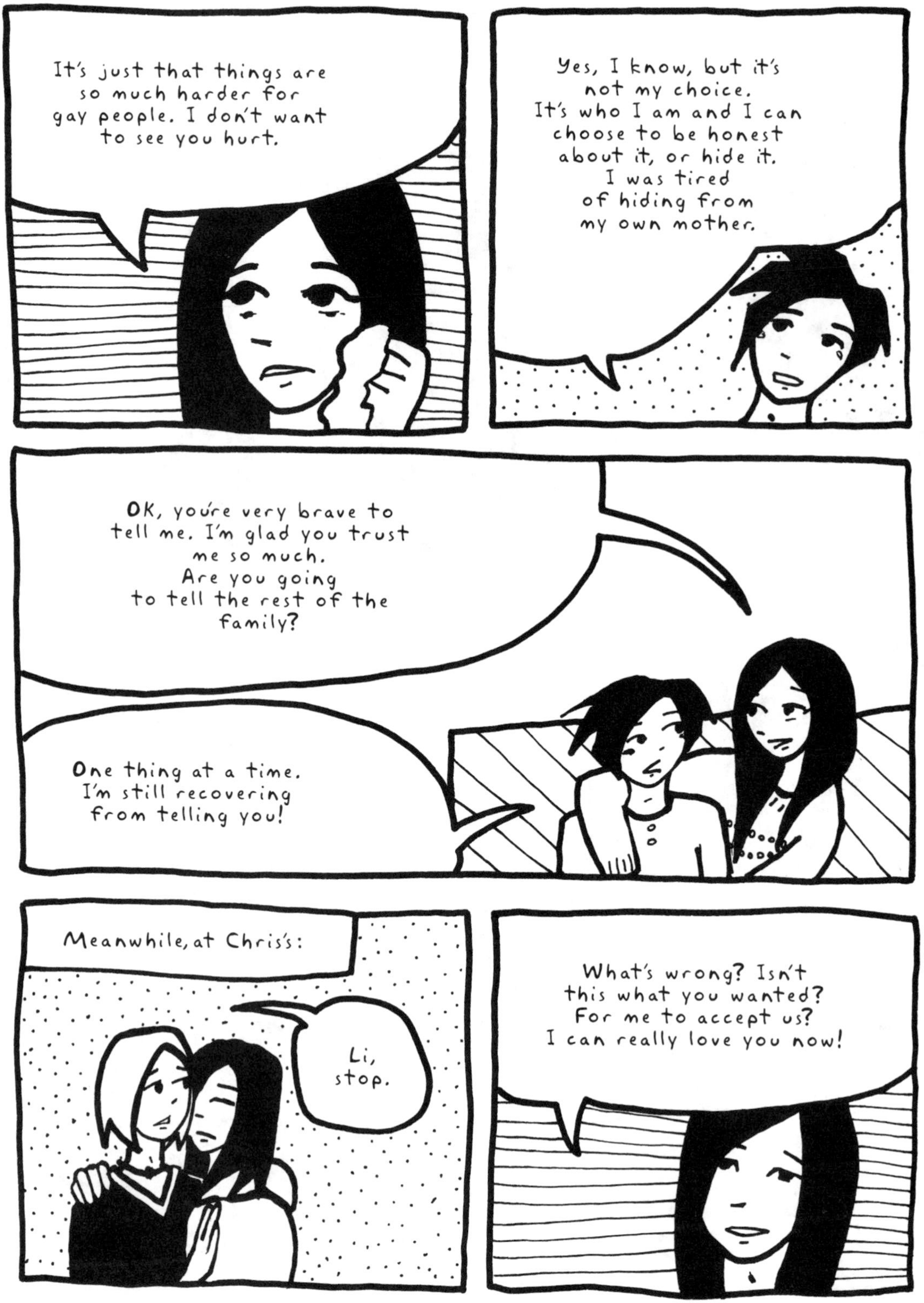
It's just that things are so much harder for gay people. I don't want to see you hurt.
Yes, I know, but it's not my choice. It's who I am and I can choose to be honest about it, or hide it. I was tired of hiding from my own mother.
OK, you're very brave to tell me. I'm glad you trust me so much. Are you going to tell the rest of the family?
One thing at a time. I'm still recovering from telling you!
Meanwhile, at Chris's:
Li, stop.
What's wrong? Isn't this what you wanted? For me to accept us? I can really love you now!

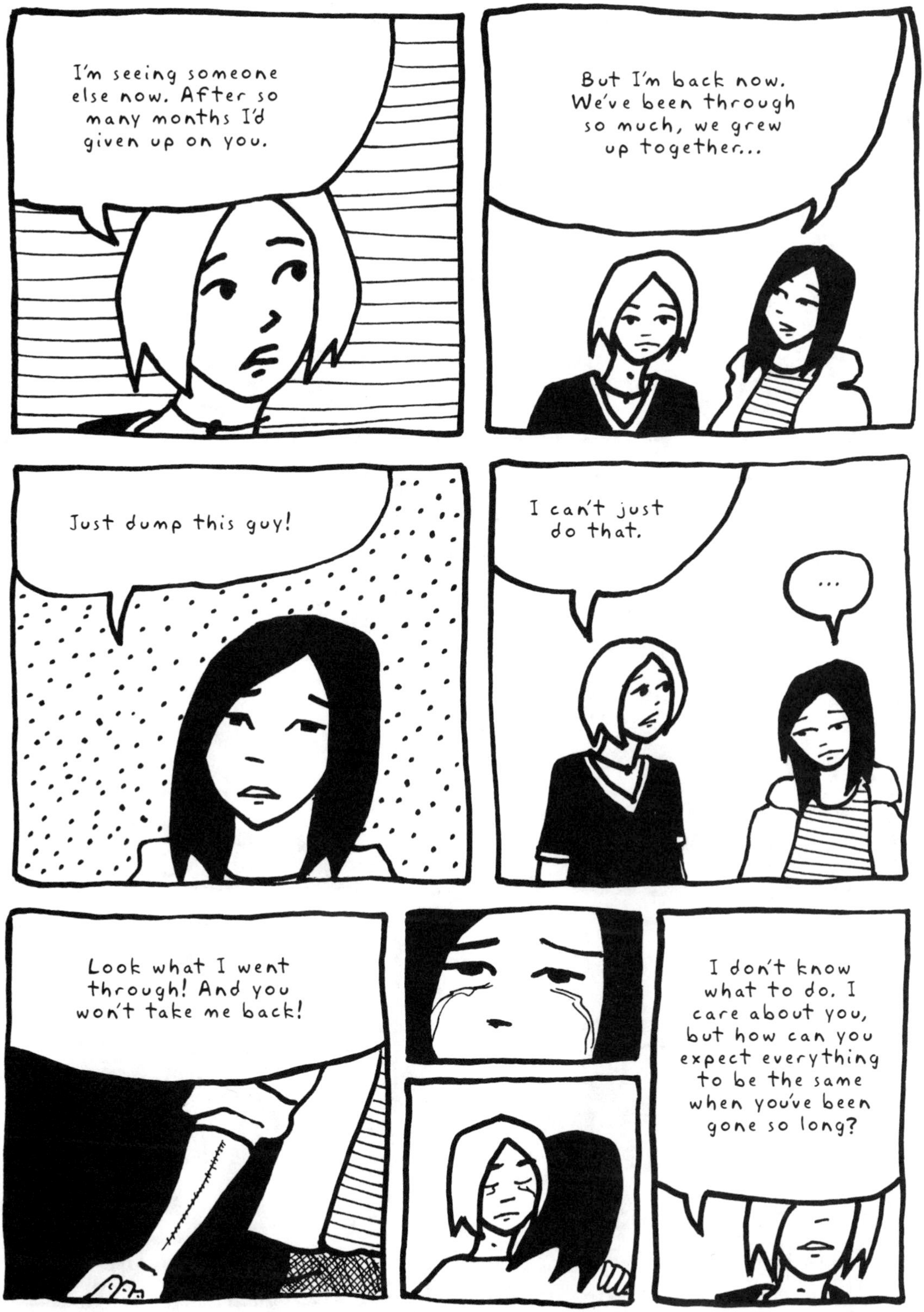
I'm seeing someone else now. After so many months I'd given up on you.
But I'm back now. We've been through so much, we grew up together...
Just dump this guy!
I can't just do that.
...
Look what I went through! And you won't take me back!
I don't know what to do. I care about you, but how can you expect everything to be the same when you've been gone so long?

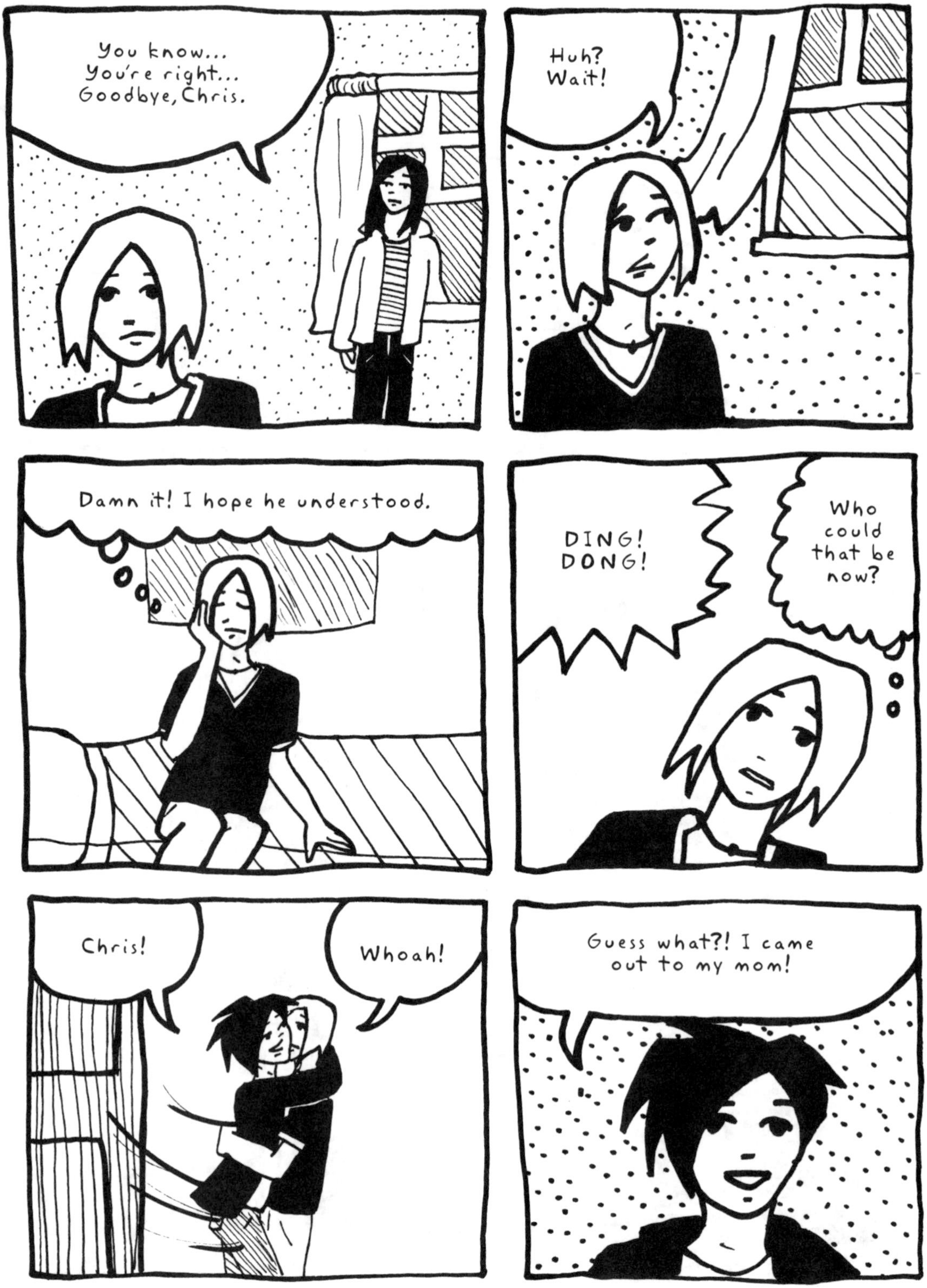
You know... You're right... Goodbye, Chris.
Huh? Wait!
Damn it! I hope he understood.
DING! DONG!
Who could that be now?
Chris!
Whoah!
Guess what?! I came out to my mom!

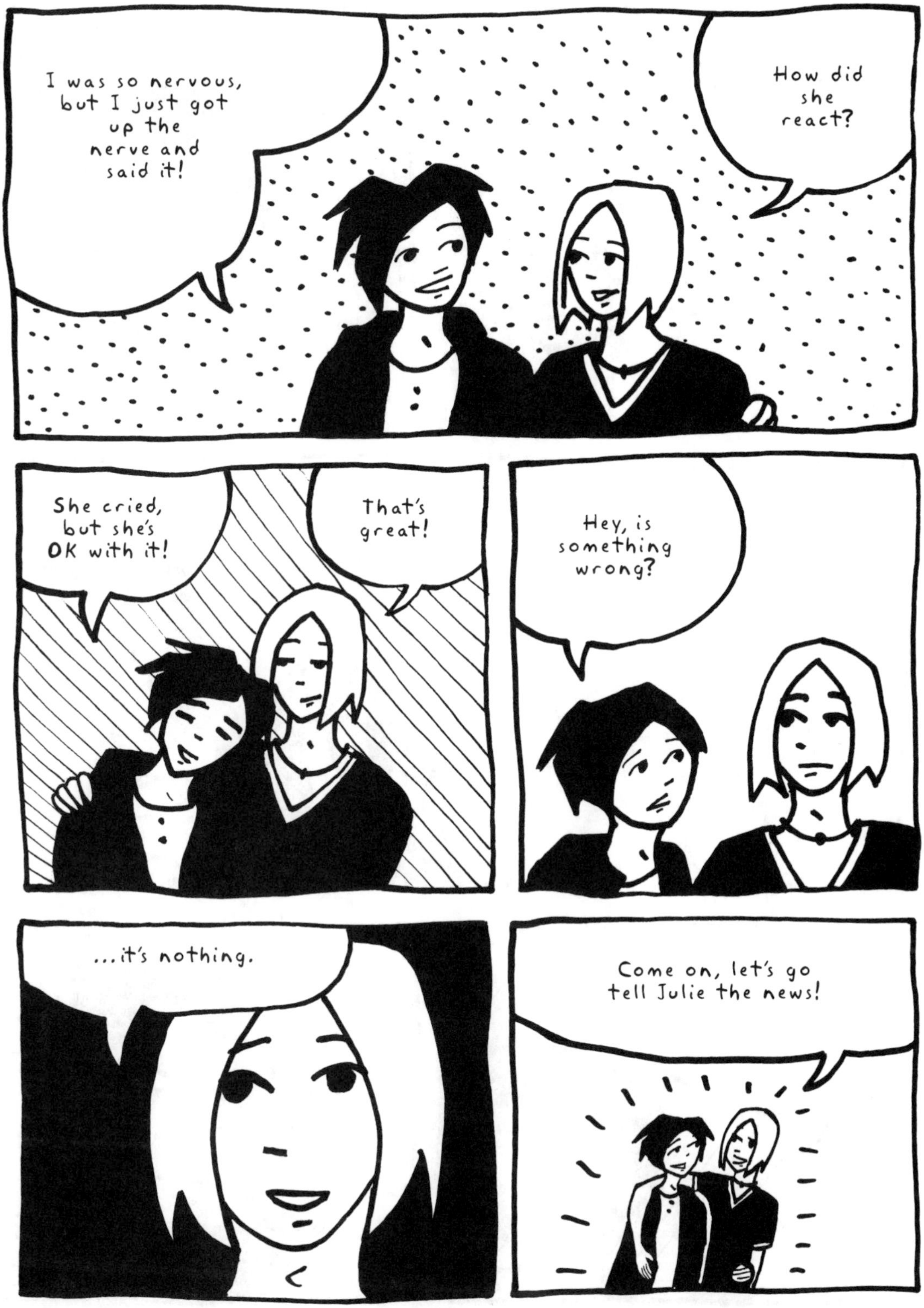
I was so nervous, but I just got up the nerve and said it!
How did she react?
She cried, but she's OK with it!
That's great!
Hey, is something wrong?
...it's nothing.
Come on, let's go tell Julie the news!

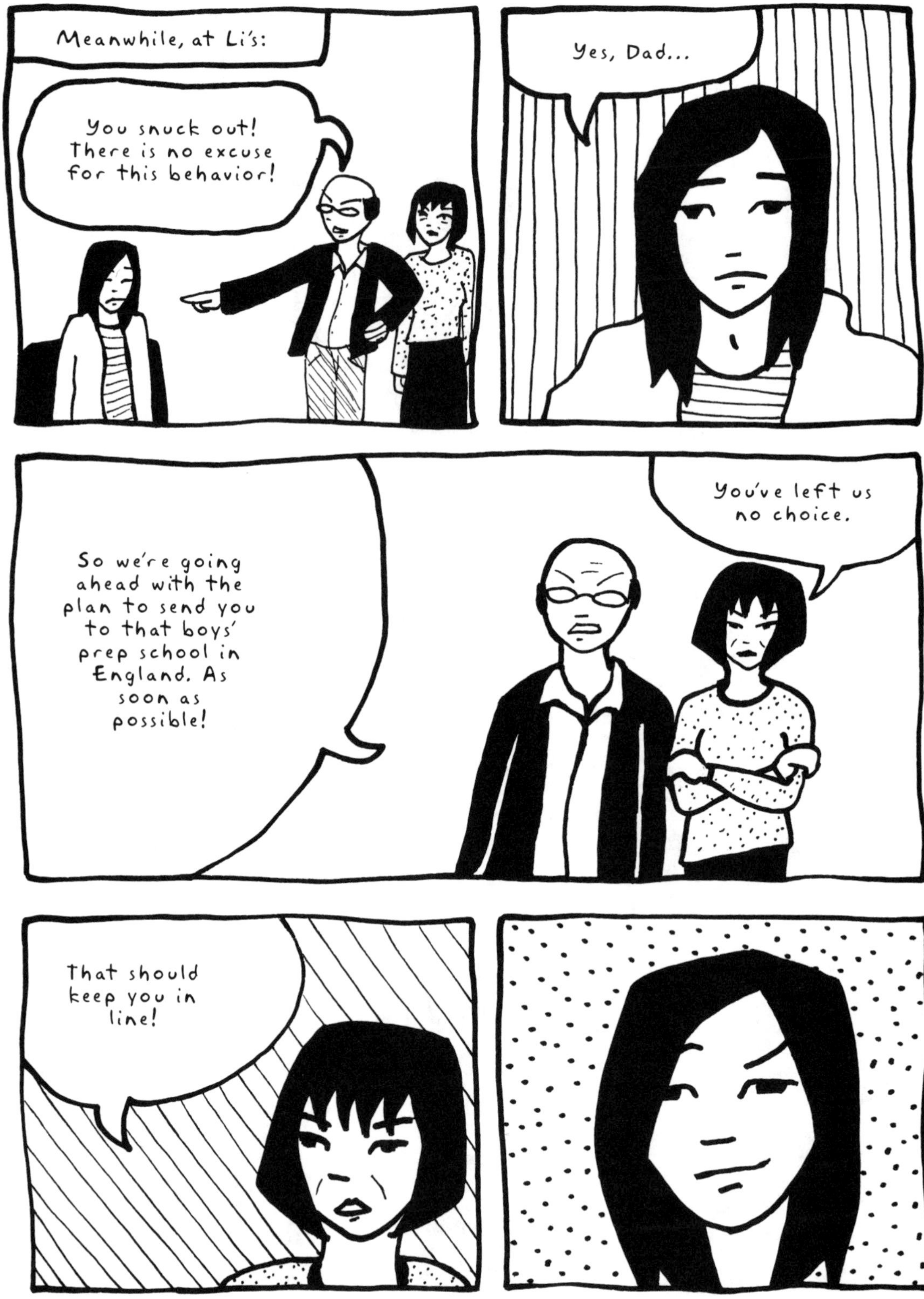

Meanwhile, at Li's:
You snuck out! There is no excuse for this behavior!
Yes, Dad...
You've left us no choice.
So we're going ahead with the plan to send you to that boys' prep school in England. As soon as possible!
That should keep you in line!

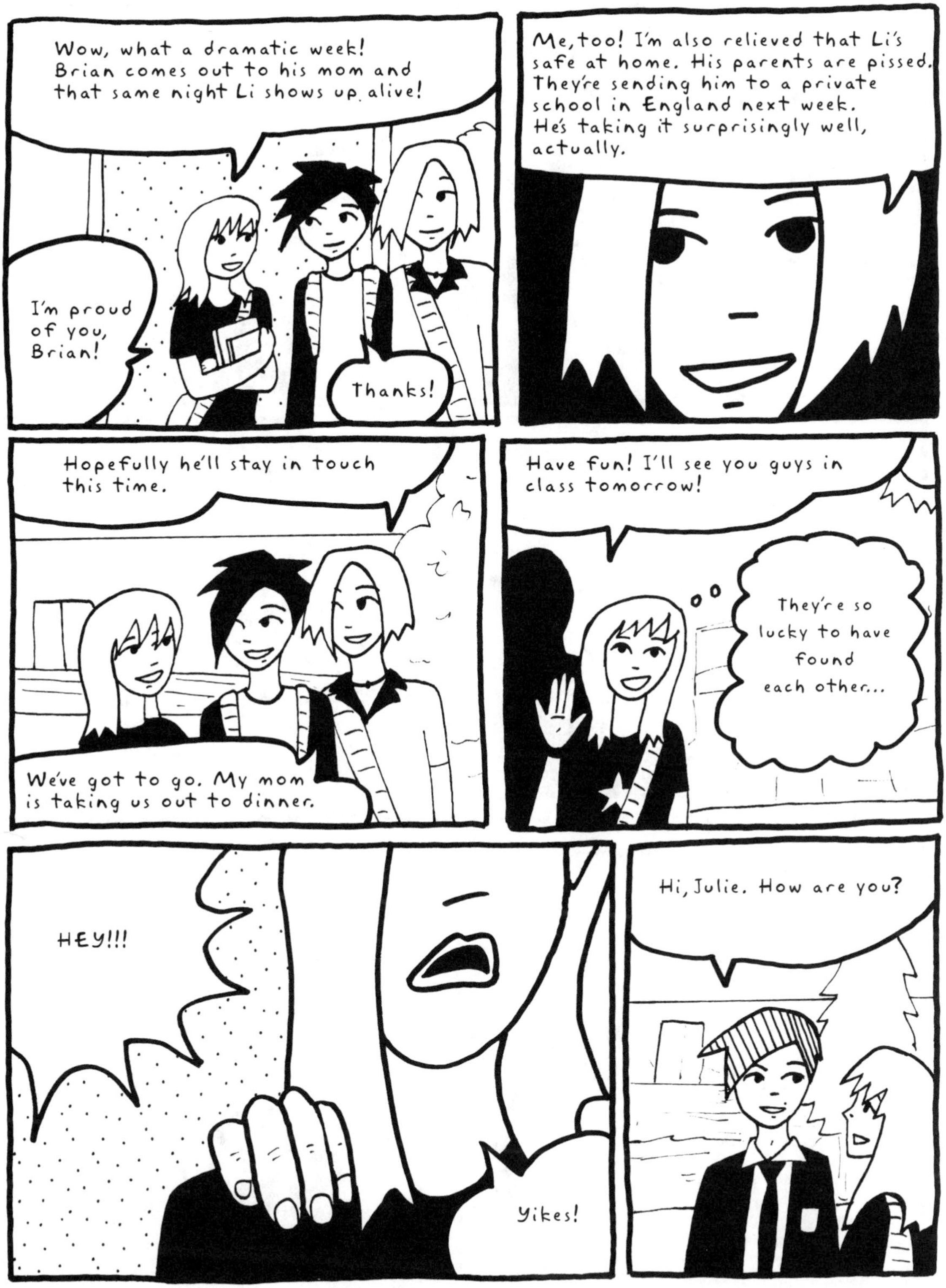

Wow, what a dramatic week! Brian comes out to his mom and that same night Li shows up alive!
I'm proud of you, Brian!
Thanks!
Me, too! I'm also relieved that Li's safe at home. His parents are pissed. They're sending him to a private school in England next week. He's taking it surprisingly well, actually.
Hopefully he'll stay in touch this time.
We've got to go. My mom is taking us out to dinner.
Have fun! I'll see you guys in class tomorrow!
They're so lucky to have found each other...
HEY!!!
Yikes!
Hi, Julie. How are you?

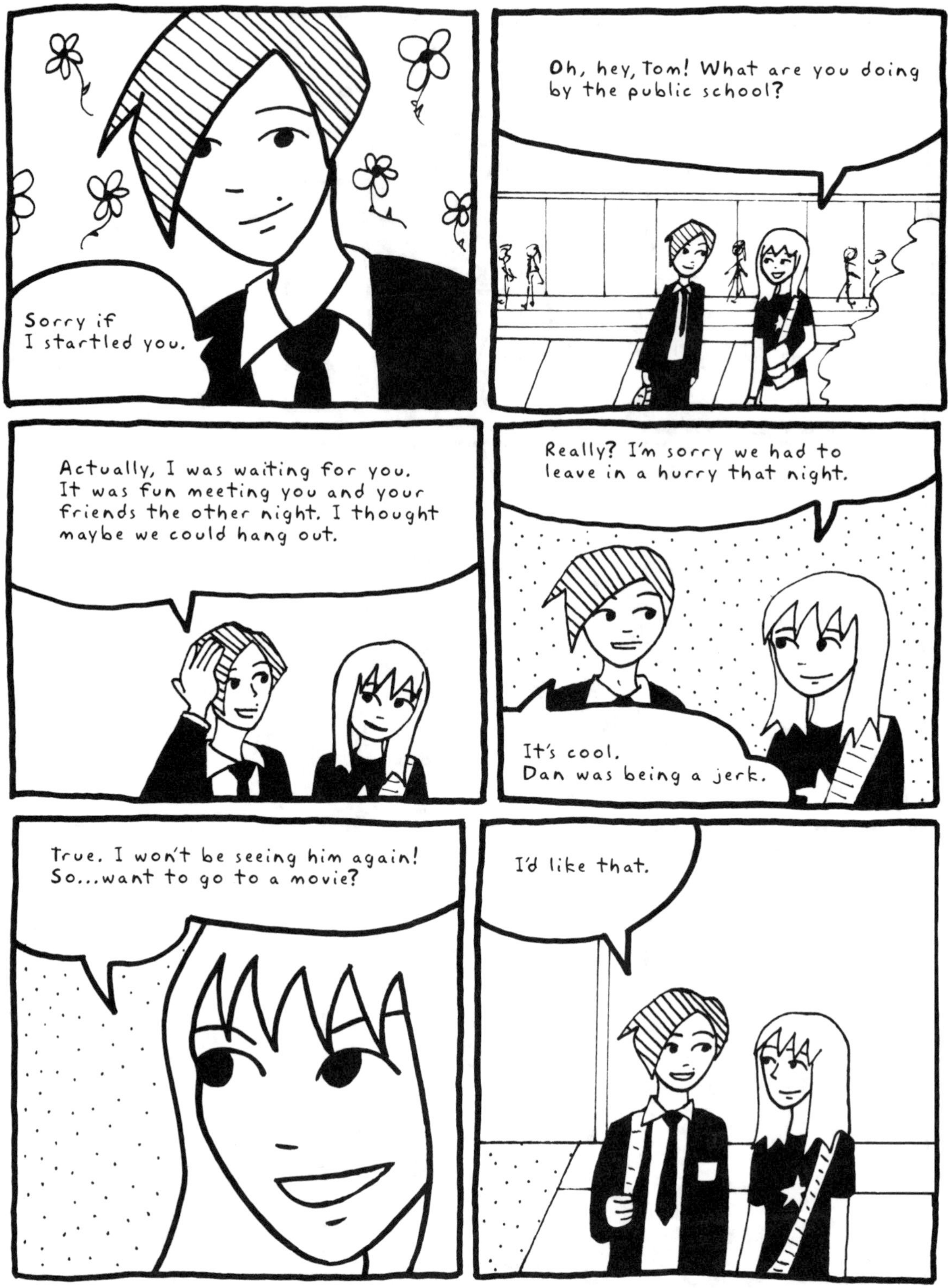

Sorry if I startled you.
Oh, hey, Tom! What are you doing by the public school?
Actually, I was waiting for you. It was fun meeting you and your friends the other night. I thought maybe we could hang out.
Really? I'm sorry we had to leave in a hurry that night.
It's cool. Dan was being a jerk.
True. I won't be seeing him again! So...want to go to a movie?
I'd like that.

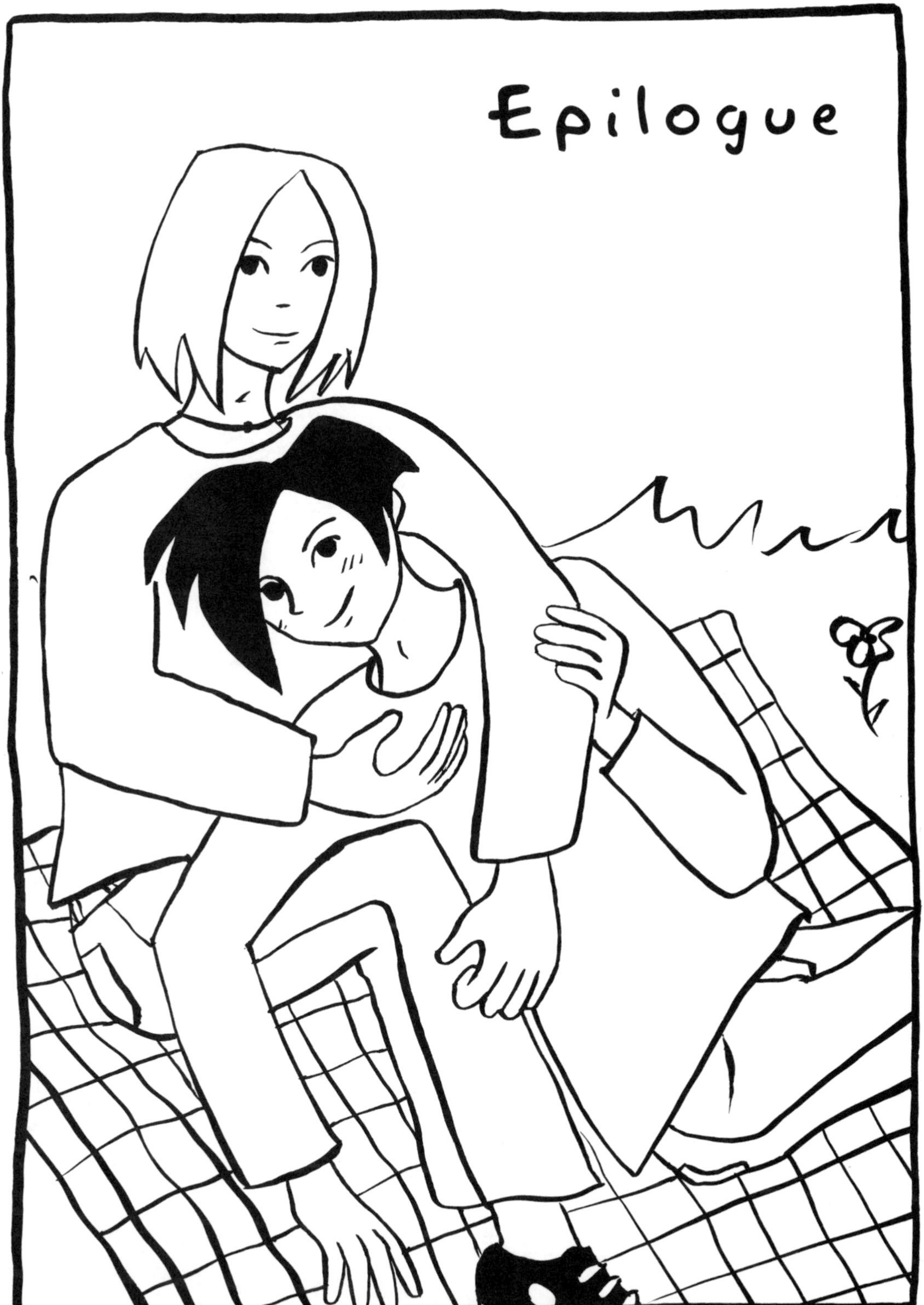
Epilogue

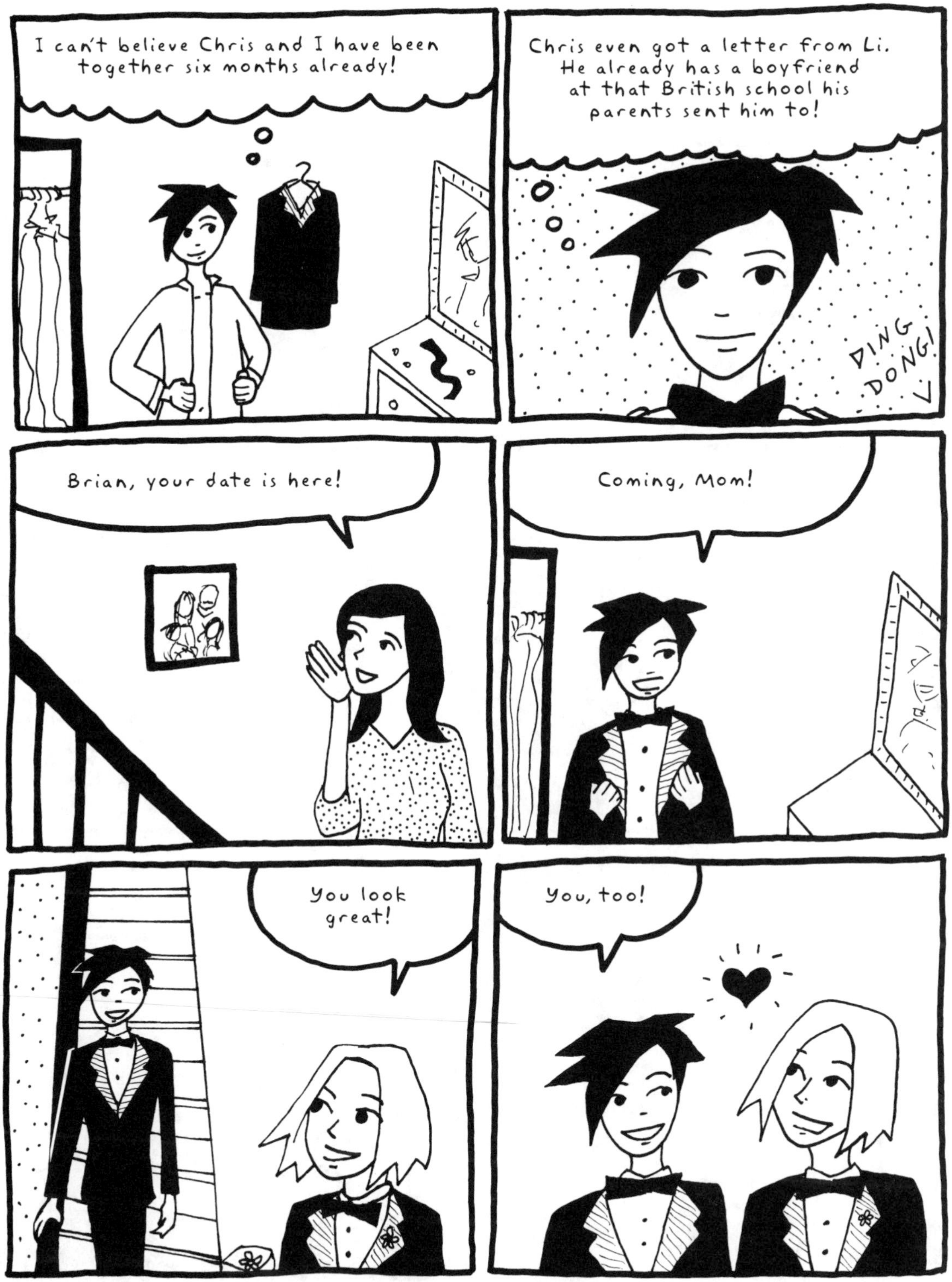
I can't believe Chris and I have been together six months already!
Chris even got a letter from Li. He already has a boyfriend at that British school his parents sent him to!
DING DONG!
Brian, your date is here!
Coming, Mom!
You look great!
You, too!

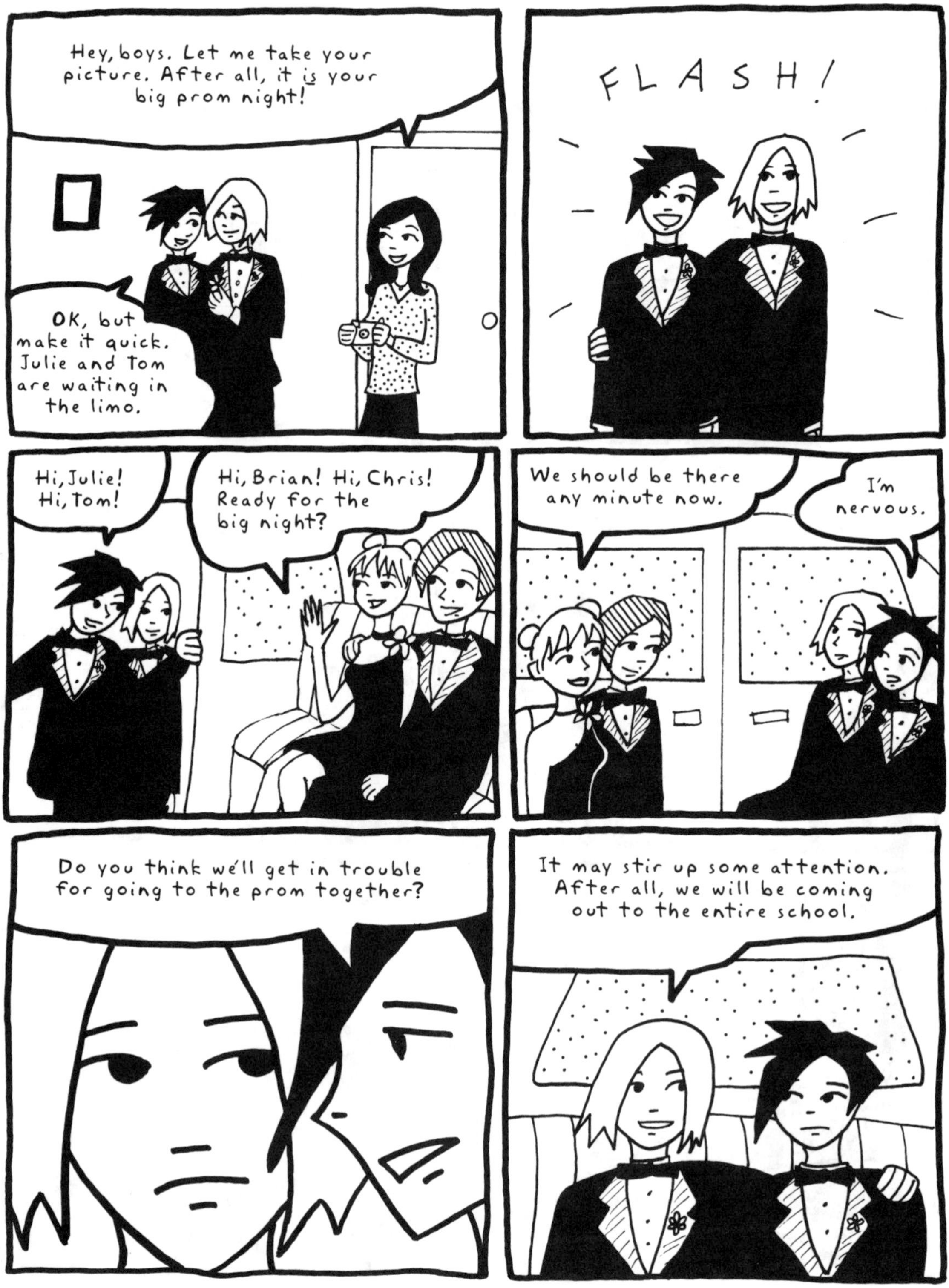

Hey, boys. Let me take your picture. After all, it is your big prom night!
OK, but make it quick. Julie and Tom are waiting in the limo.
FLASH!
Hi, Julie! Hi, Tom!
Hi, Brian! Hi, Chris! Ready for the big night?
We should be there any minute now.
I'm nervous.
Do you think we'll get in trouble for going to the prom together?
It may stir up some attention. After all, we will be coming out to the entire school.

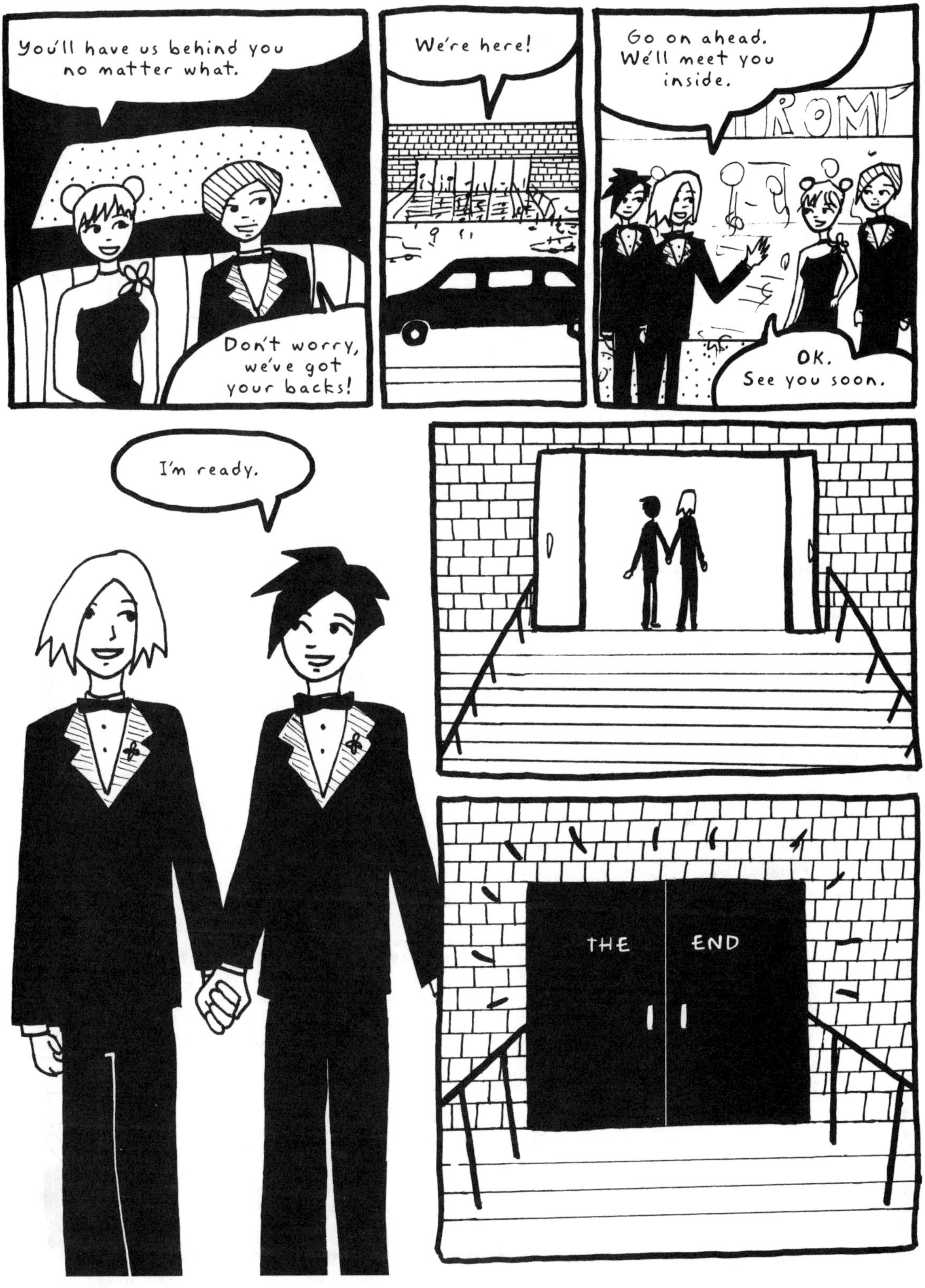
You'll have us behind you no matter what.
Don't worry, we've got your backs!
We're here!
Go on ahead. We'll meet you inside.
PROM
OK. See you soon.
I'm ready.
THE END

RESOURCES:

Trevor Talkline: A 24/7 suicide prevention helpline for gay and questioning teens
All calls are free and confidential.
1-866-4-U-TREVOR
www.thetrevorhelpline.org

Suicide Prevention: www.metanoia.org/suicide/

LYRIC (Lavender Youth Recreation & Information Center): A community center for
lesbian, gay, bisexual, transgender, queer and questioning (LGBTQQ) youth. www.lyric.org

GLBT Youth Talkline: Support line GLBT for youth.
1-800-246-7743

Gay & Lesbian National Hotline: Provides peer-counseling, information, and local
resources.
1-888-843-4564 www.glnh.org

Crisis Intervention Center: Trained volunteers and staff assist callers with a
wide variety of problems, including grief and loss, drug and alcohol problems,
mental health issues, and suicide.
1-800-999-9999

London Lesbian & Gay Switchboard [UK]: London Lesbian and Gay Switchboard aims to
provide an information, support and referral service for lesbians, gay men and bisexual
people from all backgrounds throughout the United Kingdom.
020-7837-7324

PFLAG: Parents, Families and friends of Lesbians and Gays (PFLAG) works to promote
the health and well-being of gay, lesbian, bisexual and transgendered persons, their
families and friends through: support, to cope with an adverse society; education,
to enlighten an ill-informed public; and advocacy, to end discrimination and to secure
equal civil rights.
www.pflag.org

The Hetrick-Martin Institute: Founded in 1979 in New York, the Hetrick-Martin Institute, home of the Harvey Milk School, is a non-profit, social service, advocacy and education organization serving lesbian, gay, bisexual, transgender youth; homeless and HIV-positive adolescents; and all youth who are coming to terms with issues of sexuality.
www.hmi.org

GLSEN: The Gay, Lesbian and Straight Education Network (GLSEN), through its network of 85 chapters in 35 states, works with school officials and parents to assure that each member of every school community is valued and respected, regardless of sexual orientation or gender identity.
(212) 727-0135 www.glsen.org

AVP: The Lesbian and Gay Anti-Violence Project (AVP) provides information on preventing violence against lesbians and gays and support in reporting bias crime. AVP also provides confidential legal advocacy, professional and peer counseling, as well as, national bias crime information.
(212) 714-1184 (phone) or (212) 714-1141 (24 hours)
www.avp.org

Thanks to: Sharon Denson, Irwin Deutsch, Jim Coulter, Chris
Coulter, Ed Denson, Paul Phillips, Lillian Denson, Mike Denson,
Ellen Quint, Jon Quint, Aaron Quint, Dov Quint, Irwin Deutsch,
Joanne and Ron Sanoff and the rest of my wonderful family!
I'm so lucky to have you!
Christine Soulard, Matt Loux, Jenn Keating, Pat Cash, Peter
Cummings, Friends of Lulu, Heidi MacDonald, Sara Schwartz, Marc
Wilkofsky, Sergio Baradat, Mark Smith, Fly, Andi Watson,
C.B. Cebulski, Dave Roman, Raina Telgemeier, John Green, Chris Couch,
James Brown, Holly Go Lightly, Peter Bagge, John Crossen,
Cary Portway, Joe Weary, Patrick Shannon, Jennifer Sandifer,
Ben Casey, Justina Fitzpatrick, Sherman Chen, Jamilah Bourdon,
Mayumi Shimokawa, Mike Pinto, Brian Cirulnick, Jenny Gonzalez,
P5, LisSsa Darrow, Jeremy Jusay, Mike Brisbois, Adam Dekraker,
Russ Turk, Mr. Tim, Rodney Greenblat, Yasuko Shimizu, Tony Arena,
Ron Grunewald, G.B. Jones, Tim Fish, Craig Bostick, Richard O'Connor,
Elin Winkler, Will Allison, Dean Hsieh, Dame Darcy, Alvin Orloff,
Jennifer Blowdryer, Jesse Leon McCann, Mina Monden, Lauren
Weinstein, Kate and Patrick Hambrecht, Poppy Z. Brite, Howard Cruse,
James Kochalka, Yuuko Koyama, Yuka Tejima, Trish Ledoux, Toshifumi
Yoshida, Julie Davis, Yumi Kori, Carl Horn, Jason Staloff, Derek Davis,
Ron Thomson, Chris Payne, Matt Cohen, Mike Salera, Karriem Shabazz,
Frank Lamonica, Rob Gilpatrick, Steve Grassotti, Janelle Nicol,
Andrea Suarez, David Lerner, Dick Demenus, Daniel Genalo, Don
Peterson, Bernard Nazario and the rest of the Tekserve crew!

Abby Denson has created comics for XY Magazine since 1996. She has also scripted Powerpuff Girls Comics, Simpsons Comics, Sabrina The Teenage Witch, Josie and the Pussycats, Disney Adventures, and comics for Nickelodeon Magazine. She's been playing in punk bands since she was sixteen years old. She loves her family, New York City, container gardening, rock and roll, and petting her cat.
www.abbycomix.com

Also available from Manic D Press

The Military Draft Handbook: A Brief History and Practical Advice for the Curious and Concerned
edited by James Tracy, $12.00

Good Advice for Young Trendy People of All Ages
edited by Jennifer Blowdryer, $15.00

The Killers: Destiny is Calling Me
by Jarret Keene, $12.95

Legends of Punk: Photos from the Vault
by Rikki Ercoli, $19.95

King of the Roadkills by Bucky Sinister, $9.95

In Me Own Words: The Autobiography of Bigfoot
by Graham Roumieu, $12.95

The Beautiful: Collected Poems by Michelle Tea, $13.95

Gutterboys by Alvin Orloff, $13.95

From the Inside Out: Radical Gender Transformation, FTM and Beyond
edited by Morty Diamond, $13.95

Beyond Definition: New Writing from Gay & Lesbian San Francisco
edited by Marci Blackman and Trebor Healey, $10.95

Dances with Sheep: A K Chronicles Compendium
by Keith Knight, $11.95

Fear of a Black Marker: Another K Chronicles Compendium
by Keith Knight, $11.95

Passion of the Keef: The Fourth K Chronicles Compendium
by Keith Knight, $12.95